MIXED FEELINGS

signale
modern german letters, cultures, and thought

Series editor: Peter Uwe Hohendahl, Cornell University

Signale: Modern German Letters, Cultures, and Thought publishes new English-language books in literary studies, criticism, cultural studies, and intellectual history pertaining to the German-speaking world, as well as translations of important German-language works. *Signale* construes "modern" in the broadest terms: the series covers topics ranging from the early modern period to the present. *Signale* books are published under a joint imprint of Cornell University Press and Cornell University Library in electronic and print formats. Please see http://signale.cornell.edu/.

MIXED FEELINGS

*Tropes of Love in German
Jewish Culture*

KATJA GARLOFF

A Signale Book

CORNELL UNIVERSITY PRESS AND CORNELL UNIVERSITY LIBRARY
ITHACA AND LONDON

Cornell University Press and Cornell University Library gratefully acknowledge the College of Arts & Sciences, Cornell University, for support of the Signale series.

First published 2016 by Cornell University Press and Cornell University Library

Printed in the United States of America

Library of Congress Cataloging-in-Publication Data

Names: Garloff, Katja, author.
Title: Mixed feelings : tropes of love in German Jewish culture / Katja Garloff.
Other titles: Signale (Ithaca, N.Y.)
Description: Ithaca, New York : Cornell University Press and Cornell University Library, 2016. | Series: Signale | Includes bibliographical references and index.
Identifiers: LCCN 2016036450 | ISBN 9781501704963 (cloth : alk. paper) | ISBN 9781501704970 (pbk. : alk. paper)
Subjects: LCSH: Jews—Germany—History—1800–1933. | Germany—Ethnic relations—History—19th century. | Germany—Ethnic relations—History—20th century. | Germany—Intellectual life—19th century. | Germany—Intellectual life—20th century.
Classification: LCC DS134.25 .G37 2016 | DDC 305.892/404309034—dc23
LC record available at https://lccn.loc.gov/2016036450

Cloth printing   10 9 8 7 6 5 4 3 2 1
Paperback printing   10 9 8 7 6 5 4 3 2 1

For Binya

CONTENTS

ACKNOWLEDGMENTS

This book grew out of my curiosity about a figure of speech. During years of studying and teaching German Jewish culture, I came to wonder why so many scholars characterized German-Jewish relations from the Enlightenment to the Holocaust as an (unhappy) "love affair." Is it reasonable to compare a complex historical process of social, cultural, and political integration with love, I asked? Does this trope not risk identifying the individual with the group, suggesting that emotions drive history, and downplaying questions of power and inequality? As I came to discover, however, critics draw on a long history of viewing German-Jewish cultural relations through the lens of a love affair. And so my misgivings gave way to appreciation. I wrote this book to illustrate how literary love stories comment on social processes; how the rhetoric of love underscores political demands; how philosophies of love generate new models of pluralist communities.

The book is indebted to a number of scholars who view German Jewish literature and culture as both interesting in its own right and inspiring in contemporary debates about multiculturalism, human rights, and the particular in relation to the universal. Special thanks are owed to William Donahue and Martha Helfer, who established a new forum for the field, the Biennial German Jewish Studies Workshop at Duke University. It was there, as well as at numerous conferences of the German Studies Association and the Association of Jewish Studies, that I regularly met scholars, including Abigail Gillman, Malachi Hacohen, Jeffrey Librett,

Elizabeth Loentz, Erin McGlothlin, Leslie Morris, Agnes Mueller, Anna Parkinson, Brad Prager, Todd Presner, Paul Reitter, Scott Spector, and Rochelle Tobias, whose questions and comments shaped this book. Sander Gilman and Liliane Weissberg, who have long been mentors of mine, made helpful suggestions at different stages of the project. Special thanks are due to Jeffrey Grossman, Martha Helfer, Jonathan Hess, Michael Levine, and Jonathan Skolnik, who, in addition to inspiring me through their own work, read chapters of this book in draft form. I am also grateful for the insights provided by Eva Lezzi, which turned what could have been scholarly competition into a fruitful cross-Atlantic collaboration. Stefani Engelstein has been a close friend and intellectual interlocutor for many years; I would like to thank her in particular for her comments, after reading a draft of the manuscript, on the shape of the whole in relation to the parts.

I appreciate the abundance of institutional support for this project, without which it could not have been completed. Early on in the project I received a Millicent C. McIntosh Fellowship from the Woodrow Wilson Foundation, which funded several research trips to Germany. The Dean's Office at Reed College provided generous support for conferences and summer research, as well as two Sabbatical Award Fellowships that gave me the time to write the book. Colleagues from other institutions invited me to lecture on the project, allowing me to test my ideas in front of insightful audiences at Harvard University, Dartmouth College, the University of Massachusetts Amherst, the University of Washington, the University of Missouri, the Hebrew University of Jerusalem, and the University of Hong Kong. A one-year research and teaching stint on the East Coast likewise advanced the project—thanks are due to Mark Anderson, who arranged for my visiting scholar status at Columbia University in the fall of 2008, and to Eric Rentschler, who invited me to spend the spring of 2009 as a visiting professor at Harvard University. I also wish to thank the entire faculty of Harvard's German department, as well as the graduate students of my seminar on German-Jewish love stories, for making my stay there both enjoyable and productive.

I am fortunate to teach at an institution that generously supports faculty research while encouraging professors to think about the broader implications and pedagogical relevance of their work. I think fondly of the many conversations I have had with friends and (current and former) colleagues from Reed—in workshops, over coffee, during walks—conversations that would flow effortlessly from teaching to research to life, and back: especially with Diego Alonso, Ann Delehanty, Jacqueline Dirks, Elizabeth Duquette, Ariadna García-Bryce, Ülker Gökberk, Marat Grinberg, Laura Arnold Leibman, Jan Mieszkowski, Geraldine Ondrizek, Roger Porter, Paul Silverstein, Michael Taylor, John Urang, Steven Wasserstrom, and Catherine Witt. I am also grateful to the students enrolled in different versions of my seminars on modern German Jewish writers and the literature of love who asked incisive questions, challenged my ideas, and contributed some of their own. Two of these students, Christopher Muñoz-Calene and Benjamin DeYoung, assisted me in the final phase of the manuscript preparation by checking the translations and the bibliography.

Cornell University Press has been extraordinary in their efficiency throughout the publication of this book. I would like to thank Kizer Walker, Peter Uwe Hohendahl, and the editorial board of the *Signale* series for their speedy decision-making, thoughtful suggestions for changes, and kind understanding when I had to postpone the submission of the manuscript. Marian Rogers copyedited the book with great care and dedication. Thanks are also due to Paul Reitter, who revealed himself as one of the readers for the press, for his generous reading of the manuscript.

I began this book with a buoyant spirit, as a recently tenured professor enjoying the freedom to pursue the research projects about which she cared most. I put the last touches on it while I was in deeper grief than I could ever imagine. The outpouring of love from the many communities that helped bring the book into existence was likewise crucial in sustaining me and my family through this terrible time. To all the people who brought us meals, took us out for some distraction, went with me on nature walks, or simply listened: I will be forever grateful to you—as I will be to my parents, siblings, and the members of my extended family in Germany, France, Israel, and Australia, who rallied to our support. I would also like to thank my husband, Asher Klatchko, for loving me unfailingly, for cooking delicious meals, for retaining an independent spirit—and for being able to grieve with courage and dignity. Every day I think with love and longing of our older son, Binya; I dedicate this book to his memory. Our younger son, Yona, was born while I was first developing the ideas for this book; we gave him the Hebrew name Yair, without fully knowing then how much he would grow into just that: the light of our life.

Parts of the introduction and the conclusion appeared in *Nexus: Essays in German Jewish Studies* 1 (2011). A section of chapter 1 was published in *Lessing Yearbook* 36 (2004/2005), and an earlier version of chapter 4 was in *The German Quarterly* 80, no. 4 (Fall 2007). The last section of the conclusion appeared in *Judaism, Christianity, and Islam: Collaboration and Conflict in the Age of Diaspora*, ed. Sander Gilman (Hong Kong: University of Hong Kong Press, 2014). I thank the publishers for permission to reprint this material in revised form.

A note on quotations and translations: I quote in English throughout the book. For quotations from literary texts, I often provide the page number for the German original as well. I have used published translations whenever possible. All other translations are mine.

MIXED FEELINGS

Introduction

> By and large, then, the love affair of the Jews and the Germans remained one-sided and unreciprocated.

Thus Gershom Scholem sums up his critique of German-Jewish relations in the modern age in his essay "Jews and Germans" ("Juden und Deutsche," 1966).[1] Few accounts have been more frequently cited—whether approvingly or critically—in the scholarly discussion of German Jewish culture and history. Scholem argues in the essay that the process of Jewish emancipation and acculturation that began in the late eighteenth century did not usher in a dialogue between Jews and non-Jews. Rather, it created the illusion of equality in Jews, who failed to realize that their desire for social integration lacked a German counterpart. Jews simply did not see that assimilation dissolved the communal bonds among them without truly granting them access to German society. In rather broad strokes, Scholem sketches the history of German-Jewish relations, from sporadic economic interactions before the eighteenth century to the struggle of Jews for civil and political rights to their strong identification with German culture in the nineteenth and the early twentieth centuries. And he implies that the social exclusion of the Jews persisted despite this identification, rendered them vulnerable to persecution, and ultimately culminated in the Holocaust.

Beneath the veneer of this historical narrative Scholem tells a love story—or more precisely, an unhappy love story. He speaks of longing, fervor, and passion in a way that suggests that the struggle for equal rights and the adoption of new cultural and religious practices were primarily motivated by feelings. Words such as *relationship*, *encounter*, and *intimacy* liken the interaction between

---

1. Gershom Scholem, "Jews and Germans," in *On Jews and Judaism in Crisis*, ed. Werner J. Dannhauser (New York: Schocken, 1976), 71–92; here 86. All further citations of "Jews and Germans" refer to this edition and will be included parenthetically in the text.

collectives to that between individuals. In this way, Scholem casts the process of Jewish emancipation and assimilation as an emotional drama between an impetuous lover and a reluctant beloved: the Jews' first yearning glances toward German culture and history were followed by "passionate involvement" (75) and "complete submission" (81)—and rejection from the start. Indeed, the Jews' "stormy" striving for culture and education met with resistance among non-Jews, who felt the pace of Jews' advances to be "overheated" (80–81). Scholem's rhetoric of love is problematic not the least because it shifts part of the blame for the historical outcome to the Jews. Their all-too-ardent love for German culture is said to have been self-destructive, since it blinded them to the political realities of emancipation—namely, the power imbalances it presupposed and the antisemitic backlashes it entailed. Indeed, it is striking how much power Scholem accords to love as a motivation and an explanation for broad social interactions. While he rejects the Jewish love for things German both as an experience of the past and as a model for the future, he turns the "love affair" into a master trope for the historical process of Jewish emancipation and assimilation.

Other scholars have found the trope of the German-Jewish love affair similarly compelling. In *Freud, Jews, and Other Germans*, Peter Gay makes very different claims about the situation of Jews in the German Empire in similar terms. Gay argues that the expectation of Jews around 1900 that antisemitism would disappear was not entirely misguided and that their passionate identification with German culture was based on real or perceived intellectual affinities; and he describes these affinities as a form of love. Thus Hermann Cohen, the neo-Kantian philosopher who envisioned an entwinement of *Deutschtum* and *Judentum* based on shared Greek roots, is "an instructive chapter in the Jewish love affair with German culture."[2] In its different orientations, the trope continues to be deployed with remarkable persistence in works on German Jewish history. Scholars who share Scholem's overall assessment compare the dilemmas of Jews in Nazi Germany during the 1930s to an "abusive marriage" or claim that "the unrequited love affair of Germany's Jews with their native country *led* to the unspeakable horrors of the Holocaust."[3] Others follow Gay in evoking love to counter such historical determinism. Steven Aschheim, for instance, calls for an analysis of real-life German-Jewish love affairs and marriages as "a necessary corrective to the view of all German-Jewish history, in the light of its terrible conclusion, as a history of unremitting hostility and estrangement."[4]

---

2. Peter Gay, *Freud, Jews, and Other Germans: Masters and Victims in Modernist Culture* (New York: Oxford University Press, 1978), 114.

3. John Dippel, *Bound upon a Wheel of Fire: Why So Many German Jews Made the Tragic Decision to Remain in Nazi Germany* (New York: Basic Books, 1996), xix; Michael Blumenthal, *The Invisible Wall: Germans and Jews; A Personal Exploration* (Washington, D.C.: Counterpoint, 1998), dust jacket; both quoted in Deborah Hertz, *How Jews Became Germans: The History of Conversion and Assimilation in Berlin* (New Haven, Conn.: Yale University Press, 2007), 15 (Hertz's emphasis).

4. Steven E. Aschheim, *Scholem, Arendt, Klemperer: Intimate Chronicles in Turbulent Times* (Bloomington: Indiana University Press, 2001), 41.

Why has love—and especially unhappy or one-sided love—become such a popular model or metaphor for German-Jewish relations? Among the terms that have been used to describe German-Jewish relations before the Holocaust—terms such as *dialogue*, *symbiosis*, and *subculture*—*love* intuitively seems to be the most problematic. The use of love as a model for sociopolitical integration can personalize the political, individualize the social, and romanticize power relations. This book argues that it is nevertheless an important model: historically significant, aesthetically intricate, and politically inventive. Since the beginnings of Jewish emancipation in the late eighteenth century, writers have used the idea of love to comment on the changing position of Jews in the German-speaking countries. In so doing, they generated new models of group relations that did not necessarily come to fruition at the time but that can serve as an inspiration in today's debates about pluralism and multiculturalism.

The most important primary sources for this book are literary love stories that involve partners from different religious, cultural, or ethnic backgrounds. Such love stories hark back to a literary tradition that ranges from Shakespeare's play *Romeo and Juliet*, the famous romance across social boundaries in Renaissance Venice, to Laurents's and Bernstein's musical *West Side Story*, which adapts this model to the ethnic conflicts in 1950s New York City. In both *Romeo and Juliet* and *West Side Story*, two people from opposing groups fall in love with each other. The personal relationship between them ultimately helps forge new social bonds, if only after first exacerbating the conflict between the groups and causing the death and/or desolation of the lovers. In each case, the drama begins with the lovers' ability to look beyond the other's social background, to see each other as individuals rather than members of a group. "What's in a name?" Juliet asks famously and rhetorically in *Romeo and Juliet* when she realizes that Romeo belongs to the family hers is feuding with. In *West Side Story*, the Puerto Rican Maria similarly responds to her brother's angry question about the white boy from the rival gang with whom she has fallen in love—"Couldn't you see he's one of them?"—"No, I saw only him." In both works, the drama unfolds because radical individuation is not entirely possible, because the lovers never stop being members of a social group. Love stories of the *Romeo and Juliet* type can dramatize the tension between social determination and self-actualization because their characters are both unique individuals and actors in a social world.

Mixed Feelings reads such love stories together with political and philosophical texts that invoke the idea of love to rethink the relations between different social groups. I argue that these texts together constitute a discourse of love that accompanied Jewish emancipation and assimilation in the German-speaking countries from the beginning. The focus is on romantic love, which I define as the powerful attraction between two individuals and the basis of a potentially lifelong relationship. How could the idea of romantic love become a generative force in sociopolitical debates? First, the very slipperiness of the term *love* makes it productive. Because *romantic love* shares a semantic domain with terms such as *friendship*, *family affection*, and *neighbor-love*, literary love stories can proffer a sociopolitical commentary, and political texts can mobilize the rhetoric of love. In these texts, the idea of romantic love often draws on and changes existing forms of social and religious love. Second, texts that analyze German Jewish history and identity in terms of love tend to be characterized by a heightened rhetoricity. Scholars rely on rhetorical devices such as personification (when they endow an abstraction with human features) and synecdoche (when they represent a group by one of its members) to characterize the relationship of Jews to German culture as a "love affair."

We may understand this rhetoricity in terms of a tension between what Roland Barthes calls the "figures" and the "story" of love. In *A Lover's Discourse*, Barthes describes the lover's speech as a stream of linguistic scenes, gestures, and utterances ranging from "catastrophe" to "fulfillment," from "I want to understand" to "I am crazy."[5] These are akin to figures in a choreographic sense. They both restrain and enable the lover's speech, much as a choreographic figure guides a dancer's movement, casting her into an existing pose from which she wrests a new expressive potential. According to Barthes, the love story, which is "the tribute the lover must pay to the world in order to be reconciled with it" (7), purges these disjointed elements of affect and transforms them into a whole. Barthes himself strives to undo the temporal sequence and hierarchical order of the love story—in his book he lists the figures alphabetically, as in a dictionary—and the rhetoric of love in Scholem, Gay, and others achieves a similar effect. By isolating figures of love and transposing them to new historical and political contexts, these authors mobilize the anarchic energy of figures of love, creating affectively charged texts.

My own term for this rhetorical dimension is *trope*, which I use in the two different meanings the term has acquired. *Trope* can refer to a figure of speech that is recurring, ossified, even clichéd. The phrase "German-Jewish love affair" today has become a trope in that sense, a catchy expression used by scholars and journalists to capture a complex historical process of social, cultural, and political integration. Originally, however, *trope*, which is derived from the Greek verb *trepein*, meaning "to turn," refers to a figure of speech that alters the ways in which language is used, that has the power to change the terms of a given discourse. This is the potential revealed in *Mixed Feelings*, which shows how tropes of love help create new models of group relations. In the past, writers and thinkers used such tropes to intervene in the emancipation debates and rethink the project of assimilation. Today, we can turn to their works to reexamine these central terms of German Jewish studies.

---

5. Roland Barthes, *A Lover's Discourse: Fragments*, trans. Richard Howard (New York: Farrar, Straus and Giroux, 1979), 48, 54, 59, 120.

Rethinking Emancipation and Assimilation

The concept of assimilation has long been the linchpin of German Jewish studies. Several recent studies provide a fresh perspective as they scrutinize the conceptual limitations of the term rather than assuming assimilation as a sociohistorical fact. Scott Spector, for instance, argues that the concept of assimilation remains wedded to a notion of identity that is problematic in its connotations of stability and coherence.[6] Social scientists who measure degrees of assimilation on a spectrum of identities ranging from "German" to "Jewish" hypostatize individual behavior and diminish cultural complexity. While Spector recommends discarding the term, his project in fact resonates with attempts by other contemporary scholars to rethink the term, in part by revisiting the full range of its historical meanings. In a review of early twentieth-century and contemporary scholars, Till von Rahden identifies many thinkers for whom assimilation is not equated with the disappearance of Jewish particularity but rather presents a chance for creativity and renewal.[7] Assimilation thus understood is not a passive adoption of a cultural system imagined as closed and coherent, but a creative process that involves the contestation, negotiation, and transformation of cultural symbols and practices. It is a two-way rather than a one-way street and may lead to genuinely new cultural formations. Since *Mixed Feelings* promotes this broader understanding of assimilation—in fact argues that the tropes of love that were so ubiquitous in the assimilation debates are among its key sources— I use the terms *assimilation* and *acculturation* interchangeably throughout this study.[8]

In recent years, scholars have developed a rich vocabulary of *subversion, counterhegemony, strategic reversal,* and *situational ethnicity* to capture the complexity of German-Jewish cultural interaction. In *Germans, Jews, and the Claims of Modernity*, Jonathan Hess highlights the agency of Jews in the process of integration and the polemical nature of their political interventions. He shows that Jews did not passively accept new social and cultural norms but rather actively, and often subversively, appropriated them. Other scholars emphasize the necessity of rethinking the connection between identity and agency. Thus van Rahden speaks of the "situated ethnicity" of German Jews, who laid claims to Jewish identity in some situations but not in others, and Steven Aschheim of the "co-constitutionality" of German culture. Aschheim wants to move beyond a notion of German culture as a quasi-autochthonous entity to which Jews may contribute in one way or another. He conceives of this culture as a product of the interaction between different social

---

6. Scott Spector, "Forget Assimilation: Introducing Subjectivity to German-Jewish History," *Jewish History* 20, nos. 3–4 (2006): 349–61.

7. See Till van Rahden, "Verrat, Schicksal oder Chance: Lesarten des Assimilationsbegriffs in der Historiographie zur Geschichte der deutschen Juden," *Historische Anthropologie* 13, no. 2 (2005): 245–64.

8. Many contemporary scholars in German Jewish studies prefer the term *acculturation* because it seems better suited to express the agency, creativity, and complexity involved in the sociocultural process. On this terminological shift, see Jonathan M. Hess, *Germans, Jews, and the Claims of Modernity* (New Haven, Conn.: Yale University Press, 2002), 9–10.

groups and individuals who do not necessarily act in their capacity as "Germans" or "Jews."[9] Thus far, the new approaches in German Jewish studies have paid only limited attention to the role of affects and feelings. This may be so because many contemporary scholars seek to modify David Sorkin's groundbreaking concept of a German Jewish "subculture" that emerged during the process of emancipation and acculturation. Whereas Sorkin argued that the struggle for social acceptance created new yet largely unconscious ties among assimilating Jews, recent scholarship suggests that the attempts of Jews to sustain multiple alliances were quite conscious and deliberate.[10]

Mixed Feelings introduces the notions of affect, feeling, and emotion, for which literature provides a rich archive, into the scholarly debate. In so doing, I join several other scholars engaged in bringing about an "affective turn" in German Jewish studies. Paul Reitter's genealogy of Jewish "self-hatred," for instance, reconsiders a feeling long thought to be particularly debilitating and self-destructive.[11] Reitter shows that German Jewish thinkers initially used the idea of "self-hatred" affirmatively, regarding it as a healthy antidote against complacency among Jews and non-Jews alike. My study offers a revisionist reading of the opposite feeling—love—to which I attribute an even stronger generative power. I argue that expressions of love can mark an impasse in the process of assimilation and issue in creative leaps and reversals. The obsession with love in German Jewish thought and literature does not reflect naïveté about the political realities of emancipation but rather calls attention to its unfulfilled promises—and to the creative acts their fulfillment would require.

---

9. Till van Rahden, "Weder Milieu noch Konfession: Die situative Ethnizität der deutschen Juden im Kaiserreich in vergleichender Perspektive," in *Religion im Kaiserreich: Milieus—Mentalitäten—Krisen*, ed. Olaf Blaschke and Frank-Michael Kuhlemann (Gütersloh: Kaiser, Gütersloher Verlags-Haus, 1996), 409–34; Steven Aschheim, "German History and German Jewry: Boundaries, Junctions, and Interdependence," *Leo Baeck Institute Yearbook* 43 (1998): 315–22. Other important approaches include Paul Mendes-Flohr's reflections on German Jewish "hybridity" in *German Jews: A Dual Identity* (New Haven, Conn.: Yale University Press, 1999) and Todd S. Presner's "cultural geography" of German-Jewish encounters in *Mobile Modernity: Germans, Jews, Trains* (New York: Columbia University Press, 2007).

10. See David Sorkin, *The Transformation of German Jewry, 1780–1840* (New York: Oxford University Press, 1987). Sorkin shows that (incomplete) emancipation did not necessarily lead to assimilation or nationalism, but to the establishment of independent Jewish organizations and publications. However, he emphasizes that most German Jews did not see this as a new form of Jewish collectivity at the time.

11. See Paul Reitter, *On the Origins of Jewish Self-Hatred* (Princeton, N.J.: Princeton University Press, 2012). Other scholars contributing to the "affective turn" in German Jewish studies include Scott Spector, who suggests the term *subjectivity* to capture the ambivalent and affect-laden relationship of Jews to German culture (Spector, "Forget Assmilation," 358), and Asher Biemann, who analyzes the German Jewish fascination with Italian culture in *Dreaming of Michelangelo: Jewish Variations on a Modern Theme* (Stanford, Calif.: Stanford University Press, 2012). In German-language scholarship, Eva Lezzi's *"Liebe ist meine Religion!" Eros und Ehe zwischen Juden und Christen in der Literatur des 19. Jahrhunderts* (Göttingen: Wallstein, 2013) examines representations of Christian-Jewish love in nineteenth-century German literature.

This rhetorical function can be illustrated through the example of two well-known reflections on German Jewish identity that make prominent use of the idea of love: Moritz Goldstein's "The German-Jewish Parnassus" ("Deutsch-jüdischer Parnaß," 1912) and Jakob Wassermann's *My Life as German and Jew* (*Mein Weg als Deutscher und Jude*, 1921). Goldstein and Wassermann wrote at a time when the integration of Jews into German culture and society had run into difficulties, when the rise of modern (that is, politically motivated and racially argued) anti-semitism had led to disenchantment with the ideals of emancipation and assimilation. Both Goldstein and Wassermann compared the German Jew to a rejected lover when they realized the futility of their search for a viable German Jewish identity. In what follows now, I show that the image of the rejected lover marks a certain impasse in the authors' argument about assimilation, and that it helps them conceptualize a move beyond this impasse. The trope of unrequited love allows Goldstein and Wassermann to elaborate new possibilities out of the perceived failure of Jewish emancipation.

Immediately upon its publication, Moritz Goldstein's essay "The German-Jewish Parnassus" sparked much controversy because it called Jews mere administrators of German culture, and unwanted ones at that.[12] Goldstein seems to reiterate the well-worn antisemitic topos of the Jew who necessarily remains external to German culture, who is capable of critique but not creativity. The ensuing controversy, however, has obfuscated the fact that the concept of culture undergoes a decisive change over the course of the essay. Goldstein initially espouses an idea of culture as the expression of a nation's unique spirit and calls upon the Jews to create their own Hebrew-language culture in Germany. However, he realizes that this brand of cultural Zionism offers no solution for German Jews such as himself, who are too deeply immersed in German culture to accomplish the leap into Hebrew and are therefore forced to hover in a perpetual in-between state or diaspora. This impasse leads Goldstein to reconsider the character of German culture and to arrive at an idea of what Aschheim would call "co-constitutionality": *"German culture is to no small degree Jewish culture. For Europe as a whole is probably more Jewish than is generally known"* (291; Goldstein's emphasis).

At this point in the argument Goldstein shifts into the rhetorical register of love. He enjoins the Jews to let go of the unresponsive beloved: "Our relationship to Germany is that of an unhappy love. Rather than endlessly and piteously languishing after the beloved, we should finally be manly enough to rip her, with firm determination, out of our heart—even if a piece of that heart goes with her" (292). The image of the Jew as a rejected lover completes Goldstein's conceptual shift from autochthonous to co-constitutional culture. Rather than assert a clear break, this image reclaims the truly internal relationship of Jews to German culture denied

---

12. See Moritz Goldstein, "Deutsch-jüdischer Parnaß," *Der Kunstwart* 25, no. 11 (1912): 281–94; here 283. All further citations of this article will be included parenthetically in the text.

in their initial representation as mere administrators. The heartbroken Jew seems to suffer from a melancholic attachment to a lost object with which he identifies so thoroughly that he no longer recognizes it as separate. The piece of heart that still adheres to the beloved after she has been erased from memory illustrates the powers of identification. It is only consistent that the essay, which begins with a call for a separation of German and Jewish cultures, ends with an embrace of cultural hybridity. Goldstein argues that Jewish self-affirmation will stop "the exaggerated principle of nationality" (292) and expose the international character of many cultural formations. The figure of the rejected lover both articulates and disarticulates the impasse at which German Jews find themselves.

The figure fulfills a similar function in Jakob Wassermann's memoir *My Life as German and Jew*. Wassermann, who at the time was a successful literary author, records in this work his past struggles for a social and artistic existence. Like Goldstein, he regards antisemitism as the main obstacle to a viable German Jewish identity; and like Goldstein, he gestures toward the possibility of new forms of identity. He begins his memoir by lamenting the inner disharmony that suffuses his life and his being, yet he ends it with an emphatic claim to a dual identity: "I am a German and I am a Jew, one as much and as fully as the other, neither can be unraveled from the other. I feel that in a certain sense this is new."[13] It is significant that Wassermann does not attempt to flesh out this new fusion of the Jewish and the German much further. Rather, he simply abandons his attempts to define "Jewishness" and "Germanness," which had characterized his memoir to this point.

The figure of unrequited love plays a crucial role in the leap into newness. Wassermann repeatedly invokes the Jewish love for things German in *My Life as German and Jew*, most notably in a question that precedes the passage cited above. After realizing that even his closest non-Jewish allies are unable to grasp the depth and the prevalence of antisemitic prejudice, he asks rhetorically: "Does one not feel the greatest sorrow for those one loves most deeply, though that love be entirely unrequited?" (231).[14] One example of such one-sided love is the friendship Wassermann forms in his youth with a Gentile man from an impoverished patrician family. Though never explicitly homoerotic, their relationship contains romantic elements such as irresistible attraction, courtship, jealousy, yearning, and emotional drama. At one point they live together in Zurich, where they spend all of their days and nights together, sharing meager meals and long conversations. Yet a "gulf" (76)

---

13. Jakob Wassermann, *My Life as German and Jew*, trans. S. N. Brainin (New York: Coward-McCann, 1933), 234 (trans. modified). All further citations of *My Life as German and Jew* refer to this translation and will be included parenthetically in the text.

14. Wassermann builds here on a motif he also used in his novels, which depict interreligious love affairs as a form of redemptive transgression. In his first novel, *The Jews of Zirndorf* (*Die Juden von Zirndorf* [Munich: Albert Langen, 1897]), the idea of Jewish renewal is tied up with an opening toward the non-Jewish world figured in sexual relations. The protagonist, who initially distances himself from the Jewish community but later becomes the source of its revitalization, is the offspring of a Christian-Jewish love affair.

opens between them when Wassermann relates how he once lost his job because of his employer's antisemitism. Instead of offering sympathy, the friend contends that Jews can never be fully integrated into German society, and Wassermann soon after takes leave with bitter feelings. When they meet again many years later, the friend concedes that Wassermann might be an exception in which "something like a fusion, a new synthesis" (174) occurred, but he regards this exception as a confirmation of the rule. Wassermann, in contrast, holds that the exception breaks the rule and opens up an entirely new possibility—and it is he who gets the last word, at least in the memoir. It is over and against his friend's arguments about the incompatibility of Germans and Jews that Wassermann posits the possibility of a dual identity.

Despite the difference in their political outlook, Goldstein and Wassermann concur in their use of tropes of love. In both writers, the figure of unrequited love is part of an effort to create an affective resonance, to confront antisemitic hatred with the pathos of love. Yet even more important is its function as a point of dialectical reversal. In both authors, the figure of unrequited love points to the opposite of the text's initial argument. Goldstein calls for a separation of "German" and "Jewish" cultures, but the image of the melancholic lover suggests an abiding attachment. Wassermann conjures the possibility of interreligious harmony, but the relationship with his beloved friend suggests an irreconcilable conflict. These contradictions are indicative of a more general problem the writers encounter in their argument about Jewish assimilation. Neither Goldstein's cultural Zionism nor Wassermann's advocacy of assimilation offers a persuasive solution to the dilemma of Jews whose claims to German culture remain unrecognized or unaccepted. In both writers, the image of the rejected lover serves as a placeholder for an in-between identity that seems as elusive as necessary. The figure of unrequited love gives expression to an impasse and turns it into an opportunity: the opportunity to rethink the project of assimilation.

Love and Universality

Beyond its contribution to the study of German Jewish culture, *Mixed Feelings* seeks to intervene in contemporary debates about multiculturalism, in which *love* is a contested term. On the one hand, the use of love as a model for group relations has been criticized for glossing over or even legitimizing the hegemonic force of a dominant culture. Zygmunt Bauman, for instance, argues that the literary discourse of love serves to resolve social conflicts in an idealized private sphere.[15] On the other hand, contemporary theorists such as Giorgio Agamben, Alain Badiou, and Kenneth Reinhard turn toward love in their search for new models of singularity and

---

15. See Zygmunt Bauman, *Modernity and Ambivalence* (Ithaca, N.Y.: Cornell University Press, 1991), 197–230.

universality. They define love as a mode of relating to others in their singularity, an alternative to the commodification of cultural difference in some strands of contemporary multiculturalism. One aim of this book—its presentist concern, if you wish—is to show that the work of German Jewish thinkers and writers can be a vital resource in this debate; that they offer new and incisive ideas about love as an ethical and political force in the here and now.

At this point it is necessary to preempt an objection that may be raised against my project: that a focus on love implies a Christian bias, a view of German Jewish thought through a lens external to it. As I will show, German Jewish writers deliberately and creatively appropriated a theme often associated with Christianity. They produced their own and unique visions of the role of love in the constitution of communities. *Mixed Feelings* is framed by two such visions. In the second half of the eighteenth century, Moses Mendelssohn based his argument for an unconditional emancipation of the Jews on the idea of brotherly love, which at the time had mostly Christian connotations but which Mendelssohn reclaimed as a core value of Judaism. At the beginning of the twentieth century, Franz Rosenzweig tied his call for a Jewish "dissimilation" to the Judaic idea of revelation, which he very much defined in terms of love, as an outpouring of divine love and a call to neighbor-love. Although my project reconstructs the many ways that love has been used in the debates about Jewish emancipation and acculturation, it highlights one particular strand in this discourse. *Mixed Feelings* traces a critical countertradition of German Jewish writers who mobilize tropes of love to find new ways of realizing Jewish particularity within German culture and society. This countertradition, I argue, can make germane contributions to today's debates about multiculturalism.

How can love, perhaps the most private of emotions and experiences, create new models of community? There are of course many forms of familial, religious, and political love that are directed at something beyond the individual; we can love our parents, God, a culture, or a nation. Yet contemporary theorists who revisit the idea of love have in mind something more radical—and more paradoxical—than the harnessing of emotions for social and political ends. In *The Coming Community*, Giorgio Agamben argues that the *singularity* experienced in romantic love ushers in a new kind of communality. Agamben describes in this book the foundation of a politics beyond identity and of a community devoid of essence. Only if communities are not premised on fixed identities, and political demands are not mere reflexes of group interests, can the political constitute an open space of transformation and possibility. According to Agamben, such political communities are based on human beings in their *whatever singularity*, by which he means a form of selfhood that hovers between the individual and the generic, or the particular and the universal, that is rooted in the self yet oriented toward another. It needs to be noted that the English translation "whatever" misses the crucial dimension of desire implied in the Latin word that Agamben uses—*quodlibet*, or "what pleases"—and that expresses this fundamental relationality.

Agamben's first example of relating to others in their *whatever singularity* is love, that is, an individual's intense emotional attraction to another individual. He emphasizes that we do not love someone for the qualities that s/he embodies and that could be described by adjectives. Rather, we love someone in his or her "being such as it is," a phrase that points to the inadequacy of attributive language with respect to the other's uniqueness: "Love is never directed toward this or that property of the loved one (being blond, being small, being tender, being lame), but neither does it neglect the properties in favor of an insipid generality (universal love): The lover wants the loved one *with all of its predicates*, its being such as it is. The lover desires the *as* only insofar as it is *such*—this is the lover's particular fetishism."[16] This passage recalls Roland Barthes's idea that love suspends linguistic classification—"one cannot speak *of* the other, *about* the other; every attribute is false, painful, erroneous, awkward: the other is *unqualifiable*"[17]—while pushing it further. Agamben's provocative claim is that the singularity experienced in love enables a new kind of collectivity: *whatever singularity* is the foundation of political communities that do not hinge upon fixed identities or conditions of belonging.

Love is for Agamben only one of the realms in which *whatever singularity* is revealed and witnessed; it is but an example and dropped from consideration in his further reflections on community and politics. Whereas Agamben mentions love only in passing, other theorists argue for a more fundamental connection between love and universality. Though their focus is often on neighbor-love, they retain the hallmark of romantic love—the attachment to a person in his or her singularity—which is seen as the foundation of a new form of universality. Thus Kenneth Reinhard draws on German Jewish thinkers to differentiate between Jewish and Christian conceptions of neighbor-love, and between two forms of universality that may emerge from neighbor-love: infinity and totality.

Reinhard bases this argument on the changing meaning of neighbor-love in Leviticus 19:18 ("Thou shalt not take vengeance, nor bear any grudge against the children of thy people but thou shalt love thy neighbor as thyself: I am the LORD") and 19:34 ("The stranger that sojourneth with you shall be unto you as the home-born among you, and thou shalt love him as thyself; for ye were strangers in the land of Egypt: I am the LORD your God"). The Hebrew term for "neighbor" in Leviticus 19:18 is *re'a*, a word that can mean "friend," "fellow," "neighbor," or even "another person." Its exact meaning in this passage has been subject to debate. Whereas traditional rabbinic commentaries tend to read *re'a* as "fellow Jew," exponents of German Reform Judaism, including Hermann Cohen and Ernst Simon, understand the term to mean "fellow human being." They argue that the expansion of the injunction to love one's neighbor to the "stranger" (Hebrew, *ger*) in Leviticus 19:34 makes it clear

---

16. Giorgio Agamben, *The Coming Community*, trans. Michael Hardt (Minneapolis: University of Minnesota Press, 1993), 2 (Agamben's emphasis).

17. *A Lover's Discourse*, 35; Barthes's emphasis.

that it is not limited to Jews. Reinhard generally concurs but points out that the semantic expansion is more complicated than most (and especially Christian) notions of universal love suggests. Rather than include every human in the commandment, Leviticus 19:34 extends it to one form of the human, the *ger* or "stranger," in a way that does not fully obliterate the earlier meaning of *re'a* or "neighbor." The duality of terms persists and effectively makes both me and my neighbor a stranger to ourselves. Rather than a *totality* that encompasses all human beings, Jewish universalism produces an *infinity* into which strangers can enter one by one:

> I would argue that the effect of this proximity is not to construct a category of universality so much as to bring out a certain strangeness, both in the figure of the neighbor and in the condition of the Jew who is so enjoined. . . . In the ethical space that opens in the nearness of Leviticus 19:18 to 19:34, the *ger* dwelling among Jews is "like" the Jews only insofar as they were themselves *unlike* someone else, "strangers in the land of Egypt." The parallelism of the two commandments does not imply that the injunction to love the neighbor is based on a common positive feature, practice, or ideal that all humanity shares, but rather that neighbor-love involves an element of essential *difference*, the fact that both the self and the neighbor are "strange," internally alienated from the larger group, whether that be Egypt or Israel, and that this structural parallel is the only absolute basis for their solidarity.[18]

The idea of a solidarity emerging from the shared experience of estrangement is an element of what one may call, in a variation of Derrida's phrase, a "politics of love."[19] *Mixed Feelings* approaches such a politics via erotic or romantic love, which arguably differs from neighbor-love in its intensity, exclusiveness, and bodily involvement. However, as Slavoj Žižek, Eric Santner, and Kenneth Reinhard observe in the introduction to their book *The Neighbor*, the difference is rarely an absolute one. Both Jewish and Christian commentators have noted that the Hebrew word *ahavah* used in Leviticus 19:18 and 19:34 can also refer to sexual or romantic love. Commentators have often tried to diminish a sense of inappropriate affect by reading *ahavah* as a metaphorical expression or as a reference to God's love.[20] *Mixed Feelings* eschews such distinctions and shows how stories and figures of romantic love generate new visions of living together in an inescapably pluralist world. One of my key theoretical resources here is the work of Franz Rosenzweig. As I will show in chapter 6, Rosenzweig provocatively and unapologetically

---

18. Kenneth Reinhard, "The Ethics of the Neighbor: Universalism, Particularism, Exceptionalism," *Journal of Textual Reasoning* 4, no. 1 (November 2005): 1–21; here 7. See also Reinhard's elaboration of the idea of Jewish universalism in "Universalism and the Jewish Exception: Lacan, Badiou, Rosenzweig," *Umbr(a): A Journal of the Unconscious* 1 (2005): 43–71.

19. Jacques Derrida, *The Politics of Friendship*, trans. George Collins (London: Verso, 1997).

20. Slavoj Žižek, Eric L. Santner, and Kenneth Reinhard, *The Neighbor: Three Inquiries in Political Theology* (Chicago: University of Chicago Press, 2005), 6.

links different forms of love. Taking his cue from the biblical Song of Songs, he argues that erotic love is an instantiation rather than a metaphor of divine love, which in turn inspires and informs all neighbor-love. For Rosenzweig, the ethics of neighbor-love—which for him as for Reinhard involves an infinite connectivity between singulars—is inextricably tied to the upheaval of body and soul triggered by divine love and experienced in erotic love.

The work of German Jewish writers is uniquely suited to elaborate this connection between love and difference. Part of my argument is that this sets them apart from many of their Christian or Gentile counterparts. While both Jewish and non-Jewish authors contributed to the debates about emancipation and assimilation, their writings are to some extent divided along the lines of totality and infinity, of unity and difference. As I will show, in non-Jewish authors romantic love and marriage tend to be totalizing models of integration. From Friedrich Schlegel's idea of a union of opposites to Achim von Arnim's ambivalence about Christian-Jewish love to Heinrich von Treitschke's antisemitic call for intermarriage, many non-Jewish authors equate romantic love with a reduction of differences. In contrast, many Jewish writers conceive of romantic love as an opportunity to express and negotiate differences. In thinkers such as Moses Mendelssohn, Franz Rosenzweig, and Hannah Arendt, the idea of love provides an impetus for the creation of pluralist communities. Literary authors such as Georg Hermann, Arthur Schnitzler, and Else Lasker-Schüler compose love stories that proliferate the differences between religious or ethnic groups while also forging new connections between them. (The term "German Jewish culture" has therefore two slightly different meanings in this book. It can refer either to the discursive space in which the terms of Jewish integration were negotiated—by both Jews and non-Jews—or to the cultural production of German-speaking Jews.[21])

The logic of differentiation in German Jewish writers resonates with Alain Badiou's theory of love as disjunction. A key interlocutor in contemporary debates about love, universality, and multiculturalism, Badiou emphatically rejects the Romantic idea of love as fusion in works such as "What Is Love?" and *In Praise of Love*.[22] He maintains that rather than the One, love produces the Two. When two people fall in love—an event that can in no way be predicted or precipitated—they begin to construe the world from the perspective of the Two, which in turn brings their differences to the fore. They see the world not

---

21. My definition of Jewish authorship follows Dan Miron, who emphasizes an author's existential—rather than essential—Jewishness and also takes into account his or her reception. According to Miron, an author counts as Jewish if his or her work "evinces an interest in . . . [his or her] sense of *Judesein*, being Jewish, or is being read by readers who experience it as if it showed interest and were conditioned by the writer's being Jewish." Dan Miron, *From Continuity to Contiguity: Toward a New Jewish Literary Thinking* (Stanford, Calif.: Stanford University Press, 2010), 405.

22. See Alain Badiou, "What Is Love?," trans. Justin Clemens, *Umbr(a): A Journal of the Unconscious* 1 (1996): 37–53; Alain Badiou with Nicolas Truong, *In Praise of Love*, trans. Peter Bush (New York: The New Press, 2012).

only from their own point of view but also from that of their beloved. They plan their life as a shared life, in which every event has a meaning for themselves as well as for their beloved. The loving couple experiences a unity-in-division, or a proximity-in-distance. Because love creates a structure of Twoness, it inculcates in humans the experience of difference as such. Lovers move from the singular to the universal by passing through difference. In this way love becomes "an individual experience of potential universality."[23]

As I will show, the work of German Jewish writers calls for a modification and expansion of this theory in at least two ways. First, their creative use of the idea of love challenges Badiou's clear distinction between love and politics. For Badiou love and politics are two different truth procedures, as he terms them, which differ both in reach and in effect. While love creates the Two out of the One, politics creates the one out of the many—namely, a collective that can agree on principles of justice and equality.[24] Much of what I say in this book about tropes of love as a source of sociopolitical renewal goes against such a clear distinction between private emotions and public policy. Second, Badiou defines the difference that emerges in love and guides the lovers' construction of the world quite narrowly as sexual difference. Although he tries to avoid gender essentialisms by speaking of male and female "positions," which do not necessarily have to be assumed by men and women, respectively, he is primarily concerned with sexual difference. As I will show, German Jewish thinkers and writers help push this idea in new directions by suggesting that differences of religion, class, or culture can become manifest in love. In his correspondence with his Christian lover, Franz Rosenzweig develops an intricate theory of how their love affair ultimately enhances the distance between them and anchors each of them more firmly in their respective religious tradition. This insight applies to many of the unfulfilled love stories analyzed in this book, stories in which the two partners never really come together. These stories allow religious and cultural differences to crystallize, thereby rendering them more tangible—but also newly negotiable.

Structure of the Argument

In this book, I seek to unlock the potential of the trope of the "German-Jewish love affair" by tracing its genesis around the beginning of the nineteenth century

23. Badiou, *In Praise of Love*, 17.

24. See, for instance, Badiou, *In Praise of Love*, 54. It is interesting in this regard that Badiou's critique of contemporary multiculturalism in a book on Saint Paul—who famously reduced the biblical commandments to the injunction to love one's neighbor as oneself—ultimately culminates in a vision of sameness. See Alain Badiou, *Saint Paul: The Foundation of Universalism*, trans. Ray Brassier (Stanford, Calif.: Stanford University Press, 2003); and Eric Santner's perceptive critique of Badiou's politics in "Miracles Happen: Benjamin, Rosenzweig, Freud, and the Matter of the Neighbor," in Žižek, Santner, and Reinhard, *The Neighbor*, 76–133.

and its transformation around the beginning of the twentieth century. I do not attempt a complete literary or conceptual history—the material would be too abundant and the questions too manifold—but rather focus on two transformative moments that produced particularly rich clusters of stories and tropes of Christian-Jewish love. These are moments in which new literary discourses of love developed while the position of Jews vis-à-vis German society was intensely debated: (1) Around 1800, literature actively promoted, rather than merely reflected, the rise of the Romantic love ideal and the shift from arranged to love-based marriages. In the German-speaking countries, this change in the theory and practice of love coincided with the beginnings of Jewish emancipation. Part I of this book shows how both supporters and opponents of Jewish emancipation based their arguments on tropes of love. (2) Around 1900, the rise of racial antisemitism had called into question the promises of emancipation and led to a crisis of German Jewish identity. This period saw an increase in public debates about Christian-Jewish intermarriage, which were tied up with racial discourses and concerns about procreation, heredity, and the mutability and immutability of the Jewish body. Part II of this book shows how turn-of-the-century German Jewish authors wrested love away from biologist thought and reinstated it as a model of sociopolitical integration.

In terms of methodology, the book offers a *discourse analysis* of the term *love*. I argue that the term at times became a nodal point in the discourse of Jewish emancipation, in the sense that it structured and partially fixed this discourse but also opened it up to new possibilities.[25] Each chapter traces the ways that "love" enters into the debates about emancipation and assimilation at a particular juncture in history. These are turning points at which the debates about German Jewish identity grow more intense: the Enlightenment discussion of civic equality; the Christian-Jewish encounters in the Romantic salons; the antisemitic turn of the younger Romantics; the debates about "interracial" marriage around 1900; the crisis of Jewish identity in turn-of-the-century Vienna; and the trend toward Jewish "dissimilation" around the First World War. My focus is on well-known literary works, which I situate in a broader context of political debates, philosophical essays, and less canonical literary texts, including popular plays, middlebrow novels, and feuilletons. This discourse analysis shows how love functions as a trope across the genres, disclosing a conceptual history that sheds new light on the cultural exchange between Jews and Germans—terms that should be enclosed in quotation marks because their meanings intersect and change over time. Another way of describing my approach is as a *functional analysis* of representations of interreligious and interethnic love. I ask how writers and thinkers use the idea of love—as

---

25. On the concept of the nodal point, see Ernesto Laclau and Chantal Mouffe, *Hegemony and Socialist Strategy: Towards a Radical Democratic Politics*, 2nd ed. (New York: Verso, 2014), 98–100.

a concept, a story, or a metaphor—to create new visions of cultural, social, and political integration.[26]

The book begins with the two eighteenth-century thinkers who first demanded an unconditional political emancipation of the Jews: Moses Mendelssohn, the leading philosopher of the Haskalah or Jewish Enlightenment, and Gotthold Ephraim Lessing, the influential Enlightenment thinker, dramatist, and publicist. Chapter 1 shows how both Mendelssohn and Lessing invoke the possibility of interfaith love to stake their claims to civic equality. In *Jerusalem* (1783), Mendelssohn affirmatively cites the Judaic injunction against interfaith marriage while appealing to the "brotherly love," or political goodwill, of his Christian readers. Lessing plots his famous plays on religious tolerance, *The Jews* (1749) and *Nathan the Wise* (1779), around impossible Christian-Jewish romances. The plays' logic is best described as one of incomplete sublimation, a redirection of erotic energies that never comes to a standstill and that thwarts any complacent vision of interfaith harmony. Both Lessing and Mendelssohn suggest that (what I will term) "affective kinship" may serve as a foundation of communities in which different religious groups enjoy political equality. At the same time, their awareness of the precariousness of such kinship—and of all interreligious love—enhances the appeal character of their texts.

Chapter 2 moves into the early Romantic period, when the increased social interaction between Jews and Christians in the Romantic salons led to much-discussed interfaith love affairs that found their way into literature. When in 1799 Friedrich Schlegel, the leading theoretician of German Romanticism, published *Lucinde*, the clearest example of the Romantic love ideal in German literature, it was widely assumed that the novel was based on the author's relationship with Dorothea Veit, the oldest daughter of Moses Mendelssohn. I argue that Schlegel's transformation of love into a model for society hinges upon the elision of religious difference in favor of sexual opposition, an elision that explains the striking absence of references to Jews and Judaism in the novel. The second part of the chapter reads Veit's own novel *Florentin* (1801), in which love conspicuously fails to secure the hero the sense of home and identity he desires, as a critical response to *Lucinde* and a subversion of the Romantic love ideal. In resisting the homogenizing force of romantic love, Veit continues the political project of Mendelssohn, who sought to harness the powers of love for Jewish emancipation while guarding against forced assimilation.

Chapter 3 shows how easily tropes of love can be co-opted for ideological purposes. Among the younger generation of German Romantics we find explicit literary

---

26. For a similar functional analysis of love stories in a different context, see John Urang's *Legal Tender: Love and Legitimacy in the East German Cultural Imagination* (Ithaca, N.Y.: Cornell University Press, 2010). As is appropriate for a functional or discourse analysis, I will not focus on biographical experience. I will consider an author's own experience of interfaith love only when it clearly matters, for instance, when it shapes a book's reception (as in the case of Friedrich Schlegel's *Lucinde*) or when an author explicitly reflects on real-life experience in his work (as in Franz Rosenzweig's letters to Margit Rosenstock-Huessy).

treatments of Christian-Jewish love that are at the same time undeniably antisemitic. These writers espoused a German nationalism that increasingly included xenophobic and antisemitic elements. They embraced antisemitic views to fend off the perceived dangers of industrial capitalism, while expressing their ambivalence about economic modernization through the literary motif of Christian-Jewish love. Exemplary of their thinking is Achim von Arnim, the author of a notorious anti-Jewish speech that decries the alleged superficiality and deceptiveness of Jewish assimilation. Even in his more sympathetic portrayals of Jews, Arnim engages in a form of narrative scapegoating, which becomes particularly clear when he depicts Christian-Jewish love affairs against the backdrop of an emerging German nationalism. In works such as "The Reconciliation in the Summer Holiday" (1811) and *Gentry by Entailment* (1819), stories of failing interfaith love serve to mask the contradictions that trouble Arnim's visions of social harmony and political unity.

Chapter 4 jumps to the turn of the century, when the rise of racial antisemitism has fostered a new Jewish self-awareness and rendered "interracial" love and marriage central to the public debates about German Jewish identity. I analyze three German Jewish writers of different and paradigmatic political orientations, who use love stories to diagnose the reasons for the faltering of emancipation: the assimilationist Ludwig Jacobowski, the Zionist Max Nordau, and the mainstream liberal Georg Hermann. Their works, including Jacobowski's *Werther the Jew* (1892), Nordau's *Doctor Kohn* (1899), and Hermann's *Jettchen Gebert* (1906), show how love stories potentially escape the ideological constraints of increasingly racialized models of identity. On the one hand, the love plot affords an opportunity to expose the obstacles encountered by Jews seeking integration in times of rising antisemitism. On the other hand, the open endings of most love stories and the ambiguous use of racial language allow the authors to eschew a final verdict on the success or failure of integration. The love plot, I argue, generates a host of equivocations between the social and the biological, and the particular and the universal, creating a metaphorical surplus that opens up venues to rethink the project of Jewish emancipation and assimilation.

Chapter 5 considers a locale famously fraught with questions of sex, love, and identity: turn-of-the-century Vienna. Vienna was the birthplace of psychoanalysis and a center of the crisis of modern Jewish identity, especially after the election of an openly antisemitic mayor in 1895. While Sigmund Freud maintained a resonant silence about Jewish-Gentile attractions, several bedfellows of psychoanalysis explicitly thematize such attractions. In his highly influential philosophy of sexuality, *Sex and Character* (1903), Otto Weininger rejects love as a model for Jewish-Gentile rapprochement in favor of a radical Jewish self-transformation, or rather, self-annihilation. I read Arthur Schnitzler's novel *The Road into the Open* (1908), which draws an analogy between a Gentile's uneven friendship with a Jewish writer and his love affair with a woman from a lower social class, as a critique of Weininger's philosophical tract. Whereas Weininger can accept Jewish assimilation only as a form of suicidal striving, Schnitzler depicts assimilation as a mutual, quasi-erotic exchange across open boundaries. Against Freud's conspicuous silence about and Weininger's vehement rejection of Jewish-Gentile love, Schnitzler advances a vision of Jewish integration in which Eros has a place.

Chapter 6 turns to two German Jewish modernists who produced very emphatic visions of interreligious encounters in and through love. Around the First World War, the increase of antisemitism and the trend toward Jewish "dissimilation" reopened the debates about German Jewish identity. At this time Franz Rosenzweig and Else Lasker-Schüler define love as a quasi-religious event that ushers in the possibility of political renewal. In *The Star of Redemption* (1921), Rosenzweig develops a concept of revelatory love as the foundation of a new kind of universality. Revelatory love, which is modeled on divine love and experienced in erotic love, is conceived as an act of singularization that at the same time exposes the subject to others. As such it enables neighbor-love and a new form of community, the infinitely open neighborhood. In the second half of this chapter I show that Lasker-Schüler's bold reinterpretation of biblical stories in *Hebrew Ballads* (1913) and other texts is a poetic performance of revelatory love. In contrast to earlier Romantic models, love is here a force of disjunction rather than unification, leading to a proliferation rather than a reduction of differences.

In the conclusion, I suggest that this model is still relevant in the post-Holocaust period. I show that even Scholem's "Jews and Germans," despite its explicit rejection of the past Jewish love for things German, relies on tropes of love to conjure the possibility of a future German-Jewish dialogue. Another famous German Jewish thinker, Hannah Arendt, is more outspoken in her valorization of love as a mode of sociopolitical intervention. In her biography of a Jewish *salonnière* of the Romantic era, Rahel Levin Varnhagen, Arendt affirms the love of the pariah as a form of solidarity that is rooted in shared experiences of marginalization. Finally, I turn to the decade after the 1990 unification of Germany, when the theme of interreligious or intercultural love enjoyed much popularity both in mainstream feature films and in contemporary German Jewish writers. Barbara Honigmann, for instance, dramatizes failing Jewish-Gentile love affairs to show how memories of the Third Reich continue to disrupt German-Jewish relations in the present. But this is not a negation of love as a trope of interreligious or intercultural mediation. Love remains an important trope in Honigmann, one that allows her to imagine a new kind of German Jewish diaspora.

PART I

1800

Romantic Love and the Beginnings of Jewish Emancipation

Romantic love took on a special significance in Western societies during the second half of the eighteenth century. Around this time, the increase in social mobility and individual freedom gave rise to a new ideal of love-based marriage that gradually replaced earlier practices of arranged marriage. Love came to be seen as the foundation of a person's most important relationship in life, and the selection of the right partner as paramount for one's happiness. As people began to conceive of themselves as individuals rather than as representatives of a class, they regarded love relationships as an opportunity to experience and articulate their own uniqueness. The literature of the time both reflects and promotes this process of individuation. Whereas medieval and early modern romances usually depict the encounter of two fairly stereotypical lovers, the adventures they experience and the obstacles they overcome, the modern novel is much more focused on the inner life of the literary characters. Their thoughts and feelings are at the center of the text. As Anthony Giddens argues, romantic love sets into motion a process of self-reflection and self-narration: "Romantic love introduced the idea of a narrative into an individual's life—a formula which radically extended the reflexivity of sublime love. The telling of a story is one of the meanings of 'romance', but this story now became individualised, inserting self and other into a personal narrative which had no particular reference to wider social processes."[1]

If romantic love is conceived as a deeply personal experience without immediate social meaning, it nevertheless has a social function. Giddens observes that romantic love does not take the individual out of society in the way that *amour passion* did. Rather, romantic love is a "generic social force,"[2] because it induces the individual to engage in long-term planning and reflection, which inevitably have a social dimension. The conflation of love, sex, and marriage in the Romantic love ideal is crucial in this regard.[3] Marriage domesticates erotic desire and imbues volatile emotions with the promise of permanence. The Romantic love ideal furthermore places a whole new emphasis on the marital relationship at the expense of other forms of kinship. Conceived as a personal bond based on individual choice and attraction, marriage takes primacy over all other personal bonds, especially those to one's birth family.[4] In *Love as Passion*—a work I will discuss at greater length in chapter 2—the sociologist Niklas Luhmann offers further observations about the social function of romantic love. He argues that modernity is characterized by two opposing tendencies, an increase of impersonal relations on the one hand and an intensified search for intimate relationships on the other. In this view, romantic love is a compensatory mechanism in a world of social fragmentation and social anonymity. In love and marriage, one relates to the other as an individual with a unique worldview and life story, as opposed to reducing the other to her transitory social role in places such as the factory, the department store, or the doctor's office.[5]

Mixed Feelings builds on these insights about the social function of romantic love and pushes them in new directions. I show how the idea of love as a medium of individuation helped recast the relations between different religious, ethnic, and cultural groups. The first part of this book analyzes the *discursive intersection*

---

1. Anthony Giddens, *The Transformation of Intimacy: Sexuality, Love, and Eroticism in Modern Societies* (Stanford, Calif.: Stanford University Press, 1992), 39–40.

2. Giddens, *The Transformation of Intimacy*, 45.

3. I capitalize the term "Romantic love ideal" to tie it more clearly to the intellectual movement of Romanticism, although some of its central elements were developed during the Enlightenment. The idea of romantic love, that is, of an intense emotional and physical attraction between two people, has of course existed for very a long time. However, the late eighteenth century gave birth to the Romantic love ideal, which conflates love, sex, and marriage and places the romantic relationship at the center of an individual's life.

4. Many scholars agree that the conjugal family had become more important than the consanguinal family by the end of the eighteenth century—which is not to say that consanguinal family ties no longer played any role. On the shifting functions of conjugal and consanguinal bonds, see, for instance, Stephanie Coontz, *Marriage: A History; How Love Conquered Marriage* (New York: Penguin, 2006); Ruth Perry, *Novel Relations: The Transformation of Kinship in English Literature and Culture, 1748–1818* (New York: Cambridge University Press, 2004); Günter Sasse, *Die aufgeklärte Familie: Untersuchungen zur Genese, Funktion und Realitätsbezogenheit des familialen Wertsystems im Drama der Aufklärung* (Tübingen: Max Niemeyer, 1988).

5. See Niklas Luhmann, *Love as Passion: The Codification of Intimacy,* trans. Jeremy Gaines and Doris L. Jones (Stanford, Calif.: Stanford University Press, 1998).

between representations of romantic love and the debates about Jewish emancipation, which also began in the second half of the eighteenth century. This intersection is no coincidence. The notion of civic equality and the valorization of romantic love are both part and parcel of the social transformations of modernity. Both are expressions of individualism and egalitarianism bound up with biopolitical and sociopolitical concerns. Ever since the publication of the first volume of Michel Foucault's *The History of Sexuality* it has been recognized that the Romantic love ideal developed in the context of biopolitics—that is, the state's attempt to control the population by disciplining the physical and social bodies of its inhabitants.[6] Similarly, public calls for Jewish emancipation were often tied to the expectation that the extension of rights to Jews would promote social homogeneity and boost the state's economy. With these contexts in mind, *Mixed Feelings* focuses on the sociopolitical *visions* that become possible when Jewish emancipation is discussed in terms of love.

The chapters in part I are structured around three literary-philosophical movements that helped redefine the place of Jews in German politics and society. Within little more than a generation, the discussion of Jewish rights shifted rapidly: from the first Enlightenment calls for civic equality (which would take a long time to materialize) to the Christian-Jewish interaction in the early Romantic salons (which for a brief period seemed to anticipate full equality) to the anti-Jewish turn of the younger generation of German Romantics (which is often regarded a precursor of modern antisemitism). My analysis of these three intellectual movements shows how love around 1800 becomes a generative force for thinking through broad social interactions, if not an outright model for social and political relations.

I begin with the Enlightenment, when the debates about Jewish emancipation began and the Romantic love ideal first arose, several decades before the literary movement called Romanticism took hold.[7] The authors discussed in chapter 1, Moses Mendelssohn and Gotthold Ephraim Lessing, contributed to the debates about Jewish emancipation as well as to the rise of the Romantic love ideal. Lessing's bourgeois tragedies promote the ideal of love-based marriage, and Mendelssohn's letters to his fiancée and eventual wife express his romantic feelings and rejection of conventional arranged marriage. In their writings about religious toleration and Jewish emancipation, Lessing and Mendelssohn also allude to interfaith romance, but they ultimately call for brotherly love as the appropriate affect

---

6. See Michel Foucault, *The History of Sexuality,* vol. 1, *An Introduction,* trans. Robert Hurley (New York: Pantheon, 1978). On the history of sexuality in Germany, see especially Isabel V. Hull, *Sexuality, State, and Civil Society in Germany, 1700–1815* (Ithaca, N.Y.: Cornell University Press, 1996). Hull argues that during the eighteenth century the locus of social control shifted from the absolutist state to civil society. She shows how the representatives of civil society sought to harness the sexual drive for the public good by tethering the drive to love and marriage.

7. On some convergences between Enlightenment and Romantic conceptions of love, see also Edgar Landgraf, "Romantic Love and the Enlightenment: From Gallantry and Seduction to Authenticity and Self-Validation," *The German Quarterly* 77, no. 1 (Winter 2004): 29–46.

between members of different religions. However, as I will show, the idea of inter-faith romance retains some of its power and gives their writings a greater political urgency. Chapter 2 shows how the early Romantic author Friedrich Schlegel and Mendelssohn's daughter Dorothea Veit, who became lovers and eventually married, derive new models of society from romantic love while foregoing explicit references to religious difference. The writings of the following generation of German Romantic authors call into question the idea of love as a force of socio-political innovation, however. Chapter 3 shows how Achim von Arnim depicts failing Christian-Jewish love affairs to argue for the continued exclusion of Jews from German politics and society. His use of love to foreclose rather than negotiate cross-religious identification throws into even clearer relief the progressive claims of Enlightenment and early Romantic writers.

1

Interfaith Love and the
Pursuit of Emancipation

Moses Mendelssohn and
Gotthold Ephraim Lessing

And you, dear brothers and fellow men, who follow the teachings of Jesus, should
you find fault with us for doing what the founder of your religion did himself, and
confirmed by his authority? Should you believe that you cannot *love us in return
as brothers* and *unite with us as citizens* as long as we are outwardly distinguished
from you by the ceremonial law, do not eat with you, *do not marry you*, which, as
far as we can see, the founder of your religion would neither have done himself nor
permitted us to do?

Thus begins the peroration of Moses Mendelssohn's *Jerusalem, or on Religious
Power and Judaism* (*Jerusalem oder über religiöse Macht und Judentum*, 1783), which
laid the philosophical foundations for the political emancipation of Jews in the German
states.[1] Mendelssohn, the spiritual leader of the Haskalah or Jewish Enlightenment,
outlines there the principles of a state that would grant rights to citizens
irrespective of their religious affiliation. The first part of *Jerusalem* promotes a strict
separation between church and state, and the second part shows that traditional
Judaism is fully compatible with the precepts of the secular state. The questions
in the passage just quoted are, of course, rhetorical, and their answers would spell
out Mendelssohn's vision of the position of Jews in the modern state: they would
enjoy equal rights and be able to observe the Judaic law in its entirety. Jews would

---

1. Moses Mendelssohn, *Jerusalem, or on Religious Power and Judaism*, trans. Allan Arkush (Hanover, N.H.: University Press of New England, 1983), 135 (my emphasis). All further citations of *Jerusalem* refer to this translation and will be included parenthetically in the text.

form new affective ties with their Christian neighbors while remaining identifiable, and in some ways segregated, as a group. Of particular interest in this passage is Mendelssohn's distinction between two kinds of personal bonds between Jews and Christians. Mendelssohn cites the Judaic injunction against interfaith marriage as an example of a religious law that must be respected if the idea of religious tolerance is to have any meaning. He pits such marriage against another kind of personal bond between Jews and Christians, which he places squarely within the project of civic integration: brotherly love.

Gotthold Ephraim Lessing, Mendelssohn's Christian friend and ally in the struggle for Jewish emancipation, dramatizes interfaith romance much more extensively than Mendelssohn before deflecting attention from it. Both *The Jews* (*Die Juden*, 1749) and *Nathan the Wise* (*Nathan der Weise*, 1779) feature an impossible Christian-Jewish love affair in which at least one of the partners contemplates the possibility of marriage but abandons the thought after a revelation of true identities. In *The Jews*, the traveler who has finally identified himself as Jewish explains that "fate" prevents him from marrying the daughter of the Christian baron. In *Nathan the Wise*, the Christian Templar learns that the Jewish girl with whom he fell in love was born a Christian and is, in fact, his sister. Since he cannot marry her, he has to overcome his erotic passion in favor of sibling affection—a brotherly love of sorts. The transformation of interfaith romance into brotherly love in Lessing and Mendelssohn calls to mind the larger set of oppositions often used to characterize the Enlightenment approach to Jewish emancipation: between public and private, friendship and love, males and females. The debate about Jewish civil rights took place in the semipublic sphere of journals, theaters, and learned societies, at some distance from the domesticity of marital life. Friendships between male intellectuals were a key element in the new sociability between Jews and Christians, but interfaith marriage remained anathema to the Haskalah and of limited interest to the Enlightenment at large.[2]

In this chapter, I read Lessing's and Mendelssohn's reflections on interfaith love and marriage in the light of their interventions in the debates about Jewish emancipation. The early 1780s mark a turning point in these debates, a shift from the idea of religious toleration to that of political-juridical equality for religious minorities. Under the rule of Frederick II, Prussia had practiced religious tolerance yet placed a host of administrative restrictions on Jews. The New Revised General Privilege and Regulation for the Jews in Prussia (1750) strictly limited the number of Jewish residents in the state and tightly regulated their access to professional and social

---

2. This is not to deny that the theme of marriage was important to the German Enlightenment. In fact, an article on civil marriage in the journal *Berlinische Monatsschrift* raised important questions about the relationship between state and religion and sparked the debate about the question "What is Enlightenment?" See Michael Thomas Taylor, "'Was heißt Aufklärung?' Eine Fußnote zur Ehekrise," in *Vor der Familie: Grenzbedingungen einer modernen Institution*, by Albrecht Koschorke et al. (Munich: Konstanz University Press/Wilhelm Fink, 2010), 51–95.

opportunities. Mendelssohn himself was painfully aware of the limitations imposed by Prussian laws. When he came to Berlin as a poor Talmud student in 1743, all he could obtain, with the help of a rich benefactor, was a temporary resident permit. Even later, after Frederick II had granted the famous philosopher a lifelong resident permit, Mendelssohn only held the status of an "unprivileged protected Jew," which among other things meant that he could not transmit his right of residence to his descendants. These conditions became the subject of fresh debate in the early 1780s, when key representatives of the Enlightenment took first steps toward the political emancipation of the Jews. The scholar Christian Wilhelm von Dohm made a plea for admitting Jews to citizenship in *On the Civil Improvement of the Jews* (*Über die bürgerliche Verbesserung der Juden*, 1781). The Habsburg ruler Joseph II promulgated the Edict of Tolerance (1782), which lifted a number of restrictions on the economic and cultural life of Jews.

Compared to these progressive thinkers of their time, Mendelssohn and Lessing were more radical in that they demanded an *unconditional* emancipation of the Jews. Whereas the Habsburg edict was inspired by statist rationales and ultimately reaffirmed the dominance of the Catholic Church, and whereas Dohm accepted stereotypical notions about Jewish moral inferiority (although he ultimately argued for unconditional emancipation), Lessing and Mendelssohn saw no need for Jews to change before or after they became citizens. In their view, citizenship should be independent of religious affiliation; residency should be a right of the citizen rather than a privilege granted by the ruler. The argument of this chapter is that tropes of love were crucial in articulating this political demand. While neither Mendelssohn nor Lessing promotes intermarriage as a model of integration—in fact, Mendelssohn explicitly rejects it—love more broadly understood plays a central role in their political vision. Both authors conjure affectionate ties between Jews and Christians to stake new claims to civic equality. Translating a religious into a political concept, Mendelssohn appeals to the brotherly love of his Christian readers to solicit support for Jewish emancipation. In Lessing's *Nathan the Wise*, interfaith romance leads to the discovery of a multireligious family network and, more importantly, to a notion of affective kinship as the foundation of an interfaith community (which, however, is never fully realized). I will argue that the precariousness of love in Lessing and Mendelssohn—the fact that love is often one-sided, forgotten, or conflicted—underscores the urgency of their political demand.

Brotherly Love versus Interfaith Marriage: Mendelssohn's *Jerusalem*

It is not surprising that eighteenth-century playwrights stopped short of representing Christian-Jewish intermarriage. Such marriages were not legally possible at the time, except when one of the partners (usually the Jewish one) converted. For Mendelssohn, there would have been additional theological reasons to single out marriage as an area in which the preservation of boundaries between Jews and Christians was imperative. Mendelssohn wanted to promote the cultural and political integration of Jews into German society while maintaining their religious distinctiveness, and endogamous marriage was crucial in this regard. As Benjamin Kaplan has shown, while interfaith marriages (between members of different Christian confessions) existed in the early modern period, and in fact were a major factor in the quest for religious toleration, such marriages also posed a threat to religious minorities intent on preserving their group identity.[3] One might argue that this is especially true of Judaism. In theological terms, the idea of a covenant between God and the Jewish people requires a certain degree of endogamous behavior to safeguard the coherence of the group. In practical terms, it may be more difficult to observe the Judaic law, with its manifold regulations of everyday activities from eating to praying, in a household in which one partner is not Jewish. As I will show, Mendelssohn rejects interfaith marriage as a model of integration and suggests brotherly love as an alternative.

In the one instance in which Mendelssohn mentions a (potential) Christian-Jewish intermarriage in *Jerusalem*, he argues for the right to religious difference in terms of natural rights. In a footnote spanning several pages, Mendelssohn cites a recent divorce case in Vienna. A Jew who had converted to Christianity wanted to stay married to his Jewish wife and raise their children as Christians, but his wife refused to comply (50–52). The case is mentioned in the pamphlet *The Search for Light and Justice* (*Das Forschen nach Licht und Recht*, 1782), which called upon Mendelssohn to explain his relationship to Judaism, and which in fact induced him to write *Jerusalem*. The pamphlet's anonymous author, later revealed to be August Friedrich Cranz, expresses the hope that the court would decide the divorce case "according to the principles of the wise Joseph"—in other words, reject religious difference as a ground for divorce.[4] Mendelssohn disagrees. A marriage, he argues, is primarily an agreement about the education of the future children in which both partners have an equal say—in this case, they entered into an (unspoken) agreement to raise the children as Jewish. If one of the partners later changes his or her religious views and a conflict arises, the case should be resolved in favor of the spouse who complies with the original agreement—in this case, the Jewish wife. As Susan Shapiro has shown, Mendelssohn advances here a new conception of religious tolerance while also engaging a blind spot of classical contract theory. Such theory emphasizes the voluntary character of the *social* contract, in which the individual cedes certain rights to the government, and at the same time naturalizes the *sexual* contract, by which all women are subordinated to all men.

3. Benjamin J. Kaplan, *Divided by Faith: Religious Conflict and the Practice of Toleration in Early Modern Europe* (Cambridge, Mass.: Harvard University Press, 2007), 293.

4. See Moses Mendelssohn, *Gesammelte Schriften: Jubiläumsausgabe*, ed. Alexander Altmann et al. (Stuttgart-Bad Cannstatt: Frommann-Holzboog, 1972–), 8:85.

For thinkers such as Locke and Rousseau, the power differential between men and women in marriage derives from the natural properties of each sex. Mendelssohn undoes this naturalization of gender positions. He conceives of marriage as a social contract into which men and women enter on equal terms, and of women as autonomous individuals capable of making their own decisions. A member of a religious minority, he simultaneously defends a woman's right to follow her conscience and a Jew's right to resist assimilatory pressures.[5]

The long footnote in *Jerusalem* can be read as a sign of Mendelssohn's ambivalence about interfaith marriage, and the difficulty of integrating it into his vision of Christian-Jewish relations. In his personal life Mendelssohn spearheaded new Jewish attitudes toward love and marriage as he embraced a historically new ideal of love-based marriage. He always emphasized that he and his Jewish fiancée, Fromet Gugenheim, had met spontaneously and without the help of a marriage broker. Against all conventions, he exchanged romantic letters with Gugenheim while refusing to perform traditional engagement rituals such as the sending of gifts. He emphatically saw his engagement and marriage as a personal affair of the heart.[6] Yet what if such a purely personal connection were to cross the boundaries between the religions (as would happen to Mendelssohn's daughter Dorothea, who will be discussed in the next chapter)? To be sure, the footnote in *Jerusalem* treats marriage as a contract between rational partners rather than a romantic bond between two fully individuated people. Yet Mendelssohn hints at a deep personal connection between the spouses, and at least for the converted husband—who "is said to have expressed his *desire* to retain his wife who has remained Jewish" (51; my emphasis)—this connection transcends religious difference. The very length of the footnote indicates that Mendelssohn struggles with the possibility of romantic attachments between people from different religions.

Mendelssohn's ambivalence reflects his concern about the totalizing effect of marriage as a model of interreligious rapprochement. In *The Search for Light and Justice*, Cranz expresses his hope that interfaith marriage will help tear down religious barriers. Mendelssohn senses that Cranz's pamphlet is just another public request for Mendelssohn's conversion and reads Cranz's advocacy of interfaith marriage in that light. Commenting on the same Viennese divorce case, Mendelssohn suggests that Cranz's advocacy rests on a faulty conception of tolerance: "Many

5. See Susan E. Shapiro, "The Status of Women and Jews in Moses Mendelssohn's Social Contract Theory: An Exceptional Case," *The German Quarterly* 82, no. 3 (Summer 2009): 373–94. Shapiro uses the concept of the sexual contract developed by Carole Pateman in *The Sexual Contract* (Stanford, Calif.: Stanford University Press, 1988).

6. On the romantic character of the relationship between Mendelssohn and Gugenheim, see Moses Mendelssohn, *Brautbriefe* (Berlin: Schocken, 1936); Jacob Katz, *Tradition and Crisis: Jewish Society at the End of the Middle Ages*, trans. Bernard Dov Cooperman (New York: New York University Press, 1993), 231–32; David Biale, *Eros and the Jews: From Biblical Israel to Contemporary America* (New York: Basic Books, 1992), 153, 165–66; Shmuel Feiner, *Moses Mendelssohn: Sage of Modernity*, trans. Anthony Berris (New Haven, Conn.: Yale University Press, 2010), 62–63.

thanks for all tolerance if its avowed purpose is still religious union! Because the emperor is tolerant, a wife is to be forced to live, contrary to the agreement entered into, in matrimony with a husband who wishes to bring up the children according to his changed [religious] principles!"[7] Mendelssohn adopts the perspective of the divorce-seeking Jewish wife when he views interfaith marriage as a forced assimilation to Christianity. Interfaith marriage comes to epitomize the complete union of faiths Mendelssohn rejects. Against the religious union (*Glaubensvereinigung*) that suppresses religious difference Mendelssohn pits the civic union (*bürgerliche Vereinigung*) that allows religious differences to be expressed in daily life. It is in this context that the idea of brotherly love takes center stage, as an alternative way of creating affective bonds between Jews and Christians. In the last pages of *Jerusalem*, Mendelssohn repeatedly invokes brotherly love while pleading that Jews should be accepted into the state *as* Jews.[8]

Mendelssohn performs here what Jürgen Habermas calls a "saving translation" of a religious idea into the sphere of politics.[9] The ideas of brotherhood and brotherly love hark back to the early Christians, who—similarly to the Jews of their time—conceived of their coreligionists as "brothers" with whom they shared an affective bond. Since the Middle Ages, and especially during the eighteenth century, the term "brotherly love" had become intermittently secularized and politicized, notably among the Freemasons (who called each other *Bruder* and promised to love

---

7. Quoted in Shapiro, "The Status of Women," 379–80.

8. It should be pointed out that the political ideal of fraternity, which is based on the idea of brotherly love, enacts a whole new set of exclusions, notably of women. As Stefani Engelstein has argued, the concept of fraternity points to a problem at the core of liberalism—namely, how to reconcile the citizen's identification with the state with more particularistic attachments of love and kinship. Eighteenth-century political philosophers responded to this problem by identifying women with purely personal feelings and excluding them from the sphere of politics. See Stefani Engelstein, "Civic Attachments & Sibling Attractions: The Shadows of Fraternity," *Goethe Yearbook* 18 (2011): 205–21. The logic identified by Engelstein is not readily apparent in Mendelssohn's *Jerusalem*. As Mendelssohn's footnote on the Viennese divorce case shows, his argument for civic equality for Jews goes hand and hand with the recognition of women's capacity to make rational decisions and act as autonomous individuals, a capacity that in the liberal model should enable women to engage in politics. However, at times Mendelssohn subsumes female conscience under paternal will, as when he describes the marital contract from the perspective of the Jewish wife: "She knew and expected nothing other than to take her place in a household governed by ancestral rules of life and to bear children whom she would be able to educate according to the *principles of her fathers*" (*Jerusalem*, 51; my emphasis). A few years after Mendelssohn, German Jewish playwrights associated with the Haskalah were to describe what happens when the daughter's desires diverge from the father's principles. In plays such as Aaron Halle-Wolfssohn's *Leichtsinn und Frömmelei: Ein Familiengemälde in drei Aufzügen* (1792) and Isaak Euchel's *Reb Henoch, oder: Woß tut me damit* (1793), the representation of Christian-Jewish love affairs serves to guard against the dangers of a superficial enlightenment coded as female. Jewish women who lust after Christian men and light entertainment embody a female model of assimilation that contrasts with the male model of *Bildung*. For a detailed interpretation of these plays, see Lezzi, *"Liebe is meine Religion!,"* 78–91.

9. On this concept of translation, see Jürgen Habermas et al., in *An Awareness of What Is Missing: Faith and Reason in a Post-Secular Age*, trans. Ciaran Cronin (Malden, Mass.: Polity Press, 2010), 15–23; and Judith Butler, Jürgen Habermas, Charles Taylor, and Cornel West, *The Power of Religion in the Public Sphere*, ed. Eduardo Mendieta and Jonathan VanAntwerpen (New York: Columbia University Press, 2011).

each other in a brotherly way) and in the egalitarian ideal of the French Revolution, *fraternité*.[10] However, the 1793 German *Adelung* dictionary does not mention any political usage but rather emphasizes the biblical, and specifically Christian, meaning of "brotherly love": "the love which biological brothers have for each other, or should have for each other. In a broader sense in the biblical style, the love which Christians, and in fact all humans, owe to each other: the former because of their common faith, the latter because of their common ancestor."[11] So when Mendelssohn establishes a connection between brotherly love and civil union, the work of translation is very much his own. He transfers the idea of an affective bond between coreligionists to a modern, secular, broadly inclusive state. In the passage from *Jerusalem* quoted at the beginning of this chapter, this translation is underscored through the paronomasia between *brüderlich* (brotherly) and *bürgerlich* (civil): "Should you believe that you cannot love us in return *as brothers* and unite with us *as citizens* [uns nicht *brüderlich* wieder lieben, euch mit uns nicht *bürgerlich* vereinigen zu können] as long as we are outwardly distinguished from you by the ceremonial law, do not eat with you, do not marry you, which, as far as we can see, the founder of your religion would neither have done himself nor permitted us to do?" (135; my emphasis).

Mendelssohn's invocations of brotherly love allow for subtle shifts from religion to politics, or from questions of religious tolerance to demands for civic equality, and vice versa. He first uses brotherly love to frame an argument for the political emancipation of the Jews in his 1772 preface to Manasseh Ben Israel's *Vindication of the Jews*; the preface was Mendelssohn's contribution to the debate about Dohm's *On the Civic Improvement of the Jews*. At the beginning of the preface, Mendelssohn expresses his hope for an expansion of "the rights of man" to new groups: "If it is the goal of providence that brother should love brother, then it is obviously the duty of the stronger to put forward the first proposal, to stretch out his arms, and like Augustus to cry out, 'Let us be friends!'"[12] Mendelssohn refers here to the final act of Pierre Corneille's play *Cinna*, in which the Roman emperor Augustus generously forgives his friends for their machinations and restores their friendship. The implication is that a similarly unilateral act on the part of a ruler—for example, the granting of civil rights to religious minorities—is necessary to reconcile the religions in his time. Mendelssohn voices this political demand by transposing the religious idea of "goal of providence" to the secular domain of politics and friendship. At the end of the preface, Mendelssohn writes that brotherly love should also reign *within* a religious community. Here he makes an argument that will become

---

10. Wolfgang Schieder, "Brüderlichkeit," *Geschichtliche Grundbegriffe: Historisches Lexikon zur politisch-sozialen Sprache in* Deutschland, ed. Otto Brunner, Werner Conze, and Reinhart Koselleck (Stuttgart: Klett-Cotta, 1972–97), 1:552–81.

11. Johann Christoph Adelung, *Grammatisch-kritisches Wörterbuch der hochdeutschen Mundart* (Leipzig: Johann Gottlob Immanuel Breitkopf und Compagnie, 1793), 1:1217.

12. Moses Mendelssohn, *Writings on Judaism, Christianity, and the Bible*, ed. Michah Gottlieb (Lebanon, N.H.: Brandeis University Press, 2011), 40.

pivotal in *Jerusalem*: religious congregations should use love and persuasion rather than coercion and punishment. In particular, they should extend brotherly love to dissenting members and relinquish the right to excommunicate them. Mendelssohn effectively equates the toleration of dissidents within a religious congregation and the integration of religious minorities into the state.

Mendelssohn's emphasis on brotherly love should not be dismissed as an apologetic appeal to Christian sensibilities. Rather, it is part and parcel of his effort to reclaim love as a core value of Judaism. Throughout *Jerusalem*, Mendelssohn presents the God of Israel as a God of love, and neighbor-love as Judaism's central commandment.[13] He reads the scene at Mount Sinai in which Moses seeks to see God's glory after God punished the Israelites for idolatry in terms of divine love and benevolence. He depicts the revelation of the Judaic law as an act of divine love, and divine punishment as an opportunity for self-improvement.[14] Mendelssohn valorizes the everyday practice of the law on similar grounds. Whereas both traditional Christians and modern Deists dismissed the law as a petrified ancient ritual, Mendelssohn hails it as a "living script, rousing the mind and heart" (102). Based on a complex semiotic theory according to which written language tends to fixate meaning and facilitate idolatry, he praises the law as a set of orally transmitted practices that propel people into communal interaction.[15] While writing tends to isolate its reader, the performer of a ritual law seeks out others, especially more experienced coreligionists, for help and advice. Oral instruction proceeds "from man to man, from mouth to *heart*" (119; my emphasis), creating affective ties between the members of the community that prove God to be "the God of love" (121). Mendelssohn's notion of the law as revealed and transmitted through love refutes long-standing stereotypes that pit Christian love against Jewish law.

As Jonathan Hess pointed out vis-à-vis Mendelssohn's portrayal of Jesus as a Jewish reformer, *Jerusalem* has a distinct polemical thrust. Mendelssohn's appreciation of Jesus is not a step toward Christianity, as Cranz and others would have

---

13. Mendelssohn quotes the famous Talmudic story in which the Jewish sage Hillel responds to a heathen's inquiry about the essence of the Jewish law: "Son, *love thy neighbor as thyself*. This is the text of the law; all the rest is commentary. Now go and study!" (*Jerusalem,* 102; Mendelssohn's emphasis). Mendelssohn conflates several different sources here. In the Talmud anecdote, Hillel states his so-called Golden Rule in the negative: "Do not do to your fellow what you hate to have done to you." Mendelssohn inserts the biblical injunction to neighbor-love (Lev. 19:18) into the Talmudic anecdote. See Alexander Altmann's commentary in Mendelssohn, *Gesammelte Schriften*, 8:348.

14. To that end, Mendelssohn even amends his own translation of the Bible, writing that God said to Moses, "Ich habe Dich namentlich *zu meinem Liebling* ausersehen," rather than just "namentlich ausersehen"; see Altmann's commentary in Mendelssohn, *Gesammelte Schriften*, 8:355 (my emphasis here). The English translation does not render the "love" as clearly: "I have singled thee out by name as the one favored by Me" (*Jerusalem,* 122).

15. Willi Goetschel has argued that Mendelssohn's emphasis on the oral tradition, which allows the law to be adapted to new circumstances, entails a new conception of tradition as intrinsically open and dynamic. See Goetschel, *Spinoza's Modernity: Mendelssohn, Lessing, and Heine* (Madison: University of Wisconsin Press, 2004), esp. 160–65.

it, but a way of securing for Judaism a central place in the modern world.[16] Mendelssohn's conception of brotherly love is similarly subversive in that he traces the Judaic origins of this idea and deplores its absence in contemporary Christianity. In the passage quoted above, the expression "love us in return" implies something later stated explicitly, that Jews already love their Christian neighbors in a brotherly way. It is not entirely clear what exactly the "in return" means here, either that Jews already abide by the laws of the land or that Judaism, which Mendelssohn throughout *Jerusalem* and against Christian stereotypes depicts as a religion of love and tolerance, provides what Habermas calls the "pre-political moral foundations" of the liberal state.[17] In any case, Mendelssohn highlights the discrepancy between the Jews' suitability for citizenship and their actual lack of civil rights.

Brotherly love furnishes not only a protopolitical value but also a rhetorical force, in the form of emotional appeals. In the last pages of *Jerusalem*, Mendelssohn repeatedly and emphatically addresses his Christian readers as "dear brothers" ("liebe Brüder"), although he is aware that Christians may harbor no brotherly feelings for the Jews. There are several such phatic moments in *Jerusalem*, in which he seeks to create and instill feelings he presumes to be missing in his Christian addressees.[18] Witness, for instance, his earlier comments on the revelation at Sinai. After quoting the biblical passage about God's benevolence, which is manifest even in punishment—"*The Lord . . . who preserveth His lovingkindness even to the thousandth generation; who forgiveth transgression, sin and rebellion, yet alloweth nothing to go unpunished*"—Mendelssohn interjects: "What man's feelings are so hardened that he can read this with dry eyes? Whose heart is so inhuman that he can still hate his brother and remain unforgiving toward him?" (122–23; Mendelssohn's emphasis). This is of course a rhetorical question, an appeal to readers to assume a conciliatory attitude toward their "brothers." Mendelssohn does not so much describe the effect of the biblical passage on its readers as he seeks to produce such an effect. The reader should be moved to tears in view of the benevolence of a God who gives his people the opportunity to better themselves. By alerting his readers

---

16. See Hess, *Germans, Jews, and the Claims of Modernity*, 91–136.

17. Jürgen Habermas, "Pre-political Foundations of the Democratic Constitutional State?," in *The Dialectics of Secularization: On Reason and Religion*, ed. Florian Schuller, trans. Brian McNeil (San Francisco: Ignatius Press, 2006), 19–52. It should be noted that Habermas's notion of a "saving translation" can only approximate the complex process of appropriation, contestation, and invocation that occurs when Mendelssohn speaks of brotherly love. Mendelssohn reclaims brotherly love as a core value of Judaism, indicts its absence among his Christian contemporaries, and calls it forward by directly addressing his Christian readers as brothers.

18. Mendelssohn's preface to Manasseh Ben Israel's *Vindication of the Jews* ends on a similarly emphatic appeal to "brothers," in this case, to his fellow Jews who are to extend tolerance to dissenters in their communities: "Nations are tolerating one another, and they are also showing you the love and forbearance that, with the assistance of the One who directs the hearts of men, can grow into true brotherly love. O my brothers, follow the example of love, just as you have until now followed the example of hate!" Mendelssohn, *Writings on Judaism*, 52. Here, too, the emphatic address "brothers" is meant to call forth the brotherly love that is missing in reality.

to the power of the biblical narrative, Mendelssohn hopes to inspire brotherly love in them. His emotional appeals help conjure a state in which Jews and Christians could share a sociopolitical structure while observing the boundaries set by their different religious practices.

Gotthold Ephraim Lessing's *Nathan the Wise*

As Willi Goetschel has argued, Lessing's *Nathan the Wise* pursues, by different means, the same political goal as *Jerusalem*. The play proposes the establishment of a new political order, "a model of full legal equality whereby the state (Saladin) recognizes the necessity of granting its citizens the same rights regardless of their religious affiliation."[19] It is important to note, however, that such an order is never fully realized in *Nathan the Wise*. The famous ring parable in the middle of the play relates the conflict between three brothers, each of whom believes he possesses the true ring—an analogy, Nathan explains, to the three monotheistic religions, each of which proclaims to be the true one. The brotherhood of the ring remains riven by conflict and competition; in the end, the judge can only advise the brothers to prove themselves worthy of the ring in the future. Nor is the extended family network in the play's final scene, which includes Recha, the Templar, and the Muslim rulers of Jerusalem, a persuasive model of an open and inclusive community. As several scholars have noted, Nathan's status in particular remains tenuous. Ritchie Robertson suggests that by establishing the family as a model of an interfaith community and by presenting Nathan as the only character who is not related to the others by blood, Lessing puts him into a position analogous to that of the German Jews, whose admittance to German society was not based on the idea of natural rights but contingent upon proof of their suitability for citizenship.[20]

In what follows, I will argue that the play locates the possibility of interreligious community elsewhere—namely, in the creation of new genealogical lineages through affective kinship. Set in the period of the Crusades, *Nathan the Wise* relates the budding love between Recha, the adoptive daughter of the Jewish Nathan, and a Christian Templar, who later turns out to be her brother, which makes their union impossible, because it would be incestuous. Their romance drives the plot, as it triggers Nathan's genealogical inquiry and eventually leads to the discovery of family ties between people of different religious backgrounds. I suggest that the

---

19. Willi Goetschel, "Lessing and the Jews," in *A Companion to the Works of Gotthold Ephraim Lessing*, ed. Barbara Fischer and Thomas C. Fox (Rochester, N.Y.: Camden House, 2005), 201.

20. See Ritchie Robertson, *The "Jewish Question" in German Literature, 1749–1939: Emancipation and Its Discontents* (New York: Oxford University Press, 1999), 45. The famous 1933 staging of *Nathan the Wise* by the Kulturbund Deutscher Juden highlighted Nathan's position as an outsider. The staging ended with a scene in which Nathan is left completely alone on the stage, abandoned by the others. See Barbara Fischer, *Nathan's Ende? Von Lessing bis Tabori: Zur deutsch-jüdischen Rezeption von "Nathan der Weise"* (Göttingen: Wallstein, 2000), 117–42.

nonfulfillment of this romance is crucial to the play's political vision. *Nathan the Wise* performs a process of sublimation in the Freudian sense, a redeployment of erotic energies in intellectual, artistic, or other creative activities. In particular, the many miraculous rescues are life-creating acts that come to supplant romantic love and marriage as a means of establishing affective bonds between the religions.

In *Nathan the Wise*, Lessing anticipates and radicalizes Mendelssohn's theory about the historical truth of religion. One of the central arguments of *Jerusalem* is that Judaism is grounded in a historical event—namely, the revelation at Sinai and the tradition of commentary it produced. Mendelssohn holds that the revelation and the subsequent teaching of the law inspire in Jews a passionate attachment to their religious tradition. He intimates that the revelation can also affect non-Jews, such as the readers of *Jerusalem*, in whom he seeks to arouse brotherly love by citing the biblical passage. Lessing goes even further than Mendelssohn in suggesting that people can fall in love with a different religious tradition. This is first hinted at in the ring parable, in which Nathan says: "Are [the religions] not grounded all in history, / Written or handed down?—And history / Must be accepted wholly upon faith— / Is that not so?"[21] Nathan goes on to explain that we will adopt the religious tradition of those we trust most, "our own people" (233/*278*). However, he defines "our own people" in two different ways, first as those whose blood we share and then as those who have loved us since childhood: "Well then, whose faith are we least likely / To doubt? Our own people's, surely? Those whose blood / We share? The ones who, from childhood on, gave / Us proof of their love?" (233/*278*). In what follows, I will argue that *Nathan the Wise* unfolds this duality by showing that the family that loves us is not necessarily the family into which we were born. The play invites the conclusion that just as we may love an adoptive father, we may become emotionally attached to a different religious tradition.

The Christian-Jewish Romance

In this drama of shifting identities, it is first necessary to establish that the relationship that develops between the Templar and a woman who is revealed to be of Christian-Muslim origin should be considered interreligious, and specifically,

---

21. Gotthold Ephraim Lessing, *Nathan the Wise,* trans. Bayard Quincy Morgan, in Lessing, *Nathan the Wise, Minna von Barnhelm, and Other Plays and Writings*, ed. Peter Demetz (New York: Continuum, 1991), 233. For the original German, see Gotthold Ephraim Lessing, *Nathan der Weise*, in *Werke*, ed. Herbert G. Göpfert (Munich: Carl Hanser, 1971), 2:278. Further citations from these editions will be included parenthetically in the text, with the page number in the English translation followed by the page number in the German edition in italics, as here (233/*278*). I have frequently (and silently) modified the translations, often inspired by the following translation: Gotthold Ephraim Lessing, *Nathan the Wise*, trans. Ronald Schechter (Boston: Bedford/St. Martins, 2004). Like Schechter, I use the name Recha instead of Rachel throughout my reading.

whether this attachment can be said to involve a Jew and a Christian.[22] The attraction between Recha and the Templar provides Lessing with an opportunity to rehearse and dismantle some of the arguments against the political emancipation of the Jews. The disjunctive sequence of revelations opens up a dramatic space in which the difficult education toward tolerance can be displayed, with the Templar figuring as an example of Christian prejudice and stubbornness, but also of the ability to learn. The Templar, who at first refuses even to enter the house of a Jew, changes his mind when he and Nathan establish a friendship grounded in the new sociability that, at the end of the eighteenth century, enabled the kind of encounters between Jews and Christians for which the friendship between Lessing and Mendelssohn has become emblematic. Yet when the Templar confesses his love for Recha and receives a rather tepid response from Nathan, he resents what he presumes to be Jewish exclusiveness, and falls back into his earlier prejudices against the Jews. Nor does the theme of interreligious love disappear after Recha's Christian origins have been revealed. Rather, as long as the Templar wants to marry her, still ignorant of the fact that she is his sister, she remains in the social position of a Jew. This becomes evident when the Templar contemplates the reasons for his attraction to Recha and finds that her Jewish upbringing and the character she owes to Nathan are more important than her Christian origins: "If I envision her as but / A Christian girl, bereft of all the traits / That only such a Jew could give to her: — / Speak, heart—what would she have to win your praise? / Nothing! Little!" (260/325). To be sure, the Judaism of Nathan and Recha is a rather disembodied religion, abstracted from concrete practice and reality.[23] Nevertheless, Recha's perceived Jewish identity serves to introduce the idea of a Christian-Jewish intermarriage.

The Templar's bitter comments regarding Nathan's supposed unwillingness to marry his daughter to a Christian echo the arguments against Jewish separateness that loomed so large in the Enlightenment debates about Jewish emancipation. Among non-Jews, both advocates and opponents of emancipation tended to accept the notion that contemporary Jewry was degenerate, though they disagreed about the reasons, and both regarded Jewish religious rituals and dietary laws as expressions of an unwholesome "clannishness" that hampered the integration of Jews into Christian society. While the opponents, most importantly Johann David Michaelis, regarded Jewish "clannishness" as an insurmountable obstacle to integration, even

---

22. Recha's mother was Christian, and Recha never converted to Judaism. It remains unclear whether her father, Saladin's brother Assad, converted to Christianity or remained a Muslim.

23. On Lessing's tendency to depict Jews in an abstract and disembodied manner, see, for instance, Mendes-Flohr, *German Jews*, 74. More recently, Jonathan Hess has suggested that Lessing might have been deliberately vague about the nature of Nathan's Judaism, and that this vagueness allowed nineteenth-century German Jewish writers and thinkers to assert their own views about the relationship between Jewish particularism and secular universalism. See Jonathan M. Hess, "Lessing and German-Jewish Culture: A Reappraisal," in *Lessing and the German Enlightenment*, ed. Ritchie Robertson (Oxford: Voltaire Foundation, 2013), 179–204.

the advocates, such as Christian Wilhelm von Dohm, devised a program of "civic improvement" intended to reduce the distinctiveness of Jews and Judaism.[24] The Templar's suspicion that Nathan resents the proposed marriage because he wants to preserve his genealogical line cannot but evoke this context. He ironically comments on the exclusiveness of the Jewish family tree: "Not that I have / The slightest doubt about your family tree. God / Forbid! You can trace it, shoot by shoot, clear back / To Abraham. And backward from there on / I know it too; will take my oath on it" (240/286).[25] However, the Templar's suspicions about the motives for Nathan's hesitation turn out to be unfounded; Recha and the Templar cannot marry because they are siblings and their union would be incestuous. In disproving the Templar's suspicions in this peculiar way, Lessing repudiates an important argument against Jewish emancipation, but at the same time tacitly accepts the assumption that Jewish "clannishness" has to be overcome.

Nonoccurrence of the marriage between Recha and the Templar allows Lessing imaginatively to refrain from violating the prohibition against intermarriage that at the time was upheld by both church and state, and by both Jews and Christians. In depicting incest as the obstacle to marriage, however, *Nathan the Wise* retroactively changes the nature of the transgression: the problem was not that the Templar loved a Jewess but that he loved his sister. By presenting the incest taboo as the decisive factor that separates Recha from the Templar, Lessing moves the obstacles to interfaith marriage to a more fundamental level. Lessing had resorted to a similar technique in his earlier plea for religious tolerance, the drama *The Jews* (1749). In this play a Jew traveling incognito saves a baron from a robbery at the hand of his own servants, who are disguised as Jews. The incident leads the baron to indulge in clichés of the deceitful, thieving Jew, not knowing that he is speaking with a Jew. The traveler discloses his Jewish identity only when the baron, as a sign of his gratitude, offers him his daughter's hand in marriage. The disclosure inspires in the baron shame about his earlier behavior. When he deplores his inability to thank the traveler adequately—now that marriage is ruled out—the traveler asks him to instead abandon his anti-Jewish prejudice and look more favorably upon Jews in the future. The play intimates that the learning process of the baron is an exemplary step toward a better understanding between Jews and Christians while stopping far short of staging an

---

24. See, for instance, Christian Wilhelm von Dohm, "Concerning the Amelioration of the Civil Status of the Jews," in *The Jew in the Modern World: A Documentary* History, ed. Paul R. Mendes-Flohr and Jehuda Reinharz (New York: Oxford University Press, 1980), 27–34 (see 28 and 29 for the use of "clannish"); Johann David Michaelis, "Arguments against Dohm," ibid., 36–38.

25. Later on, when he asks the Patriarch for advice, the Templar revives the age-old myth of Jews stealing Christian children to fill in the gaps in Daya's account: "And then we would be informed that the girl was not / The Jew's own daughter: he had picked her up / In childhood, bought or stolen" (*Nathan,* 248/297). The scene, which shows how easily the Templar falls back into the Christian war ideology of his times, was probably intended as a warning against the anti-Judaic sentiments in Enlightenment philosophy. See W. Daniel Wilson, *Humanität und Kreuzzugsideologie um 1780: Die 'Türkenoper' im 18. Jahrhundert und das Rettungsmotiv in Wielands "Oberon," Lessings "Nathan" und Goethes "Iphigenie"* (New York: Peter Lang, 1984), 74, 86.

intermarriage. However, the impossibility of interfaith marriage is also naturalized, or given a biological rather than a social foundation, through repeated allusions to the age of the Christian girl.[26] Because the spectator is aware throughout the play that the baron's daughter is simply too young to marry, marriage appears unrealizable from the beginning, for reasons that have nothing to do with religion. Lessing thus manages to allude to interfaith marriage while escaping from the dichotomous imperative of either carrying it out or condemning it.

The sudden disappearance of interfaith romance in *Nathan the Wise* still begs for an explanation, especially since love and marriage are explicitly referenced as ways of mitigating religious conflicts. We learn that Saladin at one point pursued a politics of intermarriage to ensure the truce between Christians and Muslims during the Crusades, hoping that his brother Melek would marry Richard the Lionheart's sister. His plans foundered over Christian demands for conversion, which is, of course, precisely what would have been demanded from a Jew who wanted to marry a Christian in Lessing's times.[27] Moreover, the social and religious injunctions against interfaith marriage did not prevent Lessing from playing with the theme in various ways. An earlier draft shows that he originally planned to end the play with two such marriages, between Sittah and the Templar and between Saladin and Recha. The couples were evidently not meant to be blood relatives, though the Templar is said to stem from Antioch in Syria, which sets his origins in greater proximity to those of his bride Sittah.[28] In the final version, Recha and the Templar are themselves the offspring of a marriage between a Christian woman and a Muslim man—at least no mention is ever made of their father's conversion to Christianity. Why did Lessing shun the possibility of ending the play with yet another interfaith marriage? And what happens to the tensions—erotic and otherwise—that have been built up in the dramatization of the impossible love story?

Like *The Jews*, *Nathan the Wise* prepares the audience for the failure of romance by suggesting that the obstacles to marriage are of an internal rather than external nature. Something seems never quite right about the love between Recha and the Templar. Their feelings for each other are noncontemporaneous—the Templar falls in love with Recha at the very moment her own feelings cool down—and prove altogether chimerical. Nathan, who figures here as the voice of the Enlightenment, early on suggests that Recha's passion for the Templar is mere *Schwärmerei* (reverie), an expression of inner torment. Rejected by the man who saved her,

---

26. The representation of yet-to-be-married women as immature and childlike is quite conventional in eighteenth-century literature, so one may argue that the barriers to interfaith marriage in *The Jews* are not truly given a biological foundation. However, the allusions to the girl's age in this play are not simply conventional but rather serve to prepare the audience for the (especially for a comedy) disappointing end.

27. See *Nathan*, 201/237–38. See also Wilson, *Humanität und Kreuzzugsideologie*, 64. On the historical background, see the annotations to *Nathan the Wise*, in Lessing, *Werke*, 2:755.

28. See Lessing, *Werke*, 2:743. Antioch was an old Christian community in Syria. Its invocation in the draft underscores the Christian—if Eastern—origins of the Templar.

Recha is torn between her head and her heart (179/*211*). Indeed, Recha's feelings are shown to be the product of a schism between imagination and reality that she gradually learns to overcome. When she first tells Nathan about how she was rescued by what she deems was an angel, she emphasizes that it was a *visible* angel, in contrast to the invisible angel that saved her father during his perilous journey to Babylon (180/*213*). Nathan's side comments then inform us that her vision is based on a misinterpretation of visual details: her taking of the sleeve of the Templar's white coat to be a wing. Recha's confused passion turns into a more tender affection once she meets the Templar again and recognizes in him a human being rather than an angel. The encounter helps her integrate visual with other sense impressions, including that of the Templar's speech, and puts an end to her *Schwärmerei*: "The sight of him, his speech, his actions have . . . / DAYA: sated you already? RECHA: Sated is not the word; / No—far from it.—DAYA: Assuaged the pangs of hunger. / RECHA: Well, yes; you could put it that way" (226/*269*). Scenes such as this one suggest that Recha had an intuitive knowledge of the true relations between herself and the Templar, which explains why the revelations of the final scene do not come as such a disappointment to her.[29]

Like *The Jews*, *Nathan the Wise* creates hope for a better society by first invoking and then disrupting the possibility of interfaith romance. If the dramatization of the budding love between Recha and the Templar teaches the reader about the difficulties faced by a Christian-Jewish couple, the transformation of erotic passion into sibling affection demonstrates how a socially unacceptable attraction turns into a socially acceptable one. In *The Jews*, the impossibility of interreligious love similarly opens up the possibility of better relations between the different religious groups in the future. The difference is that *Nathan the Wise* replaces the marital bond with an even more primal bond and presents the harmonious union of the religions as already achieved. Above I suggested that both plays naturalize contingent social norms, a strategy that brings the game of love to a halt. Yet this strategy is never entirely conclusive. In both plays the barriers to interfaith marriage are not insurmountable but rather retain a possibility on the horizon, opening up a temporal gap between desire and fulfillment. In *The Jews*, the Christian girl who is too young to marry can theoretically still do so in the future. And the incest taboo invoked in *Nathan the Wise* is a social convention rather than natural law, or more precisely, it is the law that marks the transition between nature and culture. As Claude Lévi-Strauss famously argued, the incest taboo founds the possibility of social exchange through exogamic marriage, thus making human societies

---

29. The integration of visual, aural, and tactile impressions that mitigates Recha's visual infatuation also marks other instances of cognitive intuition in *Nathan the Wise*. See Susan E. Gustafson, *Absent Mothers and Orphaned Fathers: Narcissism and Abjection in Lessing's Aesthetic and Dramatic Production* (Detroit: Wayne State University Press, 1995), 244–45.

possible.[30] The substitution of the incest taboo for the injunction against intermarriage in *Nathan the Wise*, then, situates the possibility of interfaith romance in a prehistoric past. This impression of a past withdrawn from memory is compounded by the fact that one interfaith romance—between Assad and his Christian wife—has already happened in the play and that we know next to nothing about the circumstances of that relationship. By projecting the fulfillment of interfaith romance into a remote past or an unknowable future, Lessing retains and redirects the affective energies behind such romance.

The uncontainability of desire transpires in the figurative excess of the word "fire," which throughout the play indexes the precarious nature of the love between Recha and the Templar. The fire metaphor in *Nathan the Wise* has generally been interpreted as an expression of excessive, even violent, irrationality. Indeed, the metaphor links the Templar's vehement passion for Recha to the religious fanaticism of the patriarch and to the brutal pogrom in which Nathan's wife and sons perished. However, the opposition between calm reason and violent passion never quite works in the play.[31] There is simply no way of extinguishing the fire. Recha's miraculous rescue from fire continues to incite new fires, first in her own imagination—"Her imagination still paints fire / In every scene it paints" (177/*209*)—and then in the Templar, whose unfulfilled passion for Recha is described throughout the play in metaphors of fire. It is in fact the same enlightened rhetoric that is meant to dampen Recha's exalted imagination that sets the Templar on fire. Nathan seeks to purge both of them of unwanted affects by showing them the truth behind appearances. He teaches Recha to see the real human behind the imaginary angel, and the Templar to see the universally human behind the particular group: "What is a people? / Are Jew and Christian sooner Jew and Christian / Than human being?" (214/*253*). However, this rhetorical strategy arouses new desires in the Templar, who upon establishing a friendly bond with Nathan expresses his wish to meet the wise man's daughter in the words "I'm burning with desire [*Verlangen*]" (214/*254*). The ambiguities around the word "fire" point to the limits of the

---

    30. See Claude Lévi-Strauss, *The Elementary Structures of Kinship*, trans. James Harle Bell, John Richard von Sturmer, and Rodney Needham, rev. ed. (Boston: Beacon Press, 1969), esp. 29–68, 485–97. I cannot fully explore here the significance of the incest motif in *Nathan the Wise* and other eighteenth-century literature, which is currently the focus of important research in the field. In *Sibling Action: The Genealogical Structure of Modernity* (New York: Columbia University Press, forthcoming), Stefani Engelstein argues that the literary motif of sibling incest is linked to the imagination of more democratic political principles. Michael Thomas Taylor offers an intriguing reading of *Nathan the Wise* that focuses on the interconnectedness of different forms of love and the centrality of the prohibition of incest in the play. According to Taylor, this prohibition guards against all attractions based on sameness and ultimately dismisses love as the basis of the social bond altogether. See Taylor, "Same/Sex: Incest and Friendship in Lessing's Nathan der Weise," *Seminar* 48, no. 3 (2012): 333–47.

    31. For an incisive reading of the fire metaphor, see Daniel Müller Nielaba, "'Die arme Recha, die indes verbrannte!' Zur Kombustibilität der Bedeutung in Lessings *Nathan der Weise*," in *Neues zur Lessing-Forschung: Ingrid Strohschneider-Kohrs zu Ehren am 26. August 1997*, ed. Eva J. Engel and Claus Ritterhoff (Tübingen: Max Niemeyer, 1998), 105–25.

play's pedagogic project. In dramatizing the interreligious romance and transforming it into something else, *Nathan the Wise* creates an affective space in which the audience can be educated about the proper direction and application of feelings. Yet the proliferation and dissemination of the word "fire" in the play also reveal the impossibility of ever fully domesticating erotic desire.

Affective Kinship

Both *Nathan the Wise* and *The Jews* end somewhat unconvincingly, as the promise of a society free of prejudice cannot fully compensate for the disappointments caused by the prevented marriage. The German Jewish philosopher Franz Rosenzweig once deplored the lack of children at the end of the *Nathan the Wise*, which he read as a sign of the "bloodlessness" of the idea of emancipation.[32] Indeed, by depriving the audience of the generic happy ending of comedy, *The Jews* turns into a farce. *Nathan the Wise* brings the interfaith romance to a similarly abrupt end; the transformation of the Templar's passion into sibling affection is not staged in the same tangible detail as the moderation of Recha's feelings. When faced with the fact that Recha is his sister, he exclaims: "You take from, and give to me, Nathan! / And both in full!—But no, you give me more / Than you are taking! Infinitely more!" (273/345). Helmut Schneider has read these lines against the backdrop of the Enlightenment myth of male self-creation and the attendant repression of the sexual, and in particular the birth-giving, body. According to Schneider, the ingenuity of *Nathan the Wise* is that the play does not simply suppress the contingency associated with birth and corporeality but transposes it to the spontaneity of the rescue actions and the playfulness of the dramatic structure. In the Templar's acceptance of a gift that inevitably hinges upon a loss, the concept of self-creation gives way to the acknowledgment of the irreducible exteriority of our own origin.[33]

I would suggest pushing Schneider's ideas about the displacement of sexual energies further and reading *Nathan the Wise* as a form of sublimation, a mobilization of erotic desire for a vision of coexistence of the religions. I am using the concept of sublimation here in a broad Freudian sense to designate creative acts that redirect and redeploy energies otherwise used to perform sexual acts. In Freud's dynamic model of the psyche, Eros figures as the creative force that drives the agglomeration of elements into more complex units, a process that binds energy. Whereas

32. Franz Rosenzweig, "Lessings Nathan," in *Zweistromland: Kleine Schriften zu Glauben und Denken,* vol. 3 of *Gesammelte Schriften*, ed. Reinhold Mayer and Annemarie Mayer (Dordrecht: Martinus Nijhoff, 1984), 449–53.
33. Helmut J. Schneider, "Der Zufall der Geburt: Lessings *Nathan der Weise* und der imaginäre Körper der Geschichtsphilosophie," in *Körper/Kultur: Kalifornische Studien zur deutschen Moderne*, ed. Thomas W. Kniesche (Würzburg: Königshausen and Neumann, 1995), 100–124.

the archetype of such erotic activity is human procreation, intellectual and artistic works are seen as valuable substitutes for procreation, in fact as activities that give birth to humanity at large. In *Nathan the Wise*, sublimation in this sense does not so much take place on the level of the psyches of individual characters; Recha's feelings are never of an unambiguously erotic nature, and the Templar's passion is never convincingly transformed into something else. Structurally, however, the plot and perhaps also the reaction elicited in the audience enact a societal sublimation. *Nathan the Wise* displaces creative energies from romantic love and marriage to miraculous rescues by which people are given their life anew. The play mobilizes these energies for a political project, the creation of a sociopolitical order capable of accommodating religious difference—although it is crucial that this project never takes on concrete contours.

In *Nathan the Wise*, the miraculous rescues are a form of filiation that depends on luck, chance, affect—anything but a conscious choice. The metaphor of the gift (*Geschenk*) that comes to describe the saved lives underscores the idea of the unexpected and the unpredictable (215/255). Nathan's adoption of the Christian Recha just after his own family has been murdered in a pogrom and Saladin's sparing of the Templar's life just after the Templar Order has broken the truce between Muslims and crusaders are equally spontaneous and inexplicable acts. As second-order births in which people are given their lives once again, they are also creative acts. These rescues might be understood as expressions of virtue, following the Enlightenment idea that reason and morality ultimately converge: as people help those whom they are naturally least inclined to help, they overcome their social and religious parochialisms and realize their true humanity. But the rescue actions in *Nathan the Wise* follow affective impulses to a degree that undermines the idea of reason's victory over emotions. These actions are motivated by previous losses, the memory of which returns and gives rise to a process of substitution: Saladin is overcome and moved to tears by memories of his brother when he looks at the Templar's face. The Templar, who finds little worth in his life after Saladin has effectively made him a prisoner, gives in to suicidal impulses when he rescues Recha from fire. Even Nathan, who adopts a Christian child after suffering terrible losses at the hands of the Christians, does not exclusively listen to the voice of reason, as he initially puts it. Rather, he performs a mourning ritual in the course of which he transfers the love for his murdered children to a substitute object: "All I know is this: I took the child, I bore it to my couch, / I kissed it, threw myself upon my knees, / And sobbed: O God! For seven *one* at least is back!" (257/317).[34]

Equally important is the fact that the miraculous rescues are not isolated events. Recha's rescue by the Templar is throughout the play presented as the result of the

---

34. For a reading of this scene of loss and grief, see Astrid Oesmann, "*Nathan der Weise:* Suffering Lessing's 'Erziehung,'" *Germanic Review* 74, no. 2 (Spring 1999): 131–45.

Templar's own miraculous survival. This emphasis on how one person's survival depends on another's effectively establishes new genealogical lines. There are in fact two different genealogical lines: Saladin rescued the Templar who rescued Recha, and Wolf rescued Nathan who rescued Recha. This parallelism rests on a small detail hardly ever mentioned by scholars—namely, the fact that Wolf von Filneck, Saladin's brother and the biological father of Recha and the Templar, repeatedly rescued Nathan, whom he had befriended before his death (255/*314*). The fact that Wolf was unable to rescue Nathan's family from fire compounds the impression that his rescue act was aimed at Nathan the individual and independent of family bonds. Furthermore, its very repetition casts Wolf's deed as the structural condition rather than a one-time event of Nathan's life. This observation provides a new answer to the question of whether Nathan in the final scene stands apart because he does not fulfill the criteria of belonging or stands out because he makes the family reunion possible. Seen in the light of his own repeated rescue, Nathan becomes less of an outsider and more of a link in a longer historical chain. Nathan is not so much the founder of a spiritual family or the embodiment of the idea of male self-creation, but the middle element of one of the genealogical lines established in the play.

The miraculous rescues stand for two different models of kinship. Saladin's and the Templar's rescue actions are grounded in intuitive cognition of existing kinship relations. Saladin's affective response to the Templar's face turns out to be well founded—the Templar is indeed related to Saladin's late brother—and the Templar's attraction to Recha seems a misinterpretation of a similar intuitive knowledge of blood relations. Both moments of recognition are focused on memories of the past rather than projections of the future.[35] Whereas the connection between Saladin, the Templar, and Recha is underwritten by biological kinship and suggests that the emotion at work might be unconscious love for one's relatives, the affective lineage between Wolf, Nathan, and Recha is not. Furthermore, whereas Saladin's and the Templar's deeds are referenced and narrated throughout the play, those of Wolf and Nathan receive next to no narrative elaboration or explanation. The knowledge of Nathan's adoption of Recha is withheld from most characters in the play. Nathan reveals the details of the adoption only to the friar, whom he admonishes to keep the story secret. Even less is known about the circumstance of Wolf's rescues of Nathan. We do not know why Nathan was in danger or how Wolf came to help him. Their actions form a chain of interventions that makes the final family reunion possible and at the same time points beyond the family as a model of kinship. These miraculous rescues do not reflect existing kinship relations but instead create tenuous new relations, a form of kinship-in-becoming.

---

35. The earlier draft of *Nathan* contains allusions to the Templar's memory of his mother. When he first sees Recha, who in the draft is called Rahel, the Templar believes he has seen her before, perhaps in a dream, and Nathan suggests she might remind him of his mother. See Lessing, *Werke,* 2:738.

The Politics of Love

The connections built through affective kinship, however, never translate into a sociopolitical order in which Nathan the Jew would enjoy a truly equal status. Such an order remains a possibility that is never fully realized, or, to the extent that it realized, is constantly endangered. The precarious status of Nathan's "rights" is a case in point. Nathan himself discusses adoptive fatherhood in terms of rights, and the word was likely to evoke the contemporary debate about Jewish civil rights. He bases his paternal claims to Recha on the Enlightenment view that we have a greater right to the things we acquire through virtue than to those nature bestows on us (176/*208*). In the end, however, Saladin threatens to limit Nathan's rights once again through the claims of biological kinship. After Nathan's revelation that he is Recha's and the Templar's uncle, Saladin alludes to the potential rivalry between him and Nathan: "Me, not recognize my brother's children? / My niece and nephew—not my children? / Not recognize them? Me? And let you have them?" (274/*346*).[36] The sense of rivalry stems from the different forms of fatherhood embodied by Nathan and Saladin. Whereas Nathan's claims to fatherhood depend on mutual agreement—"For should not / My daughter's brother be my child as well— / As soon as he wishes?" (273–74/*345*)—Saladin's claims do not need such consent: "(*to the Templar*): And now, you stubborn boy, now you'll have to love me! / (*to Recha*) And now I am what I proposed to be! / Whether you like it or not!" (275/*346–47*). The principle of adoptive fatherhood seems theoretically valid but practically threatened by Saladin's despotism. Nathan's position in the extended family remains tenuous because this family cannot truly accommodate the new relations built on affective kinship. The final scene underscores that Nathan's rights—Jewish rights—are to be demanded rather than assumed.

As we have seen, both Lessing and Mendelssohn register the possibility of interfaith romance while focusing their attention on other affectionate bonds between members of different religions. In that process, love becomes a future-oriented emotion, the source of actions that have yet to occur. In his calls for civic equality, Moses Mendelssohn appeals to a brotherly love he assumes to be lacking in his Christian readers. His emphatic address "dear brothers" implicitly calls on Christians to extend brotherly love to the Jews. In *Nathan the Wise*, love is similarly future oriented. We may recall here the open-endedness of the ring parable. The original ring was a token of love, a sign of a father's election of a favorite son, with the capacity to render its owner agreeable to others. Beyond that, it was an insignia

---

36. On this exchange, see Sasse, *Die aufgeklärte Familie*, 258–60. For an analysis of Saladin's despotism, see also Christiane Bohnert, "Enlightenment and Despotism: Two Worlds in Lessing's *Nathan the Wise*," in *Impure Reason: Dialectic of Enlightenment in Germany*, ed. W. Daniel Wilson and Robert C. Holub (Detroit: Wayne State University Press, 1993), 344–61.

of power and authority: whoever inherited it became master of the house irrespective of birth order. This rite of investiture no longer functions when one father loves his three sons equally and passes a ring to each of them. In a situation in which neither of the rings can prove love past or present, the judge defers to the brothers' own potential to generate love. Rather than pass a verdict, he advises them to make every effort to demonstrate benevolence and prove themselves worthy of the ring. There is a sense of urgency in the judge's final address to the brothers, a protopolitical command to free the world from prejudice: "Let each aspire / To emulate his father's uncorrupted love, / Free from prejudice!" (235/*280*).

The nonfulfillment of romantic love in *Nathan the Wise* is crucial for the political effect of the play. I have suggested that the logic of play is one of sublimation broadly understood, a redirection of erotic energies to dramatic acts of rescue and, ultimately, to the idea of politico-juridical equality between the religions. Yet sublimation also remains peculiarly open-ended. While incest prohibition restores a certain order after the possibility of interfaith romance has created much confusion and imbalance, this order becomes neither concretized nor truly stabilized. As the development of the fire metaphor shows, emotions are never fully domesticated, and erotic energies never fully inactivated in the play. Nor can the final scene of familial harmony expunge all traces of conflict between competing genealogical claims. This sense of ongoing conflict makes the play politically more provocative than any vision of interfaith harmony could be.

A comparison with subsequent plays throws the import of Lessing's representation of the potential Christian-Jewish love relationship into even clearer relief. In the years following the first performances of *Nathan the Wise*, a number of Christian supporters of Jewish emancipation wrote plays that pick up on the same motif but offer very different solutions. Two of these plays dramatize the budding love between a Christian man and a Jewish woman who conveniently turns out to to have been born a Christian but was adopted by a Jew, which enables the couple to marry. Another play juxtaposes two weddings, a Jewish wedding and a Christian one, and yet another play ends tragically with the death of the Jewish girl.[37] These plays perform what Zygmunt Bauman, following Niklas Luhmann, identifies as one major function of the modern discourse of love: they resolve the conflicts arising from shifting social relations in an idealized private sphere.[38] The plays cast domestic life as a domain that is exempt from the inequalities caused by social

---

37. See Johann Karl Lotich, *Wer war wohl mehr Jude?* (Leipzig: Friedrich Gotthold Jacobäer, 1783); Karl Steinberg, "Menschen und Menschensituationen, oder die Familie Grunau," *Deutsche Schaubühne* 4 (1792): 1–180; Gottfried Julius Ziegelhauser, *Die Juden: Eine bürgerliche Scene in einem Aufzuge* (Vienna: Johann Baptist Wallishausser, 1807); Jakob Bischof, *Dina, das Judenmädchen aus Franken: Ein tragisches Familiengemälde* (Fürth: Im Büro für Literatur, 1802). On the motif of interreligious love in these plays, see also Peter R. Erspamer, *The Elusiveness of Tolerance: The "Jewish Question" from Lessing to the Napoleonic Wars* (Chapel Hill: University of North Carolina Press, 1997), 106–9.

38. See Bauman, *Modernity and Ambivalence*, 197–230.

power (and achieve this effect only by erasing Judaism as a divisive factor) or, in the case of the last play, as a domain that *should* be exempt from such inequalities. Compared to these later plays, Lessing's transformation of erotic love into sibling affection is more provocative and open-ended. Lessing's move toward the naturalization of the social obstacles to interfaith marriage remains suspended; instead he turns love into a metaphor of social integration that cannot be confined to the private sphere of domestic life—or to any other partial domain for that matter. He contributes to the debates about Jewish emancipation by dramatizing desire rather than fulfillment, a political desideratum rather than a political program.

2

Romantic Love and the Denial of Difference

Friedrich Schlegel and Dorothea Veit

Between 1790 and 1806, at least nine Jewish women in Berlin regularly opened their houses to visitors from across the social spectrum and led spirited conversations about art, literature, and society. The most famous of these Jewish *salonnières* were Henriette Herz and Rahel Levin Varnhagen; others include Sara Levy, Marianne Meyer Eybenberg, and Sara Meyer Grotthus. Scholars have long held that the informal gatherings in their homes fostered a historically unprecedented social interaction between Jews and Christians. Hannah Arendt notes that visitors could experiment with new forms of cross-class and cross-religious sociability because of the outsider status of the salon hostesses: "Precisely because the Jews stood outside of the society [the Jewish salons] became, for a short time, a kind of neutral zone where people of culture met."[1] In recent years, scholars have cautioned against overly optimistic accounts of the egalitarianism of salon culture and painted a more differentiated picture of its form and duration.[2] They point out that the

---

1. Hannah Arendt, *Rahel Varnhagen: The Life of a Jewess*, ed. Liliane Weissberg, trans. Richard Winston and Clara Winston (Baltimore: Johns Hopkins University Press, 1997), 127.

2. Barbara Hahn speaks of "the myth of the salon" that gradually evolved after 1945. See her *The Jewess Pallas Athena: This Too a Theory of Modernity*, trans. James McFarland, (Princeton, N.J.: Princeton University Press, 2005), 42–55. Among other things, Hahn points out that the Jewish women of Berlin did not use the word "salon" for their own forms of socializing. For a detailed analysis of the "salon communication," see Hannah Lotte Lund, *Der Berliner "jüdische Salon" um 1800: Emanzipation in der Debatte* (Berlin and Boston: Walter De Gruyter, 2012).

socializing of the Jewish *salonnières* involved a greater variety of places, contexts, and modalities than previously acknowledged, and that it was an altogether precarious and transitory phenomenon. "Salon" conversations could happen at the tea tables of open houses, during dinner or dance parties, after theatrical or musical performances, and during leisurely walks in the parks and streets of Berlin. They could take the form of a dialogue, a letter, or a billet. They extended from Berlin to Weimar, Jena, and Breslau as well as to lakeside resorts, where social rules and conventions were generally more relaxed. Furthermore, the wealth of communicative forms, places, and media cannot gloss over the fact that the egalitarian encounter between people from different classes and religions was very short-lived and, perhaps, always more of an aspiration than a reality.

Part and parcel of the Christian-Jewish interaction in the Berlin salons were platonic and not-so-platonic love affairs that have long drawn the attention of scholars of Jewish history and are still debated controversially. The historian Deborah Hertz describes her own vacillation between two different views of these love affairs, as either an expression of individual freedom or a threat to Jewish communality. Hertz originally celebrated the intermarriages of a number of salon women as "a heroic protest against a strict system of arranged marriage," but subsequent research sensitized her to the costs of these rebellions to Jewish communities.[3]

The debate is of long standing. On one end of the spectrum, the nineteenth-century historian Heinrich Graetz views the salons as the beginning of the end of Jewish communal life in Germany precisely because they led to interreligious love affairs. He calls the salon of Henriette Herz a "Midianite tent," alluding to the biblical story of Midianite women who seduced the Israelites to practice idolatry.[4] Though very different in tone, Hannah Arendt's critique of the atomizing force of romance in the biography *Rahel Varnhagen* betrays a similar concern. Arendt views the affectionate bonds in the salons as an expression of a politically problematic individualism, a tendency among Jews to seek personal liberation rather than political emancipation. The historian Steven Lowenstein similarly emphasizes the loss of Jewish collectivity. He regards the increase in Christian-Jewish love affairs around 1800 as a symptom of the crisis of the Berlin Jewish community during the second stage of modernization. After the death of Moses Mendelssohn in 1786, the belief of the early Haskalah in the reconcilability of acculturation and religious orthodoxy began to wane. In the absence of attractive alternatives within Judaism,

---

3. See the foreword to Deborah Hertz, *Jewish High Society in Old Regime Berlin*, 2nd ed. (Syracuse, N.Y.: Syracuse University Press, 2005), XV. In the book itself, Hertz argues against the idealization of Christian-Jewish unions as love matches. She shows that such unions were ruled by a distinct social logic: the exchange of wealth for status. See the chapter "Seductive Conversion and Romantic Intermarriage," 204–50.

4. Heinrich Hirsch Graetz, *History of the Jews* (Philadelphia: Jewish Publication Society of America, 1895), 5:422.

Berlin Jews who were eager to join the modern age began to consider more radical departures from tradition and to ignore the social taboos against conversion and intermarriage.[5] In all of these accounts, Christian-Jewish love affairs figure as either the cause or the effect of the Jews' inability to act collectively, whether toward the preservation of tradition, in the effort for religious reform, or in the struggle for political rights.

On the other end of the spectrum, writers have celebrated such affairs as a sign of the emancipation of the individual from social norms and conventions. The relationship between Friedrich Schlegel and Dorothea Veit is perhaps the most famous of the Christian-Jewish love affairs that originated in the salons. Born Brendel Mendelssohn in 1764, Veit was the oldest daughter of Moses Mendelssohn, the famous Enlightenment philosopher discussed in the previous chapter. Her father personally oversaw her education but then married her off in 1783 to a Jewish businessman without much concern for her own opinion. In 1797, Dorothea, as she had begun calling herself, met and fell in love with Friedrich Schlegel, the pivotal thinker of the early Romantic movement. The couple started living together after Veit obtained a rabbinical divorce from her first husband in early 1799. They married only in 1804, largely because of stipulations in the custody arrangement for Veit's younger son. In many accounts, the story of Friedrich Schlegel and Dorothea Veit serves to illustrate the blessings of love-based marriage, in contrast to the presumed sacrifice of personal happiness in an arranged marriage. Commentators often dwell on Veit's plight in her first marriage to the Jewish banker Simon Veit, who is portrayed as kind and gentle, but uneducated and insensitive to the pleasures of high culture. According to these commentators, it was no wonder that she was dissatisfied with her dull husband and receptive to the charms of witty and artistic Schlegel. It was admirable, even, that she overcame her fears of social castigation and followed her heart into a relationship based on mutual love.[6]

At no moment, then, would one expect a greater confluence of the discourse of love and the debates around Jewish acculturation than during the short-lived era of the Berlin salons. But this is not exactly what happened. To be sure, the Christian-Jewish love affairs that often began in the salons found their way into literature, which at the time was instrumental in disseminating the new love ideal we still call Romantic. During the years in which their relationship developed and solidified, Friedrich Schlegel and Dorothea Veit each wrote a novel that centers on the Romantic love ideal. Schlegel's *Lucinde* (1799) is perhaps the clearest instantiation of this

5. See Steven M. Lowenstein, *The Berlin Jewish Community: Enlightenment, Family, and Crisis, 1770–1830* (New York: Oxford University Press, 1994), esp. 104–19.

6. See, for instance, Carola Stern, *"Ich möchte mir Flügel wünschen": Das Leben der Dorothea Schlegel* (Reinbek bei Hamburg: Rowohlt, 1990).

ideal in German literature.[7] Veit's *Florentin* (1801) relates to this ideal largely negatively, through the frustrated hopes of its eponymous hero.[8] However, neither novel
makes explicit references to Jews or Judaism. This omission is surprising, consider-
ing that interfaith romance is well suited to illustrate the power of romantic love,
in which claims to individuality override social determinations, and that Christian-
Jewish relationships soon afterward became emblematic of just this trend, whether
evaluated positively or negatively.

The chapter explores the disjunction between the historical significance and the
literary avoidance of interfaith love affairs around 1800. I begin by offering two different explanations for the absence of references to Jews and Judaism in Schlegel's
Lucinde. (Of course, I do not suggest that literary texts need to be read biographi-
cally. But because of the literary conventions of the time, Schlegel's novel was
read—and could be expected to be read—as an autobiographical document from
the very beginning. This invites speculation about the role of Veit's Jewishness.)
First, in early Romantic and Idealist philosophies of love, Jews come to embody a
negative principle. Thinkers such as Schleiermacher and the young Hegel pit Judaism, which they associate with a state of stasis or alienation, against the principle of
unification that is love. While Schlegel himself barely ever mentions Judaism in his
writings, his work participates in these philosophical currents and at least sets nothing against their latent antisemitism. Second, I read the absence of references to
Jewishness in Schlegel's *Lucinde* as part of a larger pattern of signification in literary love stories. Around 1800, when love becomes a privileged medium of individuation, the lack of markers of social identity, especially of such overriding markers
as Jewishness, helps create literary characters conceived as unique individuals.

The most important strand of my argument concerns the ways in which romantic love, which initially entails a withdrawal from society, generates new models of
society and politics. This happens in both *Lucinde* and *Florentin*. As I will show,
these novels wrestle with the question of how to incorporate strangers into a community, and thereby implicitly comment on the process of Jewish emancipation
and acculturation. However, they offer two quite different visions of sociopolitical
integration. Wherever Schlegel turns love into a metaphor for society, he elides differences of class and religion in favor of the sexual dichotomy between the lovers.
Differences other than gender become unspeakable as Schlegel projects the gender
dichotomy onto society at large. Against the backdrop of Schlegel's problematic
elision of difference—which would include Jewish difference—Veit's work reveals

---

7. See Paul Kluckhohn, *Die Auffassung der Liebe in der Literatur des 18. Jahrhunderts und in der
deutschen Romantik*, 3rd ed. (Tübingen: Max Niemeyer, 1966), 361–93; and Sara Friedrichsmeyer, *The
Androgyne in Early German Romanticism: Friedrich Schlegel, Novalis, and the Metaphysics of Love* (New
York: Peter Lang, 1983), 131–67.

8. Many contemporary text editions and critical essays speak of Dorothea *Schlegel*, even though her
last name at the time of the publication of *Florentin* was Veit (and her official first name still Brendel).
Veit was baptized and married Friedrich Schlegel on April 6, 1804.

its critical potential. I read *Florentin*, in which love conspicuously fails to secure the hero the sense of home and identity he desires, as a subversion of the Romantic love ideal and a critique of the political models derived from this ideal. While in *Lucinde* the polity gets reorganized along gendered lines, in *Florentin* the polity remains in a state of becoming.

Excursus: "The Jew" as Negative Principle in Philosophies of Love

The figure of "the Jew" functioned as a negative principle in the Idealist and Romantic philosophies of love that developed around 1800. The young Hegel, for instance, advances a secular version of the traditional Christian opposition between Judaic law and Christian love in his "The Spirit of Christianity and Its Fate" ("Der Geist des Christentums und sein Schicksal," 1798–1800). The work belongs in the context of Hegel's critique of Kantian moral philosophy and its concept of freedom. Against Kant's categorical imperative, which he deemed a too external law, Hegel posits love as a principle of union and the true ground of human freedom. Only love can reconcile subject and object, the spiritual and the sensual, the human and the world, the idea of individual autonomy and the need for reciprocal relationships with others.[9] In the first section of his tract, entitled "The Spirit of Judaism," Hegel uses the image of the Jew as a negative foil for these ideas. As in Kant, the Jew in Hegel is an embodiment of heteronomy. Hegel conjures a series of historical Jewish figures from Noah to Moses Mendelssohn who submit to God's command rather than recognize the possibility of human freedom. But even more important for Hegel is the purported Jewish lack of love. He describes how Abraham, the father of the Jewish nation, first cut all bonds of love to his native country and then failed to form new bonds in his chosen country. Abraham's unwillingness to wed his son to a Canaanite woman is for Hegel the most salient expression of the alienation that characterizes Jewish existence. Hegel goes so far as to call the rape of Dinah, related in Genesis 34, a mere "insult" (*Beleidigung*) and her brothers' revenge of the rape further proof of the Jewish inability to create loving bonds with their environment.[10]

Significantly, Hegel does not encourage increased social interaction between Christians and Jews, such as he most certainly witnessed in his surroundings, as a solution to the perceived problem of Jewish separateness. He alludes to the possibility of friendly and amorous bonds with Christians but immediately adds that in the past such cross-religious socializing led to dialectical backlashes. Hegel

---

9. See also Wolf-Daniel Hartwich, *Romantischer Antisemitismus: Von Klopstock bis Richard Wagner* (Göttingen: Vandenhoeck and Ruprecht, 2005), 94.

10. Georg Wilhelm Friedrich Hegel, "The Spirit of Christianity and Its Fate," in *On Christianity: Early Theological Writings by Friedrich Hegel*, trans. T. M. Knox (Gloucester, Mass.: Peter Smith, 1970), 182–301; here 188. (The translator chooses a stronger word here than the German "Beleidigung ihrer Schwester" suggests: "outraging of their sister.")

uses Judaism exclusively as a foil for his ideas about human freedom in and through love. His "The Spirit of Christianity" shows how the figure of the Jew comes to embody negative principles in German Idealism: in this case, the state of alienation that ensues from the inability to love.[11]

Closer to the home of Friedrich Schlegel and Dorothea Veit, Friedrich Schleiermacher provides another example of how Christian-Jewish love is excluded from the purview of early Romantic thought. A Christian theologian, Schleiermacher was a close friend of the couple and an ardent supporter of civic equality for the Jews. It thus comes as a surprise that, in his contribution to the debates around David Friedländer's proposal for a "dry baptism" of the Berlin Jews, he expresses reservations about interfaith marriage.[12] Schleiermacher ends his plea for abolishing the laws against marriage between members of different religions with a caveat: "It may perhaps not be advisable in most cases for a Christian man and a Jewish woman (or vice versa) to contract a marriage tie."[13] This caveat indicates the conservative thrust of his tract, the primary concern of which is the problem of conversions without true faith. Schleiermacher believes that a Jew's desire to marry a Christian is frequently the cause of such opportunistic conversions, which he fears will infuse Christianity with Judaic elements. In other words, he supports the idea of civil marriage not because he wants to ensure a separation between church and state but because he wants to prevent an infiltration of Christianity with insincere converts, or any other kind of unregulated exchange between Judaism and Christianity.[14] Fear of hybridity characterizes his essay throughout. Schleiermacher complains, for instance, about "Jews who wish

---

11. On the figure of the Jew as a negative principle in German Idealism, see Michael Mack, *German Idealism and the Jew: The Inner Anti-Semitism of Philosophy and German Jewish Responses* (Chicago: University of Chicago Press, 2003). See also Martha B. Helfer, *The Word Unheard: Legacies of Anti-Semitism in German Literature and Culture* (Evanston, IL: Northwestern University Press, 2011). Helfer argues that between 1750 and 1850, German-language writers developed a new, "latent" antisemitism that has been largely ignored by scholars. Although she focuses on literary authors, her argument about the subtle presence of anti-Jewish constructions around 1800 also applies to many philosophers of the time.

12. See Schleiermacher's response to David Friedländer's *Open Letter to his Reverend, Provost Teller, Councillor of the Upper Consistory in Berlin* (1799). Friedländer, one of the leaders of the Berlin Jewish community, had become frustrated with the slow progress of Jewish emancipation and proposed that a number of Berlin Jews should convert to Protestantism under special conditions. In order to gain entrance into German society, they would accept Christianity as a rational religion without fully espousing all of its practices and rituals. Schleiermacher rejected Friedländer's (anonymous) proposal and in so doing touched upon several issues pertaining to the relationship between state and religion. See their exchange in David Friedländer, Friedrich Schleiermacher, and Wilhelm Abraham Teller, *A Debate on Jewish Emancipation and Christian Theology in Old Berlin*, ed. and trans. Richard Crouter and Julie Klassen (Indianapolis: Hackett Publishing, 2004).

13. Friedländer, Schleiermacher, and Teller, *A Debate on Jewish Emancipation,* 100.

14. See also Hess, *Germans, Jews, and the Claims of Modernity,* 169–204. According to Hess, Friedländer's proposal, which is usually read as a document of opportunistic assimilationism, is an attempt on the part of Jews to enter German society on their own terms. In contrast, Schleiermacher allows for no internal reform of Judaism and seeks to bring the reform of Judaism under the purview of the state.

to have their children circumcised and at the same time baptized. There are now already amphibians whose nature might be difficult to determine."[15]

In *On Religion: Speeches to Its Cultured Despisers* (*Über die Religion: Reden an die Gebildeten unter ihren Verächtern*, 1799), Schleiermacher construes Judaism as a remnant of the past and practicing Jews as incapable of change. In these speeches, Schleiermacher formulates the Romantic view of religion as a personal experience rooted in feelings. At the same time, he is invested in the preservation of existing religious communities and anxious about the potential dilution of Christianity. And while he ostensibly values religious pluralism, he embraces an evolutionary model of religious history according to which Judaism has lost its vitality and significance as a religion: "Judaism is long since a dead religion, and those who at present still bear its colors are actually sitting and mourning beside the undecaying mummy and weeping over its demise and its sad legacy."[16] Schleiermacher does not seem to believe in the possibility of new dynamic developments within Judaism. In Hegel, Jews cannot love; in Schleiermacher, they cannot develop. Both constructions effectively exclude Jews and Judaism from the new philosophies of love around 1800. They render Christian-Jewish love unthinkable even where—or perhaps especially where—their authors support Jewish emancipation and hail love as a secular principle of unification. In what follows, I suggest that the philosophy of love in *Lucinde* similarly hinges upon the negation of Judaism, or its transformation into an unspeakable difference.

Love as a Medium of Individuation: Friedrich Schlegel's *Lucinde*

Lucinde is the Romantic love novel par excellence. A capricious mix of letters, dialogues, narratives, and aphorisms, the novel depicts the love experiences of its male protagonist, Julius, and the fulfillment he finds in his relationship with the artistic and free-spirited Lucinde. There are no explicit references to Jews and Judaism in *Lucinde*, and yet Schlegel would have realized that his readers were likely to import ideas about Judaism into the text. It was well known that Schlegel wrote *Lucinde* under the direct influence of his love affair with Dorothea Veit. Although he had had plans for a novel since 1794 (and at that time may have had an earlier lover in mind), he began writing *Lucinde* during a crucial stage of his love affair with Veit, while she was negotiating a divorce from her first husband.

Most contemporaries read this biographical background into *Lucinde*, and they had good reasons to do so. The late eighteenth century saw a change in the relationship between literature and life, a blurring of the boundary between them. As

---

15. Friedländer, Schleiermacher, and Teller, *A Debate on Jewish Emancipation,* 89.
16. Friedrich Schleiermacher, *On Religion: Speeches to Its Cultured Despisers*, trans. and ed. Richard Crouter (New York: Cambridge University Press, 1996), 114–15.

authors included personal elements in their works and used details recognizably culled from their own life, literature began to make plausible claims to the representation of real-life experience.[17] The reception of *Lucinde* bears witness to this shift in literary conventions. The appearance of the novel caused a public scandal because it was thought to reveal intimate details from the author's life. Although the book can hardly be called pornographic, by either our standards or those of its time, its open discussion of intimacy challenged the established distinction between high literature and popular erotica. Even friends and supporters worried that *Lucinde* revealed too much about the couple's private life to the public. And Veit herself wrote to Schleiermacher: "With regard to Lucinde—yes, with regard to Lucinde!—Often my heart becomes hot and then cold again [when I consider] that the innermost will be turned outward—that which was once so sacred and homely [*heimlich*] to me will now be divulged to all the curious, all the haters."[18]

Veit does not seem to have worried that her Jewishness would be among the personal details to be exploited by the book's enemies. But this happened at least some of the time; reviews of *Lucinde* could take on a decidedly antisemitic tone. One critic who wrote derisively about the work's sensuality explicitly referred to "Madam Veit" as a member of the Jewish nation and a daughter of Moses Mendelssohn.[19] The writer Johann Daniel Falk, who satirized the eroticism of both *Lucinde* and Schleiermacher's commentary on the novel, cast Jewish women as the most enthusiastic audience of these works.[20] As Ludwig Marcuse comments: "The impropriety of *Lucinde* was intensified by the fact that the anarchy of the bedroom included the mixing of the races; taking umbrage at sexuality and at Jewishness became one and the same thing."[21] While Marcuse aptly sums up one strand of *Lucinde's* reception, I suggest that we take the couple's silence on the subject of Veit's Jewishness, and the absence of references to Judaism in *Lucinde*, seriously. This silence cannot be reduced to fear of antisemitic reverberations. It is more likely that Schlegel did not dwell on Jewishness because he sought to describe the development of individuality outside of social determinations, and because he segregated love from social identifiers other than gender.

For the early German Romantics love and marriage were mostly synonymous, and both were to be wrested away from social conventions and institutions. Schlegel belongs to the "metaphysicians of marriage," as Adrian Daub has aptly called the German Idealists and Romantics who collectively redefined marriage around

17. See Luhmann, *Love as Passion*, 135.

18. Dorothea Veit to Friedrich Schleiermacher, April 8, 1799, in *Friedrich Schlegel: Kritische Ausgabe seiner Werke*, ed. Ernst Behler, with the collaboration of Jean-Jacques Anstett and Hans Eichner (Paderborn: Schönigh, 1958–) 24:266. Hereafter cited as *KA*.

19. [Daniel Jenisch], *Diogenes Laterne*, published anonymously (Leipzig 1799), 374.

20. See Johann Daniel Falk, "Der Jahrmarkt zu Plundersweilern" (1800/01), in *Die ästhetische Prügeley: Streitschriften der antiromantischen Bewegung*, ed. Rainer Schmitz (Göttingen: Wallstein, 1992), 81–114, and the editor's commentary, 368–93.

21. Ludwig Marcuse, *Obszön: Geschichte einer Entrüstung* (Munich: Paul List, 1962), 70.

1800.[22] Thinkers such as Fichte, Hegel, and Schleiermacher conceived of marriage as a union that is grounded in itself and structured in reference to itself and therefore requires no legitimization through tradition, state, or church. "Almost all marriages are simply concubinages," Schlegel writes in *Athenäum* fragment 34, implying that marriage is invalid without a deep spiritual and physical bond between the partners.[23] If such a bond exists, its confirmation through church or state is unnecessary.

In theory, a Christian-Jewish love affair could be a perfect illustration of this idea of marriage. Because interfaith liaisons were a social taboo, and interfaith marriages a legal impossibility, they could illustrate the powers of romantic love and bolster Schlegel's critique of the institution of marriage. Indeed, one of the very few times that Schlegel brings up Veit's Judaism in his letters is in the context of his critique of conventional marriage. He expresses relief that he cannot formally marry Veit because her family is opposed to baptism, which at the time would have been required for marriage.[24] In Schlegel's view, the lack of institutionalization in their relationship guarantees the authenticity and the freedom of their love. Of course, what is an accomplished fact in the novel—Lucinde is ostensibly free from familial or communal ties—was an ongoing drama in real life, in which Veit only gradually broke away from her husband, her family, and her religion. *Lucinde* glosses over any such process, creating the fiction of an individual who always already exists outside of conventions, institutions, and social structures.

Niklas Luhmann's theory about the function of love in modern society sheds further light on the process of individuation in *Lucinde*. According to Luhmann, modern societies are characterized by functional differentiation rather than hierarchical stratification. Whereas in premodern times a person's place in the social hierarchy defined most aspects of his or her life, in modernity people are presumed to have the ability to move between different social spheres and assume different roles within them. This leads to a certain chasm between impersonal relationships—in which one relates to the other in one's social role or function—and personal relationships—in which one relates to the other as an individual with a unique worldview and life experience. The simultaneous increase of social anonymity and personal intimacy endows love with new purposes and functions. In premodern times love was primarily a form of social solidarity; now it is a medium of individuation, a highly personal, unfathomable experience. Modern lovers define and

---

22. Adrian Daub, *Uncivil Unions: The Metaphysics of Marriage in German Idealism and Romanticism* (Chicago: University of Chicago Press, 2012).

23. Friedrich Schlegel, *Friedrich Schlegel's "Lucinde" and the Fragments*, trans. Peter Firchow (Minneapolis: University of Minnesota Press, 1971), 34.

24. See Friedrich Schlegel to Novalis, December 17, 1798, in *KA* 24:215. In an earlier letter, Schlegel had already mentioned that formal marriage ("die verhaßte Ceremonie") with Veit is neither desirable nor possible, without giving an explicit reason. See his letter to Caroline Schlegel, November 27, 1798, in *KA* 24:202.

validate themselves through another person who shares their experience and perception of the world. That is why they are looking for a soul mate, someone who truly understands them rather than embodies merit, beauty, or virtue. In this way love counteracts social fragmentation and affords an experience of the self as whole, coherent, and authentic.

The love story in *Lucinde* is all about individuation thus understood. The relationship between Julius and Lucinde is a highly personal experience that occurs in a social vacuum. The lovers first meet outside of society and are free of external commitments. Although the novel goes into great details about Julius's life, we hear of no familial or social obligations on his part. Lucinde, too, "had renounced all ties and social rules daringly and decisively and lived a completely free and independent life."[25] Love in *Lucinde* is also self-referential in the way Luhmann theorizes. Julius hardly ever describes Lucinde's appearance or character. He is drawn to her not because of her qualities—such as being blond, smart, musical, and so on—but for the experience of love, for the ways in which she validates him and his view of the world. What first attracts Julius to Lucinde is the impression of "wonderful similarity [*Gleichheit*]" (98/53) between them. His love deepens as he realizes how similar they are in disposition, perception, and experience. The moment he tells her about his past life, this life comes together as a coherent story for the first time. When he talks to her about music, her responses seem to echo his own innermost thoughts. Their mutual mirroring culminates in moments of absolute, wordless understanding.

Luhmann observes that eighteenth-century literature untethers the individual from his social background and divests him of social attributes, thereby producing a "semantic void" around the individual.[26] This semantic void is only gradually filled over the course of the century. Early eighteenth-century literature already intimates that someone's social standing is less relevant for personal relationships such as love and friendship. Late eighteenth-century literature substantiates the abstract idea of the individual by depicting the development of personality through art, travel, education, and conversations. This observation offers one explanation for the narrow referential range in *Lucinde*: as a social attribute, Jewishness was so overdetermined that it would have been impossible to ignore if it appeared in the text. *Lucinde* shows that in the case of Christian-Jewish love relationships, the semantic void around the individual had to be rather forcefully created before it could be filled with new meaning.

---

25. Schlegel, *"Lucinde" and the Fragments*, 98. For the original German, see Schlegel, *Lucinde*, in *KA* 5:53. Further citations from these editions will be included parenthetically in the text, with the page number in the English translation followed by the page number in the German edition in italics, as here (98/*53*).

26. Luhmann, *Love as Passion*, 132. On the creation of this semantic void in *Lucinde*, see also Lezzi, *"Liebe ist meine Religion!,"* 126–27.

The Sociopolitical Vision of *Lucinde*

The absence of social signifiers in *Lucinde* should not divert our attention from the social dimension of the novel, which describes the emergence of a new kind of community out of the lovers' dyad. While presenting his literary characters in relative isolation from their social environment, Schlegel projects a new model of social life based on love, an alternative to a society experienced as alienating and oppressive.

Love in *Lucinde* is first and foremost a dialectical process. Julius sums up the process of love as one in which every division leads to a higher unity, every estrangement to greater harmony: "Let men or words try to bring misunderstanding between us! That deep pain would quickly ebb and soon resolve itself into a more perfect harmony" (49/*12*). By depicting love as learned behavior, part of a longer developmental process that requires a measure of distance and reflection, Schlegel opens the door for expanding love into a model of society. Lucinde is not Julius's first love but the culmination of all his previous experiences with love. Similarly, he does not instantaneously fall in love with Lucinde but discovers his affection for her gradually over a period of time. In this process, misunderstandings and periods of estrangement eventually draw the lovers closer together. The discussion of jealousy in the section "Fidelity and Playfulness" ("Treue und Scherz") provides an example of this. Julius recounts how on the night before he felt awkward and inadequate at a social event and began a flirtatious conversation with another woman, thereby making Lucinde jealous. However, her jealousy dissipates when he launches on a series of philosophical reflections on the origins and the groundlessness of her feeling. He maintains that in a true marriage infidelity is impossible because one loves a unique individual rather than an exchangeable type, and that a man who playfully loves other women by flirting with them brings form to the chaos of society.

Whenever Schlegel turns love into a model or metaphor of society, he tends to elide differences of class, nationality, or religion in favor of the sexual opposition between the lovers. Initially conceived as pure individuals, Julius and Lucinde increasingly become representatives of their genders and trigger reflections on the character and roles of men and women. Feminist critics have long argued that *Lucinde*'s theory of gender is not as protofeminist as once believed.[27] While the novel presents woman as man's equal partner, it also delimits gender roles and reinstates male dominance. Subscribing to the idea of gender complementarity that became

---

27. See especially Sigrid Weigel, "Wider die romantische Mode: Zur ästhetischen Funktion des Weiblichen in Friedrich Schlegels *Lucinde*," in *Die verborgene Frau: Sechs Beiträge zu einer feministischen Literaturwissenschaft* (Berlin: Argument, 1983), 67–82; and Barbara Becker-Cantarino, "'Feminismus' und 'Emanzipation'? Zum Geschlechterdiskurs der deutschen Romantik am Beispiel der *Lucinde* und ihrer Rezeption," in *Salons der Romantik: Beiträge eines Wiepersdorfer Kolloquiums zu Theorie und Geschichte des Salons*, ed. Hartwig Schultz (New York: Walter de Gruyter, 1997), 22–44. On the history of the idea of gender complementarity, see also Stefani Engelstein, "The Allure of Wholeness: The Eighteenth-Century Organism and the Same-Sex Marriage Debate," *Critical Inquiry* 39, no. 4 (Summer 2013): 754–76.

dominant during the late eighteenth century, Schlegel defines masculinity as search-ing activity and femininity as plant-like passivity. This essentialist theory of gender allows Schlegel to conceptualize love as a dialectical process that progressively joins opposites into more complex unities. Dialectical thinking requires that difference be understood as opposition, and Schlegel's conception of male and female sexual characteristics establishes just such an opposition. This opposition is dynamic rather than static—sexual role reversals and Julius's confusion about his sexual orienta-tion repeatedly blur the boundaries between the sexes—which is why the dialectical process can continue.[28] In this process other differences of class, religion, and so on are collapsed into the sexual opposition. Love in *Lucinde* is the androgynous union of sexual opposites whose polarity is maintained because gender is depicted as the main, perhaps the only, source of difference between Julius and Lucinde.

Here a caveat is necessary. As many critics have pointed out, Schlegel is vacil-lating between two formative principles, those of dialectics and of *Kunstchaos*, or ordered chaos. This duality emerges most clearly in his conceptions of Romantic irony, famously defined as a "permanent parabasis" (*KA* 18:85) that disrupts artistic illusion through acts of literary self-reflection. Schlegel first advances a concept of irony as progressive movement and dialectical fusion of opposites, a concept that is linked to his ideal of Romantic poetry as "progressive, universal poetry."[29] But he also proposes a second concept according to which irony interrupts this progressive movement. This form of irony is linked to what he calls paradox or chaos; accord-ing to one critic, "Paradox involves a relation between elements that are different but not oppositional. . . . Paradox slips into the structureless concept of chaos pre-cisely because, in the absence of opposition, there can be no dialectical synthesis of parts to give order and purpose to the difference between them."[30] As another critic put it, this kind of irony "says not so much the *opposite* to what is meant as some-thing *other than* is stated."[31] *Lucinde* repeatedly hints at the production of chaotic differences through Romantic irony. For instance, Julius recounts how a chance occurrence interrupted his attempt to write up his education to love and how he strived to integrate this *Zufall* into his writing in order to produce "the most beauti-ful chaos of sublime harmonies and fascinating pleasures" (45/9).[32]

---

28. On allusions to homosexuality in *Lucinde*, see Martha B. Helfer, "'Confessions of an Improper Man': Friedrich Schlegel's *Lucinde*," in *Outing Goethe and His Age*, ed. Alice Kuzniar (Stanford, Calif.: Stanford University Press, 1996) 174–93.

29. Schlegel, *"Lucinde" and the Fragments*, 175.

30. Kari Weil, *Androgyny and the Denial of Difference* (Charlottesville: University of Virginia Press, 1992), 45–46. Weil builds here on Peter Szondi's and Paul de Man's different conceptions of Romantic irony. See Peter Szondi, "Friedrich Schlegel and Romantic Irony, with Some Remarks on Tieck's Com-edies," in *On Textual Understanding and Other Essays*, trans. Harvey Mendelsohn (Minneapolis: Univer-sity of Minnesota Press, 1986), 57–73; and Paul de Man, "The Rhetoric of Temporality," in *Blindness and Insight: Essays in the Rhetoric of Contemporary Criticism*, 2nd rev. ed. (Minneapolis: University of Minne-sota Press, 1983), 187–228.

31. Lilian R. Furst, *Fictions of Romantic Irony* (Cambridge, Mass.: Harvard University Press, 1984), 12; Furst's emphasis.

32. On the Romantic concept of chaos, see also Jocelyn Holland, "*Lucinde*: The Novel from 'Noth-ing' as Epideictic Literature," *Germanisch-Romanische Monatsschrift* 54, no. 2 (2004): 163–76, esp. 166;

Love, too, may produce differences that are chaotic rather than dialectic. While the love between Julius und Lucinde creates an androgynous union of sexual opposites, it also generates new differences between the lovers: "At the beginning, nothing had attracted him so much and struck him so powerfully as the realization that Lucinde was of a similar, or even of the same mind and spirit as he was; and now he was forced to discover new differences every day. To be sure [*zwar*], even these differences were based on a fundamental similarity, and the more richly her character revealed itself, the more various and intimate did their communion become" (101/56). Are these newly discovered differences opposites that can be sublated in synthesis? Or are they more elusive differences that are given expression without being integrated into a new whole? The qualifying *zwar* (to be sure) at the beginning of the second sentence, which describes a dialectical process in which differentiation leads to a higher unity, introduces a certain ambiguity. *Zwar* has historically been used to affirm an assertion, especially when placed at the beginning of a sentence. However, since the seventeenth century *zwar* more frequently expresses a concession or exception; it is usually followed by a phrase containing *doch* or *aber* (but) that points beyond the exception.[33] This second meaning resonates in the passage above, in which *zwar* raises the expectation that the differences will persist in some way. While Schlegel hints at the presence of chaotic differences, however, he never names or elucidates them.

A remainder of chaotic difference continues to inhabit the text in the form of the *Fremdes* (foreign) that disrupts the union of the lovers and that, as I will argue, can be read as an allusion to Judaism. Initially, society itself is the main source of the *Fremdes*. The first perfect union between Lucinde and Julius, the moment in which their minds and bodies merge effortlessly, ends abruptly when other members of their party enter the room: "Softly he said 'magnificent woman!'—and just then some accursed guests came into the room" (98/54). The German original contains some interesting ambiguities that are not easily reproduced in English: "Leise sagte er *herrliche Frau!* als die fatale Gesellschaft unerwartet hereintrat." Schlegel draws here on the double meaning of *Gesellschaft* as "party" or "society" to indicate how society disrupts the harmony between the lovers. Among other things, the sudden intrusion of *Gesellschaft* undoes the linguistic synthesis of femininity and masculinity in the locution *"herrliche Frau,"* which, if broken down into syllables, is a chiasmic structure. Externalized as law or internalized as prejudice, society figures in *Lucinde* as the main source of heteronomy, or the inability of people to posit their own moral laws. In the narrative middle section "Apprenticeship for Manhood" ("Lehrjahre der Männlichkeit"), we learn that Julius's first love was a young girl who resisted his attempts at seduction "more

and Bianca Theisen's entry "Chaos—Ordnung," in *Ästhetische Grundbegriffe: Historisches Wörterbuch in sieben Bänden*, ed. K. H. Barck (Stuttgart: Metzler, 2000), 751–71.

33. See Jacob Grimm and Wilhelm Grimm, *Deutsches Wörterbuch* (Leipzig: S. Hirzel, 1854–1961) 16:949–54. (For the URLs for *Deutsches Wörterbuch* and a few other older sources used in this book, see the bibliography.)

out of a belief in some foreign [*fremdes*] law than out of a feeling on her own part" (79/38).[34] The girl's deference to a law that is foreign to her indicates her lack of maturity, which is why Julius's brief relationship with her is only the first step on his Romantic ladder of love.

The association of the *Fremde* with law and society, with external commands rather than internal feelings, evokes the stereotypical distinction between Judaic law and Christian love. As we have seen in the example of Hegel, the new philosophies of love around 1800 revived and secularized this distinction. I would argue that this association is also present in *Lucinde*, if only in an indirect, supplemental manner. In a crucial passage of *Lucinde*, Schlegel associates the social law with India, a country that would soon occupy a central place in his thought. In 1808 he published *On the Language and Wisdom of the Indians* (*Über die Sprache und Weisheit der Inder*), a book that effectively substitutes Sanskrit for Hebrew as the primal language of mankind and the foundation of European culture. Already at the time that he wrote *Lucinde*, India had mostly positive connotations for Schlegel, who liked to picture Veit as an Oriental woman of Indian origins, and India itself, in *Lucinde*, as a place conducive to sweet passivity (66/27). But the association of India with the social law is more complicated and more ambivalent. Schlegel first establishes it in a letter to Novalis, in which he speculates that after his death Veit would follow him just as Indian widows do, a custom he cites approvingly as an example of intuitive religiosity:

> If [Dorothea] lost me, she would *follow the Indian custom*, out of true religiosity and without sensing that it is extraordinary or even that it is right. . . . The religiosity of her feeling is all the more decisive due to the fact that her reason is still numb from sorrow and she has no conceptions.[35]

In *Lucinde*, Schlegel elaborates this thought when he has Julius describe how a true marriage culminates in the couple's wish to die together and how Lucinde would follow him into death if he were to die before her. He again cites the Indian custom, but this time only as a contrast to a suicide imagined as voluntary and redemptive:

> I know that you wouldn't want to outlive me either. You too would follow your rash husband into the grave, and willingly and lovingly descend into the flaming abyss

---

34. Trans. modified. Other examples of an internalized social law are Julius's "distrust" (86/43) and "prejudices of society" (87/44) that prevent him from finding fulfillment in one of his earlier love relationships.

35. *KA* 24:215 (my emphasis). The letter is from December 17, 1798. The mention of Veit's "religiosity" is all the more interesting since this is one of the very few letters in which Schlegel mentions Veit's Jewishness, i.e., the fact that she is the daughter of Mendelssohn and that Schlegel cannot marry her because Veit's baptism would be an insult to her family.

into which *an insane law forces Indian women* and, by its rude intention and command, desecrates and destroys freedom's most delicate shrines

(48/11; my emphasis)

In Schlegel's letter to Novalis, the Indian custom stands for intuitive religious feeling; in *Lucinde*, it stands for a particularly stringent religious law. The positive vision of a woman's unification with her dead husband is now supplemented by a reference to the "insane" law that "forces" Indian widows into death. Schlegel further shifts from *Gebrauch* (custom) to *Gesetz* (law), thus pitting the habit-forming power of tradition against the abstract force of law. The formulation in *Lucinde* is in fact reminiscent of Hegel's attack on Jewish heteronomy in "The Spirit of Christianity," in which he claims that the Jews' dependency on strict external laws makes "their action . . . the most impious fury, the wildest fanaticism" (204). The mania of fanaticism that describes Jewish law in Hegel is applied to India by Schlegel, at a time when he was beginning to project Indian culture into the place of origin once reserved for Judaism. The veiled allusion in *Lucinde* is symptomatic of Schlegel's treatment of Judaism, its transformation into an unspeakable difference that remains outside of the dialectical play of opposites.

Another incarnation of chaotic difference is the figure of the *Fremder* (stranger or foreigner) into which the *Fremdes* repeatedly morphs, especially when the lovers come into contact with others. The figure of the stranger in *Lucinde* crystallizes two kinds of ambiguities—namely, whether the misunderstandings between the lovers are of an internal or external nature, and whether the differences they generate can truly be integrated into a greater whole. Witness the discussion of jealousy, in which Julius blames his behavior on the presence of a stranger with whom Lucinde had a conversation Julius was too shy to interrupt. It remains ambiguous whether the stranger caused the estrangement or whether the estrangement originated within the lovers, who did not yet understand the totality of their union (71/32). The function of the foreigners in the social circle that forms around Julius and Lucinde is similarly ambiguous. The lovers' dyad keeps evolving, in part because of its inner formative principles and in part because of the influx of foreigners (*Ausländer*). Yet it is unclear whether the presence of foreigners is the cause or the effect of the circle's renewal. While the foreigners initially seem but a supplement to the innate principle of *Bildung* (cultural development) that propels the self-renewal of the community, the narrative focus is increasingly on them:

> Gradually [Julius] attracted many excellent people to his side, and Lucinde united them and kept them going and in this way a free society came into being—or rather, a big family, which because of its cultural development [*Bildung*] never grew stale. Deserving foreigners also had access to the circle. Julius didn't speak to them often but Lucinde knew how to entertain them. She did it in a way that their grotesque universality [*groteske Allgemeinheit*] and cultivated commonality [*ausgebildete Gemeinheit*]

amused the others, so that there was never a pause or dissonance in the spiritual music whose beauty consisted precisely in its harmonious variety and change. In the social arts, besides the grand, ceremonious style, there should be a place too for merely charming mannerisms or passing fancies.

(102–3/57; trans. modified)

This a prime example of how the love relationship between Julius and Lucinde, originally a self-referential structure that develops in opposition to society, generates new forms of community. The foreigners, who have the potential to irritate but in fact amuse the community, remain without name or further specification. While the narrator does not elaborate on the nature of their difference, several of their features, including their status as insider-outsiders, invite an association with Jewishness. The foreigners are described as difficult for Julius to talk with, suggesting that there is a language difference, such as that between German and Judeo-German, or another source of cultural estrangement. They are also portrayed as grotesquely cosmopolitan, a common stereotype of the Jew, and simultaneously as completely parochial, an attribute often given to Jews following Dohm's indictment of Jewish "clannishness." This latter aspect is indicated by the word *Gemeinheit*, which around 1800 was mostly synonymous with *Gemeinde* (community) and was only beginning to acquire its modern meaning of "meanness" and "vulgarity." In some Northern German dialects, *Gemeinheit* also referred to the members of a specific community who did not belong to a guild or another professional association, a group of outsiders.[36] Lucinde seems to have a special affinity to the foreigners, as she weaves them into the harmonious whole of her and Julius's social circle, thereby creating an ordered chaos. The description of the foreigners is quite negative, and yet through Lucinde their difference becomes part of an aesthetic harmony. In other words, Lucinde is a bridge between the cultures. The whole passage exemplifies the neutralization of unsettling differences in the novel, both in the sense that they cease to have a negative impact and in the sense that they can no longer be named or specified.

In another crucial passage, Julius turns Lucinde herself into a stranger, or a carrier of unspeakable difference. This occurs in a letter in which he responds to the news of her pregnancy. While the letter promises an even closer bond between the lovers—a child—it also indicates their current separation, which leads Julius to reflections on the *Fremdes* that distances the lovers from each other:

Misunderstandings are good too in that they provide a chance to put what is holiest into words. The foreign [*Fremdes*] that now and then seems to come between us is not

---

36. See s.v. *Gemeinheit,* in Grimm, *Deutsches Wörterbuch* 4.1.2:3255–56; and Johann Christian Adelung, *Grammatisch-kritisches Wörterbuch der hochdeutschen Mundart* (Vienna: Bauer, 1811), 3:561–52.

in us, in either of us. It is only between us and on the surface, and I hope you will take advantage of this opportunity to drive it completely away from you and out of you.

(109–10/*64*; trans. modified)

Significantly, Julius first locates the *Fremdes between* the lovers and then *within* Lucinde. What has been hovering on the surface is now at the center of her being, defines her being. By transforming Lucinde into a stranger, Julius invests her with both the capacity and the responsibility to overcome that otherness that can never be clearly mapped onto an opposition. His hope that she will eventually succeed in driving the *Fremdes* out of herself indicates his attempt to elide any differences that cannot be accommodated by the model of sexual opposition. Julius's reassessment can also be read more psychologically, as a half-conscious acknowledgment of a disavowed truth. Julius tries to locate the difference first outside and only later inside Lucinde. He wants to expel the *Fremdes* but finds it so negative that he can only belatedly acknowledge its presence within her. Read in this way, the passage betrays a repressed hostility toward signs of Lucinde's Jewishness.

The attempt to elide differences other than gender difference culminates in a key passage toward the end of the novel. It has often been noted that the ending of *Lucinde* is politically surprisingly harmless, even reactionary. The novel begins with the ideal of free love and ends with the norm of the bourgeois nuclear family based on a gendered division of labor. A decisive moment in this conservative turn is Julius's vision of an ideal society organized on the model of marriage: "All mankind should really be divided into only two separate classes: the creative and the created, the male and the female; and in place of this artificial society there should be a great marriage between these two classes and a universal brotherhood of all individuals" (108–9/*63*). Julius combines here two ideas of society that are at odds with each other: the gendered model of marriage and the egalitarian ideal of fraternity. Tellingly, the latter appears to be a mere afterthought of the marriage model and its implied gender ideology. In Julius's view, the equality of individuals hinges upon the polarization and hierarchization of society. Individuals can meet eye to eye only once they have been divided into polar opposites—the masculine and the feminine—which also imply a hierarchy—the active versus the passive. The context of the passage is also significant. Julius invokes the marriage model of society after complaining about the depravity of the urban masses; he imagines better social relationships in the countryside, yet finds that these, too, are marked by *Gemeinheit*. (The word *Gemeinheit*, which Schlegel used earlier to describe the foreigners' communality, here takes on its more modern meaning of "vulgarity" and "meanness.") In other words, even though the passage quoted above echoes the fighting slogan of the French Revolution ("universal brotherhood"), it ultimately has a conciliatory purpose. It distracts from the sources of social unrest and helps suppress Julius's misgivings about class differences. This passage points to the limitations of the political vision in *Lucinde*. Rather than a democratic order in which differences of class, religion, and ethnicity do not matter, Schlegel conjures a homogeneous society in which such differences can no longer be expressed.

A Stranger to Love: Dorothea Veit's *Florentin*

Not long after the publication of Schlegel's *Lucinde*, Dorothea Veit wrote her own novel about the Romantic love ideal, titled *Florentin*. The composition of the novel happened at a time of personal transition. Although Veit seems to have experienced the divorce from her first husband as liberating, the postdivorce period led to struggles for recognition. She initially rented an apartment of her own in Berlin, but soon moved with Schlegel to Jena, where the couple shared a household with Friedrich's brother August Wilhelm and his wife, Caroline. Veit soon again felt like an outsider. Caroline Schlegel, the daughter of Johann David Michaelis, in his time one of the most outspoken opponents of Jewish emancipation, began to show condescension toward Veit. A dose of antisemitism seems to have been a matter of course for Caroline, who once described Veit as follows: "She has a . . . Jewish appearance, posture, etc. She does not appear pretty to me, her eyes are large and ardent, but the lower part of the face is too haggard, too strong."[37] Writing itself was a site of linguistic and cultural transition for Veit. She belonged to a generation of assimilating German Jews who were still exposed to Judeo-German (or Western Yiddish) at home. Although her father Moses Mendelssohn advocated the use of High German (his new translation of the Bible was, among other things, meant to instruct Jewish youth in proper German), the family employed the traditional vernacular in conversations and correspondence.[38] Veit's remark to Schleiermacher about an earlier draft of *Florentin*—"The devil always reigns in those places where the dative or the accusative should reign"[39]—testifies to her occasional struggles with German grammar as well as her self-consciousness about these struggles.

At the time Veit was living with Friedrich Schlegel, unmarried and penniless, and sought to support her procrastinating lover financially by producing translations and easily marketable literature: "But I cannot push him and urge the artist down to the craftsman . . . what I can do lies within these limits: affording him peace and winning our bread myself, humbly as a craftswoman, until he is able to do so."[40] Like all of Veit's

---

37. Quoted in Liliane Weissberg, "Nachwort," in Dorothea Schlegel, *Florentin: Roman, Fragmente, Varianten*, ed. Liliane Weissberg (Berlin: Ullstein, 1987), 218.

38. David Sorkin has corrected the myth that Mendelssohn completely rejected the use of the Yiddish language. See Sorkin, *Moses Mendelssohn and the Religious Enlightenment* (Berkeley: University of California Press, 1996), 54, 175 n. 3.

39. Veit to Schleiermacher, August 1800, in *Dorothea v. Schlegel geb. Mendelssohn und deren Söhne Johannes und Philipp Veit: Briefwechsel*, ed. J. M. Raich (Mainz: Franz von Kirchheim, 1881), 45. On Veit's linguistic situation, see also Liliane Weissberg, "Schreiben als Selbstentwurf: Zu den Schriften Rahel Varnhagens und Dorothea Schlegels," *Zeitschrift für Religions- und Geistesgeschichte* 47, no. 3 (1995): 231–53; here 251–52.

40. Veit to Schleiermacher, quoted in Dorothea Schlegel, *Florentin*, ed. Wolfgang Nehring (Stuttgart: Reclam, 1993), 303.

work, *Florentin* was published under the name of Friedrich Schlegel, who in this case was designated "editor" (the author was left anonymous). Veit's self-effacing remarks and behavior helped create an image of her as a mere helpmeet to Schlegel, a submissive woman willing to give up her own aspirations for the man she loved. For Hannah Arendt, Veit's life exemplifies the attempt on the part of so many Jewish women to assimilate through love, an attempt that muted every impulse to face the contradictions of Jewish existence and demand real social change.[41] In recent years, however, feminist critics have rediscovered *Florentin* and read it as a critique or subversion of *Lucinde*, especially its construction of femininity and masculinity.[42] In what follows, I will continue this line of thought and show that *Florentin* calls into question the Romantic love ideal enshrined in *Lucinde*. Veit uses set pieces of the Romantic code of love to expose it as a code, and to explore its workings and its failures. Out of this critique grows a sociopolitical vision quite different from Schlegel's. Veit explicitly links the search for romantic love to the quest for sociopolitical integration, which would include a fatherland, and dramatizes the failures of both.

The Critique of Romantic Love

Florentin offers a critique of both the cultural ideal and the literary code of romantic love. The novel's eponymous hero is a traveler, arriving seemingly out of nowhere in woody hills where he courageously rescues a count named Schwarzenberg and is invited to stay with the count's family. He develops a friendship with the count's daughter Juliane and her fiancé, Eduard—a relationship triangle that blurs the lines between love and friendship. Just as in *Lucinde*, the middle section of *Florentin* consists of a long narrative of the hero's childhood and youth, but in this case the narrative poses more riddles than it solves. Florentin spent the first years of his life on an island in social isolation, interrupted only by occasional visits of two mysterious men and a woman whom he called mother. Later he was brought up to become a monk, a prospect he detested. At some point he learns that the girl he believed to be his sister is not his sister, and embarks on a series of journeys to Italy, England, and Germany. These journeys are a quest for his origin, destination, and

---

41. See Arendt, *Rahel Varnhagen*, 108.
42. See Inge Stephan, "Weibliche und männliche Autorschaft: Zum *Florentin* von Dorothea Schlegel und zur *Lucinde* von Friedrich Schlegel," in *"Wen kümmert's wer spricht": Zur Literatur und Kulturgeschichte von Frauen aus Ost und West*, ed. Inge Stephan, Sigrid Weigel, and Kerstin Wilhelms (Cologne: Böhlau, 1991), 83–98; Martha B. Helfer, "Dorothea Veit-Schlegel's *Florentin*: Constructing a Feminist Romantic Aesthetic," *The German Quarterly* 69, no. 2 (Spring 1996): 144–60; Barbara Becker-Cantarino, "'Die wärmste Liebe zu unsrer litterarischen Ehe': Friedrich Schlegels *Lucinde* und Dorothea Veits *Florentin*," in *Bi-Textualität: Inszenierungen des Paares*, ed. Annegret Heitmann et al. (Berlin: Erich Schmidt, 2001), 131–41; Barbara Becker-Cantarino, "Dorothea Veit-Schlegel als Schriftstellerin und die Berliner Romantik," in *Arnim und die Berliner Romantik: Kunst, Literatur und Politik*, ed. Walter Pape (Tübingen: Max Niemeyer, 2001), 123–34; Elena Pnevmonidou, "Die Absage an das romantische Ich: Dorothea Schlegels *Florentin* als Umschrift von Friedrich Schlegels *Lucinde*," *German Life and Letters* 58, no. 3 (July 2005): 271–92.

love alike. When pondering what might put an end to his restless vagabond existence, Florentin conjures the image of a female companion who will share with him a secluded life in the forest.[43] Later he describes his yearning for love to Eduard and Juliane in quintessentially romantic terms, such as love for love's sake and togetherness unto death:

> You see, dear ones, I require little, you will probably not believe how little. But it seems to be a big demand, for I never found it fulfilled. Nothing but a lovable woman who loves me as I love her, who believes in me, who is mine simply for the sake of love and without any other purpose, who opposes no prejudice and no wicked habit to my happiness and wishes, who tolerates me as I am and does not succumb under the burden, who could bravely go through life with me, and if it must be, go to death with me.
>
> (30–31/*39–40*)

Florentin's yearning for love is never fulfilled, at least not in the novel as published. Nor does romantic love work for anyone else in the novel. The plot is structured around Florentin's triangulation of a quintessentially romantic love relationship, that between Eduard and Juliane. Their encounters are replete with mutual gazes, the promise of permanence, and moments of wordless communication: "The blessedness of love closed their lips; they didn't speak and yet said everything to each other" (79/*90*). Florentin's arrival, however, brings out disharmonies and discontents between Eduard and Juliane, neither of whom is mature enough to marry. Juliane's aunt Clementina, the novel's authority on love and marriage, advises postponing the wedding, and her belated blessing of the union sounds more like a presentiment: "'God bless you, my dear children! May you never experience the sorrows of love!'" (147/*153*). In an unpublished addendum to the novel, titled "Dedication to the Publisher" ("Zueignung an den Herausgeber"), Veit is even clearer about the doom of this marriage. She explains why she did not choose a conventional ending such as the hero's marriage: "Married? Can we appease ourselves with that? Do we not see in Eduard and Juliane that all sorrow and all confusion often begins from that point on" (154/*158*). There are ample hints throughout the text that the marriage between Eduard and Juliane will at best delay their individual development and at worst make both of them unhappy.

Florentin features several relationships that bear one or more hallmarks of romantic love but turn out to be deficient or fail altogether. People fall in love against their parents' wishes (Manfredi) and against conventions (Betty), both

---

43. See Dorothea Mendelssohn Veit Schlegel, *Florentin: A Novel*, trans. Edwina Lawler and Ruth Richardson (Lewiston, N.Y.: Edwin Mellen Press, 1988), 2. For the original German, see Schlegel, *Florentin: Roman, Fragmente, Varianten*, 12. Further citations from these editions will be included parenthetically in the text, with the page number in the English translation followed by the page number in the German edition in italics, as here (2/*12*).

typically signs of individual choice, yet their love does not arise freely and spontaneously. Rather, Manfredi is talked into love by Florentin, who enlists his help in the rescue of his sister, and Betty feels morally bound to Walter, who evidently seduced her in pursuit of money. Even Count and Countess Schwarzenberg fail to persuade as a model of harmony in love. Their marriage at first appears to be an illustration of the Romantic theory of gender complementarity, as they form an androgynous whole. The external sign of such complementarity is the couple's estate, which blends the antique elements favored by the Count with the modern comforts cherished by the Countess, with the effect that "the serious will of the master of the house was tempered by the obliging inclination of its mistress" (8/17). However, the harmony between the old and the new in the manor is questionable, or at least not discernible to outsiders. As Eduard notes, the mixture of styles may actually deserve the mockery it receives: "'Those who have not had the opportunity to know the interior find it strange and allow themselves much derision about the mixture of outmoded and modern taste. And it does look strange [*befremdend*] enough'" (17/27). Although Eduard then assures Florentin that the furnishings are indeed well matched, they cannot persuasively represent marital harmony. They are at best unstable and unreliable signs of perfect love. By highlighting the difficulty of deciphering the signs of love, Veit exposes the new code of romantic love as a code, that is, a system of signs that may or may not be recognized.

Florentin draws attention to a contradiction at the heart of the Romantic love ideal—namely, its dual function as a social code and as a medium of individuation, only one of which it acknowledges. As Luhmann writes, romantic love is not "a feeling, but rather a code of communication, according to the rules of which one can express, form and simulate feelings, deny them, impute them to others, and be prepared to face up to all the consequences which enacting such a communication may bring with it" (20). However, romantic love has to disavow its own status as a social code because it promises the experience of individual uniqueness. This contradiction has implications for the literature of love. On the one hand, literary texts are the main vehicles of the new love code, as they model the intimate encounters people seek in real life. On the other hand, the Romantic love ideal poses a challenge for literature because it relies so much on indirect communication, on glances rather than words, and on a sense of preexisting understanding. Consequently, literary texts often mark the advent of love by silence; the breakdown of language comes to prove the authenticity of feelings. Many great literary works give expression to this duality. One of the founding texts of romantic love, Goethe's *The Sufferings of Young Werther* (*Die Leiden des jungen Werther*, 1774), dramatizes speechless moments of intimacy—as when Werther finally gets to kiss Lotte—while exposing the scripted character of love—as when Werther has a copy of Lessing's *Emilia Galotti* on his desk.

Florentin's narration of his past love experiences exposes this codification of love. When he makes mention of a "wife" in Rome, and Juliane and Eduard react with incredulity, he evokes Schlegel's distinction between conventional and true marriage:

> "The sums, which were completely sufficient for my modest way of life, were turned over to my wife."
>
> "To your wife?" Juliane called in surprise; "probably just your housekeeper?"
>
> "No, to my wife!"
>
> "What? You're married? [*Wie? Sie sind verheiratet?*]"
>
> "You really trusted yourself to marry? [*Wirklich getraut?*]" Eduard asked.
>
> "She probably trusted [*traute*] me, and I trusted [*traute*] her too much."
>
> (63/73)

Florentin plays here with the ambiguity of the German word *trauen*, which means either "to trust" another person or "to get married" in front of a priest or other authority. In the episode that follows he persistently refers to himself as a husband and to his companion as his wife even though they never formally married. This recalls the Romantic idea of "true marriage," which according to Schlegel is above formal rituals and speech acts such as wedding vows. A conventional marriage is an external bond cemented by the church; a true marriage is a union based on feelings of love. Florentin's pun captures this train of thought: if the partners trust (*trauen*) each other, they do not need to formally wed (*trauen*) each other. However, the optimistic belief that love can be founded on trust alone turns out to be wrong. Florentin is elated when his "wife" gets pregnant, but she aborts the baby because she fears losing her beauty and possibly Florentin along with it. This fear is not entirely unfounded, since it was her beauty that sparked Florentin's love. But, as we can infer from his later confession to Eduard and Juliane, he really wanted something else from her: by becoming a father, he sought to secure a home, an identity, a fatherland. The falling out between Florentin and his "wife" results from this misunderstanding regarding their expectations from love. The assumption that love can dispense with external scripts and rely on unspoken agreements turns out to be disastrous. The relationship built on trust rather than explicit agreement throws Florentin into disappointment, anger, even attempted murder.

Along with the idea of wordless concord between the lovers, *Florentin* dismantles the notion of circular self-validation through love. In *Lucinde*, the pieces of Julius's life finally come together when he recounts his life story to his beloved. In finding Lucinde, Julius ultimately finds himself. This self-affirmation may explain why Schlegel's novel, despite all its emphasis on fragmentation and progression, has such a centered form, with shorter prose pieces symmetrically arranged around the long narrative of Julius's education in love in the middle of the book. In other Romantic novels, such circularity is often figured as a journey that ultimately leads the protagonist back to his home and origins—and to a lover known from childhood. The famous lines "Where are we really going? Always home" from Novalis's *Henry of Ofterdingen* (*Heinrich von Ofterdingen*, 1800) come to mind, as does Ludwig Tieck's *Franz Sternbald's Wanderings* (*Franz Sternbalds Wanderungen*, 1798), the hero of which was supposed to end at his point of departure, the city of Nuremberg, and find the girl he first met as a six-year-old and whose image stayed with him ever since. A similarly circular structure informs *Florentin*, which aims at returning the protagonist to his family and at reestablishing an order that can be presaged from the beginning. Florentin's intuitive knowledge about his future wife—"'My eye has not yet seen her, but I know her'" (2/*12*)—suggests such a hidden connection between his past and his future. He may have found this connection in Juliane, about whom he at one point exclaims half-seriously: "'Of what help is it that I found everything that I want united in one person? She is the loving bride of the happy man over there!'" (30/*39*). Raised by her aunt Clementina, who is possibly Florentin's mother, Juliane is a sister figure for Florentin. *Florentin* thus gestures at structural sibling incest, a popular motif in Romantic literature.[44] The sibling relation creates the kind of similarity of situation and experience that draws couples such as Julius and Lucinde together. But unlike Lucinde, Juliane remains a one-dimensional character and Florentin's love for her does not come to fruition. The novel ends rather abruptly with Florentin's departure from the wedding of his friends: "Florentin was nowhere to be found" (147/*153*). This laconic ending, which hints at no possible continuation or closure, frustrates the Romantic desire for a love that returns us to our selves and our origin.

The Quest for Sociopolitical Integration

Florentin reestablishes the connection between love and sociopolitical identity severed in other Romantic works of literature. Florentin, who in the first pages of the book is persistently referred to as "the traveler" or "the stranger," is the outsider par excellence. Wherever he goes, he does not quite belong. In socioeconomic terms, Florentin moves within the upper classes, yet since his biological parents are unknown, his own class origins remain in question. When asked whether he is a "von Florentin"—that is, a member of the nobility—he asks to add the title Baron to his name because its original meaning is what he wishes to be—"a man" (25/*34*).[45] That is, he claims the title of a nobleman only to vacate its linguistic function as a marker of social class. Read against this backdrop, Florentin's lack of clothes befitting his

---

44. Veit hints at this relationship between Clementine and Florentin in a manuscript that is now lost. See Weissberg, "Nachwort," 226. On the literary motif of sibling incest and the fantasies about religious and cultural difference it expresses, see Stefani Engelstein, "Sibling Incest and Cultural Voyeurism in Günderode's *Udohla* and Thomas Mann's *Wälsungenblut*," *The German Quarterly* 77, no. 3 (Summer 2004): 278–99.

45. Etymologically, the word *baron* can be traced back to the Frankish *baro*, which meant "man, free man."

social status, which he cites as a cause for his abrupt departure from Eduard and Juliane's wedding, is not a marginal detail. Rather, his lack of insignia to signal his social status reveals the uncertainty about his class background. The same uncertainty characterizes Florentin's cultural affiliation. Although born and raised in Italy, Florentin seems to have a special affinity to things German, which attracts him to German artists in Rome (63/72) and to German friends who "claimed to find something completely German about me" (60/70). Oddly enough, he evidently learned the German language twice: first from the German-born priest who oversees the education of the young boy (39/48), and later as a young man during a stay in Switzerland (71/82). This twofold beginning makes it difficult to locate his acquisition of German in time, thus enhancing the ambiguity of his relationship to German culture: has Florentin assimilated to German culture, or has he always belonged to it?

Critics disagree about whether the lack of a clearly defined social identity presents a problem for Florentin, and whether this lack identifies him as Jewish. Some argue that Florentin's social ostracism marks him as both Jewish and effeminate.[46] According to him, he has always been an outsider. Already in his youth, he was a freethinker and defied authorities. He also calls himself "the poor one, the lonely one, the ostracized one, the child of chance" (85/95) and speaks of a "curse" (115/124) that lies upon him. However, as Liliane Weissberg points out, Florentin does not seem to suffer much from his predicament. He is an outsider who is also an insider, a protean figure who belongs everywhere and nowhere. Unlike many assimilating Jews, he experiences neither language difficulties nor social prejudice. He fits into each new surrounding with an ease that contrasts with Veit's own struggle for social acceptance. Florentin is a cosmopolitan who encounters friendship and support wherever he goes, in part because he never travels far from the social class in which he was raised.[47] The question of whether Florentin's lack of a clearly defined identity is a problem, and whether it reflects Veit's own assimilation struggles, ultimately remains unanswerable. What matters is that this lack becomes the novel's major theme and, moreover, is tied up with the quest for love.

The notion that love can bestow any kind of social, cultural, or political identity goes against the understanding of love as a medium of individuation. According to Luhmann, love in the Romantic period validates an individual's unique perspective and experience of the world rather than establishing his or her social identity. In fact, the self that emerges in and through love defines itself in opposition to social classifications. Romantic literature promotes this process of individuation by stripping its characters of social attributes. In contrast, *Florentin* rejoins the quest for love to

---

46. See, e.g., Becker-Cantarino, "'Die wärmste Liebe'"; and Stephan, "Weibliche und männliche Autorschaft."

47. See Weissberg, "Schreiben als Selbstentwurf," 246. Weissberg suggests that the absence of social barriers in the novel may be read as wish fulfillment on Dorothea's part. Indeed, in one of her letters, Dorothea expresses the hope that her sons would become cosmopolitans.

questions of cultural, social, and political identity, primarily through Florentin's conspicuous lack of such an identity. The novel further raises the stakes of romantic love by calling attention to biological reproduction, and by linking reproduction to citizenship. In that regard, too, *Florentin* differs from other Romantic literature, which tends to stay focused on the lovers and to circumvent the question of their offspring. Indeed, it has been argued that early Romanticism favors mental over biological procreation, in part because a child is something too particular in its own right to serve as a proof of the lovers' union.[48] In *Lucinde*, for instance, actual children play hardly a role. In a letter to Lucinde, Julius greets the news of her pregnancy enthusiastically, regards the child as the completion of their marriage, and fantasizes about its future education. His next letter, however, mostly records his despondent reaction to news of her recent illness, raising the question of what may have happened to the fetus. There is vague talk about a child in the last section of the novel, "Dalliance of the Imagination" ("Tändeleyen der Fantasie"), a dreamlike scene that transfigures childhood play into artistic productivity. An earlier section of the novel describes at length the child Wilhelmine, but she is a mere allegory of literary wit and chaos.

Compared to *Lucinde*'s privileging of artistic production, *Florentin* is more concerned with biological reproduction. Florentin himself is preoccupied with his biological origins. Throughout the novel he is searching for the true relatives who would replace imposed relatives, including the woman whom he "had to call . . . mother" (34/42) in this childhood. His wish to father a child—that is, to replace his family of origin with a family of his own—explains his terrified reaction to the abortion undergone by his Roman lover. In a discussion of his plans to emigrate to the American colonies, Florentin expresses his hope that fatherhood will secure him a fatherland. We may recall here how fraught questions of marriage, procreation, and intergenerational transmission were for Jews at the time. Veit's father, Moses Mendelssohn, one of the most famous philosophers of his time, never held a legal status high enough to transmit his right of residence to his children. This was one of the reasons he married his daughter off at the age of nineteen to a suitable man: a successful banker and, perhaps even more important, a Prussian Jew in possession of a writ of protection. And while her divorce evidently did not endanger Veit's residence status, she was still considered a foreigner and forced to pay a special "Jew toll" when crossing one of the many borders separating the German states.[49] Florentin's plan to become naturalized by becoming a father is thus highly resonant:

"To America?" called Eduard.

"Your fatherland doesn't hold you?" the Count asked.

---

48. See Daub, *Uncivil Unions*, 157–70.

49. The issue of a special pass for Veit and the costs associated with it came up in 1800, when Schlegel and Veit made plans to visit Schlegel's sister in Dresden. See the letters by Schlegel, Veit, and Schleiermacher, as well as the editor's endnotes, in *KA* 25:105, 132, 139, 472, 476, 481.

"Where is my fatherland?" Florentin called in a sadly bitter tone, then immediately said half jokingly, "as far back as I can remember, I was an orphan and a
stranger on earth, and thus I intend to call the land where I will first be called father
my fatherland."

(6/16)

At a time when the struggle for Jewish civil rights gained traction and was
accompanied by warnings against those Jews "who do not view the state as their
fatherland,"[50] Florentin's view can only be politically provocative. If Romantic
writers appropriated the birth metaphor to describe their own artistic production,
Florentin suggests that he can create his own sociopolitical identity by fathering a
child. This process of creation, however, is not within anyone's control, not even
Florentin's. Although Florentin can actively pursue integration—by seeking a
woman and begetting a child with her—there is a moment of unpredictability:
he will have to wait for his child to call him "father" before he can call a country
"fatherland." The reversal of the normal temporal sequence emphasizes the newness of the political order that can accommodate Florentin. A fatherland is usually
something one inherits from one's father, and indicates a tie to the past, rather than
something conferred by one's child that indicates a tie to the future. It can also be
both of these things at the same time, indicating continuity over generations, but
here it is an indicator of change. For Florentin, the rights associated with a fatherland do not derive from an existing order but from something yet to be created.

Florentin's quest for sociopolitical integration through love and procreation
remains unfulfilled, at least within the novel as published. In Schlegel's *Lucinde*,
love is a medium of infinite progression, yet there is also a sense of closure; Julius
has found himself in Lucinde and completed his education toward love. The circular form of the novel, which groups letters, fantasies, and other manifestations of
Julius's subjectivity around the narration of his development, is a stylistic expression of closure. In contrast, *Florentin* is more fundamentally fragmentary and
open-ended. As Inge Stephan notes, Veit's novel is an unfinished *Bildungsroman* in
reverse, one that leads back to the hero's origins but never reaches its destination.[51]
While love in *Lucinde* founds the possibility of the protagonist's further development and constant expansion of his social circle, Florentin remains without love,
a wandering stranger suspended between an unknown past and an indeterminate
future. He never begets the child he expects to bestow on him a fatherland. In the
unpublished "Dedication to the Publisher," Veit hints that Florentin will eventually found a family and a new nation in the American colonies. Yet the "Dedication" also suggests that the open-endedness of the novel is indeed programmatic;

---

50. Friedländer, Schleiermacher, and Teller, *A Debate on Jewish Emancipation*, 104. Schleiermacher
demands that the Jews give up their messianism in order to recognize their new fatherland.
51. See Stephan, "Weibliche und männliche Autorschaft," 94.

even here, national and political belonging remain a matter of uncertainty for Florentin—and a matter of conjecture for the narrator:

> For me the book is finished here, for Florentin's influence doesn't extend any further. Furthermore, we know that, in fact, he no longer made merry with seriousness but truly executed his decision, that which was for him his destiny, scorned the advantages, the fineness of culture, and *returned* to his beloved wilds. He was the leader and the *first one* of an entire nation that honored him like a divinity. Once again the family saw him in its settlements as the delegate of his people. He proudly *returned* when they wanted to persuade him to stay. Since that time we know nothing more about him. Perhaps he is still living and tells his grandchildren about the disastrous miracles and brilliant misery of the Europeans.
>
> (154/*158–59*; my emphasis)

This passage shows just how ambiguous Florentin's relationship to his new nation in the colonies is: Does he arrive at a new place or return home? Does he found a new nation or restore the unity of an existing one? His position as the "first one" of the tribe suggests that he founded the nation, as does the fact that his new compatriots revere him like a divinity. But the mention that Florentin "*returned* to his beloved wilds" creates the same ambiguity we noticed earlier with respect to his relationship to German culture, to which he may have assimilated or always already belonged, and the Schwarzenberg family, to which he may be unknowingly related. Veit's comment that the end of the novel coincides with the end of Florentin's influence on the family only enhances this ambiguity. It suggests that Florentin is not the individual agent of a *Bildungsroman* but a mere catalyst of changes in the novel's social world. As such he recalls the figure of the Jew as a social catalyst we first encountered in Lessing's *Nathan der Weise*. Florentin's position is as ambiguous as Nathan's; he may be on the outside or at the very center of the new social formations he helps create.[52] Veit hints at Florentin's future life in the colonies, suggesting that he may ultimately have obtained the fatherhood and the fatherland he has been seeking. But she presents this as a conjecture on her part and refrains from *telling* the story of his marriage and procreation in the colonies—all the while insisting that *Florentin* is a history rather than a novel, that she reports upon rather than creates her characters. Taken together, these two assertions release Florentin from authorial control and make him *structurally unidentifiable*.

---

52. Jeffrey Librett observes that Florentin resembles both the traveler in Lessing's *Die Juden* and the Templar in Lessing's *Nathan der Weise*. Interestingly, neither character can marry the girl he met through his rescue action, yet for opposite reasons: the Jewish traveler is too different from the Christian girl, and the Templar is too similar to his sister Recha. By alluding to Lessing, *Florentin* merges the figure of the stranger and the figure of the brother. See Jeffrey S. Librett, *The Rhetoric of Cultural Dialogue: Jews and Germans from Moses Mendelssohn to Richard Wagner and Beyond* (Stanford, Calif.: Stanford University Press, 2000), 187–88.

Eva Lezzi has argued that by shrouding Florentin's origins in enigmas, Veit ironically anticipates and strategically deploys the reader's desire to decipher the protagonist's identity. Rather than out her characters as Jewish, Veit playfully exposes the undecidability of all identity and the futility of any attempt to fixate identity.[53] While this is a pertinent reading, it does not address *Florentin*'s first decisive step, which is to rejoin the search for love and the quest for a social identity. By reestablishing this connection, Veit's novel goes beyond the Romantic paradigm of love as a medium of individuation. As we have seen, in Schlegel's *Lucinde*, class, religion, and nationality do not matter for the experience of love. The absence of social markers creates a semantic void around literary characters conceived as unique individuals. This semantic void may explain the scarcity of literary representations of Christian-Jewish love affairs around 1800, the social reverberations of which would be too difficult to ignore. *Florentin* does not fill this semantic void by restoring the markers of a social, cultural, or national identity. Rather, the novel conjoins the yearning for love and the quest for identity and dramatizes the failure of both.

Reading *Lucinde* and *Florentin* as commentaries on the process of Jewish emancipation and acculturation does not mean to restore the "missing" references to Jews and Judaism, but to attend to the modes of their absence. The novels represent two different modes of such absence. In Schlegel's *Lucinde*, the transformation of love into a model of society hinges upon the disavowal of differences, whether religious or socioeconomic. Love can serve as a model of society precisely because the protagonists have been divested of all social attributes. Lacking markers of a certain class, religion, or nationality, Julius and Lucinde become first individuals and then representatives of their gender, the opposition of which is projected onto an ideal society. In contrast, Veit invokes love as a medium of integration into an existing society, and as such has it fail conspicuously. While Florentin is in no way positively identified as a Jew, he is in the process of adapting to a new culture and society, just as Veit herself and many other Jews at the time were. The inconclusiveness of this process in *Florentin* can be read as a call to restore a similar open-endedness to the historical process of Jewish acculturation. Rather than instrumentalize love for a project of social integration, *Florentin* suggests that society itself has to change in ways that have yet to be determined. The political progressiveness of Veit's novel becomes especially clear when compared with the works of the younger generation of German Romantics, whose anti-Jewish attitudes are well known. As I will show in the next chapter, the later Romantic writer Achim von Arnim dramatizes failing Christian-Jewish love stories to a radically different end: to bolster his antisemitic view that Jews can never be integrated into German society.

---

53. See Eva Lezzi, "'. . . ewig rein wie die heilige Jungfrau . . .' Zur Enthüllung des Jüdschen in der Rezeption von deutschsprachigen Romanen um 1800," in *Juden und Judentum in der deutschsprachigen Literatur*, ed. Willi Jasper, Eva Lezzi, Elke Liebs, and Helmut Peitsch (Wiesbaden: Harrassowitz, 2006), 61–86.

3

Figures of Love in Later Romantic Antisemitism

Achim von Arnim

The defeat and occupation of Prussia by Napoleonic troops in 1806 gave a new impetus to German nationalism, which had initially drawn on ideas of collective self-determination by Kant and Herder but now increasingly incorporated anti-French and anti-Jewish elements. Rising antisemitism explains, among other things, why Prussia's military defeat spelled the end of most of the Berlin salons hosted by Jewish women. While the salon of Rahel Varnhagen and other Jewish *salonnières* fell out of favor, the younger generation of German Romantics began to frequent the salons of mostly noble Gentile women. Varnhagen writes in early 1808: "At my 'tea table' . . . I sit with nothing but dictionaries; I serve tea no oftener than every week or ten days, when Schack, who has *not* deserted me, asks for some. That is how much everything has changed! Never have I been so alone."[1] Yet it is at this moment, when Christian-Jewish social interaction is once again on the decline, that interfaith love affairs become a popular literary theme in younger authors such as Achim von Arnim. While Enlightenment thinkers tended to deflect attention from interfaith love and marriage, and while early Romantic writers avoided explicit references to Jews and Judaism, later Romantic authors place Christian-Jewish love stories at the center of several texts that reflect on the changing position of Jews in

1. Quoted in Arendt, *Rahel Varnhagen*, 176; Varnhagen's emphasis.

German culture and society—and that are undeniably antisemitic.[2] What does the peculiar use of figures of love in these texts tell us about the form and function of Romantic antisemitism?

Although few dispute that anti-Jewish attitudes were prevalent among the younger generation of German Romantics, scholars have found it difficult to determine the scope and the character of their antisemitism. This difficulty arises because the hallmarks of Romantic antisemitism are inconsistency and ambivalence, a simultaneous fascination with and rejection of Jews and Judaism. Nothing illustrates this better than the life and work of Achim von Arnim. Arnim had attended the same Jewish salons he condemned during the dinners of the Christian-German Table Society (Christlich-Deutsche Tischgesellschaft), of which he was a cofounder and which excluded Jews from membership. He scorned both Orthodox and assimilated Jews but appreciated some elements of Jewish culture and religion, especially its mystical strands. His literary references to the Kabbalah have been read as a sign of syncretistic openness to different religious traditions.[3]

Arnim's contradictory attitude toward Jews and Judaism emerges most clearly in a series of writings he completed in 1811, just before the promulgation of the 1812 Prussian emancipation edict, which he opposed. In the prose fragment "Reconciliation in the Summer Holiday" ("Die Versöhnung in der Sommerfrische"), Arnim advocates a model of gradual emancipation in which the granting of political rights to the Jews would only follow their religious conversion and cultural assimilation. In line with earlier Enlightenment thinking, he supports the social integration of the Jews on the condition that they adapt to the economic, cultural, and religious norms of their Christian surroundings. His drama *Halle and Jerusalem*, in which the only positive Jewish character has successfully overcome his Judaism, further illustrates this presumed necessity of radical Jewish transformation. At the same time, Arnim expresses paranoid anxieties about the actual success of assimilation, especially in his notorious speech "On the Distinguishing Signs of Jewishness" ("Über die Kennzeichen des Judenthums"), which he delivered at the Table Society in the spring of 1811. The speech attempts to restore to Jews a

2. It is customary to distinguish between three phases of German Romanticism: *Frühromantik* (ca. 1795–1804), *Jüngere Romantik* or *Heidelberger Romantik* (ca. 1804–15), and *Spätromantik* (ca. 1815–48). Although this chapter is primarily concerned with the second phase, its arguments also apply to the third phase, and I therefore speak more broadly about "later"—i.e., post-1806—Romanticism. On the relationship between Romantic antisemitism and German nationalism, see also Marco Puschner, *Antisemitismus im Kontext der Politischen Romantik: Konstruktionen des "Deutschen" und des "Jüdischen" bei Arnim, Brentano und Saul Ascher* (Tübingen: Max Niemeyer, 2008).

3. See, for instance, Gunnar Och, "'Gewisse Zauberbilder der jüdischen Kabbala'—Zur Aneignung kabbalistischer Stoffe bei Achim von Arnim und Clemens Brentano," in *Kabbala und die Literatur der Romantik: Zwischen Magie und Trope*, ed. Eveline Goodman-Thau, Gert Mattenklott, and Christoph Schulte (Tübingen: Max Niemeyer, 1999), 179–95; and Detlef Kremer, "Kabbalistische Signaturen: Sprachmagie als Brennpunkt romantischer Imagination bei E. T. A. Hoffmann und Achim von Arnim," ibid., 197–221.

visibility that he believed had disappeared because of their alleged "rare skill of hiding,"[4] which involved only superficial rather than essential changes.

One way of explaining these contradictions is in terms of a clash between different belief systems that Arnim espouses simultaneously. On the one hand, the notion of Jewish mutability informed both Christian calls for conversion and the Enlightenment idea of human perfectibility, with its corollary belief that Jews are especially in need of improvement. On the other hand, this model of transformation conflicts with a historically new sense of Jewish physical, and therefore immutable, difference. Indeed, scholars tend to regard later Romantic antisemitism as a transitional phenomenon on the route from traditional Christian anti-Judaism to modern antisemitism or, alternatively, from the eighteenth-century beginnings of Jewish emancipation to the nineteenth-century backlash against it. Modern antisemitism is here defined as (1) an expression of the socioeconomic fears caused by modernization, (2) a corollary of political ideologies, especially nationalism, that seek to unify populations, (3) a racial ideology that posits the existence of indelible physical differences between "Jews" and "Aryans," and (4) a hostility directed against assimilated Jews, whose claims of a German identity it denies. Measured by these standards, later Romantic antisemitism is often found to be almost but "not yet" fully modern. There is some consensus among scholars that despite its modern economic and political motivations, later Romantic antisemitism is not a full-fledged racial ideology and does not legitimize anti-Jewish violence.[5]

The attempt to situate Arnim's view of Jews and Judaism on a linear trajectory toward the rise of modern antisemitism and sort out its elements accordingly is problematic for several reasons. It not only promotes a sense of historical determinism but also obscures insights into how the heterogeneous elements effectively worked together. In this chapter, I draw on psychoanalytically inflected theories of ideology to offer a new explanation of the apparent inconsistencies of Arnim's antisemitism. Slavoj Žižek's concept of the "social fantasy" and Homi Bhabha's notion of "colonial mimicry" both stipulate that ideologies can incorporate a great

---

4. Achim von Arnim, "Über die Kennzeichen des Judentums," in *Werke in sechs Bänden*, ed. Roswitha Burwick et al. (Frankfurt am Main: Deutscher Klassiker, 1989–94), 6:362–87; here 363. All further citations of this speech refer to this edition and will be included parenthetically in the text.

5. See Gisela Henckmann, "Das Problem des 'Antisemitismus' bei Achim von Arnim," *Aurora* 46 (1986): 48–69; Heinz Härtl, "Romantischer Antisemitismus: Arnim und die Tischgesellschaft," *Weimarer Beiträge* 33, no. 7 (1987): 1159–73; Rainer Erb and Werner Bergmann, *Die Nachtseite der Judenemanzipation: Der Widerstand gegen die Integration der Juden in Deutschland 1780–1860* (Berlin: Metropol, 1989); Wolfgang Frühwald, "Antijudaismus in der Zeit der deutschen Romantik," in *Conditio Judaica: Judentum, Antisemitismus und deutschsprachige Literatur vom 18. Jahrhundert bis zum Ersten Weltkrieg*, pt. 2, ed. Hans Otto Horch and Horst Denkler (Tübingen: Max Niemeyer, 1989), 72–91; Peter Philipp Riedl, "'. . . das ist ein ewig Schachern und Zänken . . .': Achim von Arnims Haltung zu den Juden in den Majorats-Herren und anderen Schriften," *Aurora* 54 (1994): 72–105. More recently, Wolf-Daniel Hartwich has argued in *Romantischer Antisemitismus* that Arnim's anti-Jewish images are just as cruel as those of racial antisemites (185) but remain firmly lodged in a framework that is "transformatory" rather than "exterminatory" (26).

deal of inconsistency and ambivalence without losing their effectiveness. These post-Freudian theories shed new light on Arnim precisely because ambiguity and ambivalence proliferate in his writings around the motif of interreligious love. As I will show, romantic attachments are the means by which Arnim figures the possibilities and the limits of Christian-Jewish rapprochement. I will also argue that interfaith love stories fulfill a distinct function in Arnim's political thought, which combines German nationalism with a critique of rising industrial capitalism. Arnim wrote several texts that either stage the emergence of a German community that excludes Jews or depict the corrosion of such a community through French occupation and rising industrial capitalism. These texts include the openly antisemitic speech "On the Distinguishing Signs of Jewishness," the unpublished prose fragment "Reconciliation in the Summer Holiday," and the complex novella *Gentry by Entailment* (*Die Majorats-Herren*). In each of these texts, the dramatization of failing Christian-Jewish love affairs serves to gloss over the tensions that trouble Arnim's visions of social harmony and political unity.

"On the Distinguishing Signs of Jewishness"

Slavoj Žižek's theory of ideology shares with other projection theories the conviction that "the Jew" of the antisemites is an imaginary construct that serves to mitigate the internal conflicts of Christian communities. Yet he goes beyond the classic projection theory in claiming that not only the scapegoat but also society itself is imaginary.[6] According to Žižek, the antisemitic image of "the Jew" both embodies and disavows the structural impossibility of society and masks the contradictions in the holistic images that hold a particular society together. This idea has a particular bearing on Romantic nationalism and its vision of the yet-to-be-established national community. It explains, for instance, why antisemitism played such a crucial role during the formative phase of the Christian-German Table Society, when its rules of sociability were still in the process of being defined. The Table Society was to be a countermodel to the early Romantic salons, many of which had been hosted by educated Jewish women and, as we saw in the last chapter, functioned as sites of Christian-Jewish rapprochement. In addition, the Table Society was to serve as a model for the future German nation.[7] Yet as such it was riddled by tensions. There

---

6. For a classic projection theory of antisemitism, see Gavin I. Langmuir, *Toward a Definition of Anti-semitism* (Berkeley: University of California Press, 1990). Langmuir distinguishes between anti-Judaism, which in all its faulty overgeneralizations is rooted in a real religious conflict, and antisemitism, which lacks all foundation in reality and is based on pure fantasy. According to Langmuir, antisemitism thus defined arose during the Middle Ages, when Christians first launched blood libels and other fantastic accusations against the Jews to contain the internal conflicts of their own communities.

7. See Susanna Moßmann, "Das Fremde ausscheiden: Antisemitismus und Nationalbewußtsein bei Ludwig Achim von Arnim und in der 'Christlich-deutschen Tischgesellschaft,'" in *Machtphantasie Deutschland: Nationalismus, Männlichkeit und Fremdenhaß im Vaterlandsdiskurs deutscher Schriftsteller des 18. Jahrhunderts*, ed. Hans Peter Herrmann, Hans-Martin Blitz, and Susanne Moßmann (Frankfurt am Main: Suhrkamp, 1996), 123–59; here 144.

was, for instance, significant confusion among participants about the relationship between Prussian patriotism and German nationalism and about the dominant role of Protestantism within the future German nation. In his "Founding Song of the German Table Society" ("Stiftungslied der deutschen Tisch-Gesellschaft"), Arnim glorifies the beginnings of the Prussian state but is quite vague about its connection to the Reformation. He makes sure that the attribute "Christian" does not become too narrowly defined as Protestant, presumably because he perceives the necessity of unifying all German states in the fight against Napoleon.[8] Yet the tension between German nationalism and Prussian patriotism persists.

In Arnim's work, the figure of the Jew comes to mask this and other tensions inherent in his attempt to define and perform a German national community. As Žižek argues, ideology operates not only by abstracting historically contingent predicaments into eternal conditions but also through the opposite gesture, that is, by transforming a structural impasse into an empirical obstacle.[9] This is perhaps nowhere clearer than in Arnim's notorious speech "On the Distinguishing Signs of Jewishness." The overt purpose of the speech is to provide a rationale for the exclusion of Jews from the Christian-German Table Society; yet in so doing it first creates the Jew as a distinct and recognizable figure.[10] Arnim is mainly concerned with two purportedly Jewish traits: "secrecy" (*Heimlichkeit*), which allows Jews to infiltrate Christian spheres from which they are excluded, and "curiosity" (*Neugierde*), which makes them want to trespass into such spheres to begin with. Arnim's focus on these two traits reflects the historical moment of his writing, that is, the first phase of the acculturation process in which Jews adapted to the language, clothes, and customs of their Christian surroundings. His characterization of Jews as outwardly malleable and inwardly obdurate shows how this process gave rise to a new set of anti-Jewish stereotypes as well as a desire to restore visibility to the Jews. Arnim states that the "peculiarities" of Jews are "still by no means scientifically defined" (363) and goes on to provide a comprehensive catalogue of purported Jewish characteristics using pseudoscientific methods of observation and experiment.

"On the Distinguishing Signs of Jewishness" produces the figure of the Jew in a scene that conjures an alternative to biological procreation in general and to interreligious sex in particular. This occurs when Arnim shifts from observation

---

8. See Stefan Nienhaus, *Geschichte der deutschen Tischgesellschaft* (Tübingen: Max Niemeyer, 2003), 12–13. The poem is in Arnim, *Werke*, 5:761–63.

9. See Judith Butler, Ernesto Laclau, and Slavoj Žižek, *Contingency, Hegemony, Universality: Contemporary Dialogues on the Left* (New York: Verso, 2000), 100–101.

10. Apparently Arnim initially advocated the inclusion of baptized Jews in the Table Society but was voted down by the majority of its members. In a speech from January 18, 1815, he argues that such an inclusion can help recent converts overcome their Judaism more completely. See Jürgen Knaack, *Achim von Arnim—Nicht nur Poet: Die politischen Anschauungen Arnims in ihrer Entwicklung* (Darmstadt: Thesen, 1976), 135. Arnim's speech has sometimes been read as a sign that his antisemitism was more tempered than that of most members of the Table Society. I argue that it is precisely this demand for total Jewish transformation, against which all actual Jewish assimilation is measured and judged insufficient, that makes Arnim's antisemitism so pernicious.

to experiment, or from the description of Jewish characteristics to the creation of conditions meant to produce such characteristics. He proposes a chemical experiment—meant to be humorous, but actually extremely gruesome—that would decompose a Jew into his elemental parts, among them "4 parts of Christian blood, secretly gained through sinful mixing" (383). He then describes how he would construct a new body by exchanging those parts for equal parts of money, creating a Jew who is at least momentarily clearly identifiable as a Jew. This reconstruction is an act of purification, a separation of Jewish and Christian blood that undoes imagined sexual relations between Christians and Jews. The stylistic changes in this passage show that it is also a form of discursive production. Arnim begins his description of the experiment in the subjunctive and the style of a recipe—"Take [*man nehme*] this or another Jew" (382)—but ends it in the past indicative and the form of a report—"The Jew was reconstructed just as fast has he had been dismantled" (383). The experiment's transformation from a hypothetical to an actual event indicates that Arnim's speech performs rather than merely describes the production of the pure Jew.[11]

The Jewishness of the newly constructed Jew manifests itself in his propensity for witticism and irony when the narrator engages him in a conversation about the battle at Jena ("das große Landesunglück," 383) and the death of the queen. The first reference is to the 1806 battle against Napoleon that ended in a devastating defeat of the Prussian army. The second reference is to the popular queen Luise, who in 1810 unexpectedly died at the age of thirty-four and was greatly mourned throughout Prussia. The cult of Luise, which had begun during early Romanticism and was carried on by Arnim and others, was central to Prussian patriotism and its idea of a loving bond between ruler and subjects.[12] The cult even intensified after Luise's death, when a public emphasis on the king's feelings of grief drew ruler and subjects closer together. All Prussians were meant to identify with the mourning king and act like members of an organic community rather than subjects of an absolute state. The Jew in Arnim's speech slights the symbols of Prussian unity by making fun of the military defeat and commenting that the queen "was a woman like all others" and that he himself "had also lost one" (383). In other words, the pure Jew from which "4 parts" of Christian blood have been extracted is unable to participate in the Prussian community of love.

---

11. On Arnim's attempt to counter the figure of the "secret Jew" through the production of the "pure Jew," see also Birgit R. Erdle, "'Über die Kennzeichen des Judenthums': Die Rhetorik der Unterscheidung in einem phantasmatischen Text von Achim von Arnim," *German Life and Letters* 49, no. 2 (April 1996): 147–58; here 154.

12. On this political program of love, see Wolf Kittler, *Die Geburt des Partisanen aus dem Geist der Poesie: Heinrich von Kleist und die Strategie der Befreiungskriege* (Freiburg: Rombach, 1987), 162–75; and Nienhaus, *Geschichte der deutschen Tischgesellschaft*, 105–8. One of the events frequently recorded in history books is the personal interview Napoleon held with the pregnant queen after the defeat, which, however, did little to change the emperor's harsh policy toward Prussia.

One of the most striking features of Arnim's speech is that it openly admits its own failure. If Arnim sets out to establish clearly distinguishable signs of Jewishness, he constantly defeats his own purpose by revealing similarities rather than differences between Jews and Christians. He takes note, for instance, of the special affinity between Jews and Christian scholars. Even more importantly, Arnim concedes that Jewish identity might be a mere product of Christian projection and that he is unable to come up with a list of truly reliable markers of Jewishness. In the end he can only express his wish for the discovery of such markers and call into question the existence of commonalities among all Jews: "But what can Spinoza, Mendelssohn, and my noble Jewish friends have in common with Judas Iscariot?" (387). To be sure, the notion of the exceptional Jew is a known antisemitic tactic that typically serves to highlight the deficiencies of the average Jew. But this takes nothing away from the fact that Arnim is remarkably open about the ultimate foundering of his "scientific" project.

To understand the logic behind this self-avowed failure we may return to Arnim's imaginary production of the "pure" Jew. Arnim notes that the reconstructed Jew's cheerfulness would make him a valuable addition to the Table Society were his jokes not so misguided: "He would serve as great entertainment for the cheerful company at table, if only his jokes did not mostly hit the wrong spot, like a friendly squeeze in the place one has been bled" (384). Again, this is an interesting criticism because it suggests that Jews are providing critique through irony, locating weak spots and highlighting their existence in jocular ways that might come uncomfortably close to later Romantic ironic texts.[13] At this point Arnim quickly shifts to yet another stock idea of medieval antisemitism, the idea of a peculiar Jewish stench or *foetor judaicus*. He proposes various experiments to identify the sources and the exact chemical composition of this odor. However, rather than producing the desired formula of Jewish difference, Arnim's ruminations on the theme lead to another striking admission of the projective character of antisemitism: "I am firmly convinced that if a Christian cannot stand the smell of roses, then all Jews smell of roses to him" (385). This sentence highlights the futility of Arnim's attempt to isolate and name Jewish characteristics; it suggests that no Jewish essence exists, that "the Jew" simply is whatever the Christian dislikes. Why does this open acknowledgment of an ideological gesture not affect Arnim's overall ideological message?

Here Žižek's concept of social fantasy proves helpful. Žižek emphasizes that ideology operates not only through the construction of knowledge but also through the manipulation of affects and fantasies. Ideology critique therefore needs to be composed of two different strategies: a symptomatic reading that reveals the mechanisms of condensation and displacement by which antisemites blame social

---

13. See also Günter Oesterle, "Juden, Philister und romantische Intellektuelle: Überlegungen zum Antisemitismus in der Romantik," *Athenäum* 2 (1992): 55–91. Oesterle points out that Arnim and Brentano attempt to fend off the reproach that Romantics are close to the Jews.

conflicts on Jews; and a second procedure that "aims at the kernel of *enjoyment*, at articulating the way in which—beyond the field of meaning but at the same time internal to it—an ideology implies, manipulates, produces a pre-ideological enjoyment structured in fantasy."[14] A symptomatic reading explores the gaps, fissures, and inconsistencies of an ideological proposition in order to elicit its truth—namely, the motives behind its symptomatic distortions. Fantasies are resistant to such interpretive procedures because they do not so much cloud people's thoughts as structure their affective engagement with reality. This is why they can be fully cognizant of their ideological biases and still function in the reality these biases help create. Žižek cites contemporary cynicism as an example of how the open avowal of ideological delusion might render ideology only more effective: it does not matter that we know what we are doing as long as we are still doing it.[15] What is necessary is to thwart the enjoyment procured by the image of the Jew, who both embodies and denies the impossibility of a social identity. "Fantasy is basically a scenario filling out the empty space of a fundamental impossibility, a screen masking a void. . . . As such, fantasy is not to be interpreted, only 'traversed': all we have to do is experience how there is nothing 'behind' it, and how fantasy masks precisely this 'nothing.'"[16]

Such an exposure of a void emphatically fails to happen in Arnim's "On the Distinguishing Signs of Jewishness." To traverse the social fantasy would mean to confront the deadlock of social identity, in this case, of a Prussian patriotism that is both part of and at odds with German nationalism. It would mean to ask why one needs the Jews in order to uphold the possibility of a nonantagonistic society. It would require a space and a medium in which the answer to this question could register and transform actual behavior. In Arnim, however, the recognition of ideological delusion leads only to a further proliferation of antisemitic images. The sadistic laughter his speech was apt to provoke evinces its reliance on fantasy and enjoyment.[17] The rhythm of the text captures its logic of avoidance. Each time Arnim arrives at an insight that threatens to undermine his argument about the existence of immutable Jewish characteristics—such as his recognition of Jewish-Romantic affinities, of bilateral assimilation, of projection mechanisms—he quickly drops the subject and produces an even more grotesque anti-Jewish accusation. His cascade of antisemitic invectives even includes a version of what Nietzsche calls the metaphysical gesture par excellence, the transformation of multiple and contingent *Schulden* (debts) into a single and necessary *Schuld* (guilt).[18] Arnim repeatedly notes

14. Slavoj Žižek, *The Sublime Object of Ideology* (New York: Verso Books, 1998), 125.
15. See Žižek, *The Sublime Object*, esp. 28–30.
16. Žižek, *The Sublime Object*, 126.
17. In recent years, scholars have persuasively rejected earlier attempts to downplay the speech's antisemitism by emphasizing its private and satirical character. Oesterle argues that the speech's humor proceeds from fantasies of extinction to actual annihilation to pure cynicism. See Osterle, "Juden, Philister und romantische Intellektuelle," 63.
18. See Friedrich Nietzsche, *On the Genealogy of Morality*, trans. Maudemarie Clark and Alan J. Swensen (Indianapolis: Hackett Publishing, 1998), 39–41.

that the financial debts of Christians to Jews are at the root of anti-Jewish hostilities. These include his own anti-Jewish resentments as well as the pogroms of the past: "How many thousands have had to atone, purportedly for their crimes, but in reality to erase the dues in the book of debt in which the Christians owed them too much" (385–86).[19] Whereas this statement seems to imply a fault on the part of the Christians, Arnim proceeds to describe the alleged Jewish machinations that force Christians into debts. In shifting the emphasis back from Christian *Schulden* to Jewish *Schuld*, he effectively retracts his earlier insights into the displacement mechanisms that fuel the persecution of Jews.

The Quest for a German Community: "Reconciliation in the Summer Holiday"

If the antisemitism of "On the Distinguishing Signs of Jewishness" is all too obvious, things are more complicated in Arnim's literary texts, some of which feature quite sympathetic Jews who seem to deserve the love they receive from Christians. The prose fragment "Reconciliation in the Summer Holiday," probably written during the spring and summer of 1811, includes a remarkably empathetic portrayal of a Jew who attempts but ultimately fails to integrate into Christian society.[20] The text stages a temporary reconciliation between Christians and Jews by means of a Christian-Jewish love affair, as opposed to the deliberate undoing of such affairs in Arnim's "On the Distinguishing Signs of Jewishness." The idea of love as a bridge between different cultures, religions, and nations is also evident in the text's original purpose. Arnim wrote "Reconciliation in the Summer Holiday" as a frame narrative for his 1912 novella collection, which contains among others *Isabella of Egypt* (*Isabella von Ägypten*) and *Maria Melück Blainville*. These novellas feature exotic strangers who at least some of the time appear superior to Christians. It has been argued that Arnim's fascination with such strangers and their eroticism counteracts his nationalism. In Arnim's life and literature, the erotic charge of the "dark" Southern world leads to a cultural and religious exogamy that thwarts any attempt to draw clear lines between national or ethnic groups.[21] However, I will

---

19. See also the "Herr von Falkenstein" episode in the poem in the middle part of the speech (372).

20. The text, which Arnim never published, has sometimes been read as his attempt to work through the so-called Itzig affair. Moritz Itzig, the nephew of a Jewish *salonnière*, challenged Arnim to a duel after Arnim had shown up without invitation and behaved inappropriately at a soiree hosted by his aunt. Arnim rejected the challenge because of Itzig's Jewishness, whereupon Itzig attacked him physically in a bathhouse and later received a relatively light sentence at court. These events left Arnim profoundly shaken and seem to have alternately tempered and exacerbated his antisemitism.

21. See Hildegard Baumgart, "Arnim's 'Judengeschichte': Eine biographische Rekonstruktion," in *Arnim und die Berliner Romantik: Kunst, Literatur und Politik*, ed. Walter Pape (Tübingen: Max Niemeyer, 2001), 71–94; here 88. For a more critical view, see Sara Friedrichsmeyer, "Romantic Nationalism: Achim von Arnim's Gypsy Princess Isabella," in *Gender and Germanness: Cultural Productions of Nation*, ed. Patricia Herminghouse and Magda Mueller (Providence: Berghahn Books, 1997), 51–65; and Dorothea E. von Mücke, *The Seduction of the Occult and the Rise of the Fantastic Tale* (Stanford,

argue that "Reconciliation in the Summer Holiday" still uses the figure of the Jew to disavow the tensions inherent in a vision of social harmony. The interreligious love affair serves primarily to deflect attention from the text's rather troubled effort to picture the emergence of a broader German alliance against Napoleon.

Set in Tyrol during the Napoleonic wars, "Reconciliation in the Summer Holiday" centers on the figure of a Jew who comes to fill the voids left by war. Raphael Rabuni buys the house of a nobleman who fell on the battlefield, and gains the love of the Christian girl Therese, whose fiancé, Joseph, is thought to have suffered the same death. The narrator, a non-Tyrolean who comes for a visit, appeases Therese's brother-in-law Sebastian, who until then has been strongly opposed to her attachment, and brings about a temporary reconciliation: "We drank the wine and toasted to eternal reconciliation, to a happy outcome, where human wisdom is silent due to God's mercy, and finally to a brotherly feeling [*brüderliches Du und Du*] among all of us and to an enjoyable communal life in the summer holiday."[22] Things begin to unravel quickly, however, when Joseph unexpectedly returns with a Bavarian enemy turned friend. Meanwhile, another young soldier and potential suitor of Therese named Artur kills Raphael out of a misguided sense of military honor. In the end the text becomes increasingly disjointed and cryptic; it comes across as a somewhat strained attempt to conjure a harmonious society that includes both Tyroleans and non-Tyroleans but excludes Jews.

Raphael's unhappy love and ultimate death do not come as a surprise to the reader. His short and skinny build, nervous mind and fragile health, which contrast with Joseph's tall stature and unbridled physical power, made him a rather unsatisfying substitute all along. After Joseph's return, Raphael retrospectively appears to have been a foreign intruder in the life of Therese, who "had completely returned to her national nature [*vaterländische Natur*], so much so that she barely thought about his foreign influence any longer" (596). The text leaves little doubt that in marrying Joseph, Therese returns to her true home and origins. Her shifting attachments illustrate the biblical maxim quoted in the text—"What God wants and what he has joined together let no man put asunder" (596)—as well as Arnim's inverted version of it—"Let no man bind together what Heaven has separated, Jews and Christians" (587). Arnim evidently seeks to underscore this point by emphasizing Raphael's inability to assimilate to his Christian environment, at

---

Calif.: Stanford University Press, 2003). Von Mücke shows that in both *Isabella of Egypt* and "Reconciliation in the Summer Holiday" sexuality becomes part of a "semiotics of blood" that serves to differentiate between ethnic groups and create a sense of cohesion within each group (202). More recently, Martha Helfer has offered a compelling reading of *Isabella of Egypt* that focuses on the ambiguous status of "Jewishness" in the text. Helfer shows that the text tropes its gypsy heroine in various ways as Jewish and never fully effaces the signs of Jewishness, not even from its concluding vision of a unified Germany. See Helfer, *The Word Unheard*, 57–77.

22. Achim von Arnim, "Die Versöhnung in der Sommerfrische," in *Werke*, 3:541–609; here 579. All further citations of "Die Versöhnung in der Sommerfrische" refer to this edition and will be included parenthetically in the text.

least during his life. Although Raphael makes an earnest attempt to become completely Christian, he harbors lingering doubts about the Christian gospel. In the insert "Conversation about the Naturalization of the Jews" ("Gespräch über die Einbürgerung der Juden"), he criticizes the superficiality of most Jewish conversions and at the same time admits his own inability to fully embrace the Christian faith. Only after his death and the *Nottaufe* (emergency baptism, 599) that precedes it does Raphael's face display the signs of redemption through faith for which he has been longing. Raphael's failure to find social integration through love differs from the failure depicted in Veit's *Florentin*. While Florentin is just as unable to secure himself a place in society as Raphael, he is neither clearly marked as a Jew nor does he become a carrier of negativity in the way Raphael does.

The failure of interreligious love in "Reconciliation in the Summer Holiday" is significant because it provides a foil against which the German-German reconciliation can take shape. For Therese's fiancé, Joseph, returns to his hometown together with Max, a Bavarian soldier who saved his life. The scene in which Max and Joseph almost die together as enemies and reemerge as friends recalls Arnim's cherished idea of a profound crisis that leads to renewal.[23] It also alludes to the ways that the Napoleonic wars antagonized the German-speaking countries. A military ally of Napoleon, Bavaria acquired Tyrol in 1805. In 1809 Tyroleans rose against Bavarian rule in a famous revolt that was quelled after some months. When Bavaria finally began to shift alliances and pull its troops out of Tyrol in 1813, Arnim hailed the liberation of Tyrol in a newspaper article: "Which country is worthier of being returned to its beloved old lord and its old, free constitution than this one, which was the first among the German peoples to serve as a bloody example of the strength which loyalty and faith provide? It has shown that peoples cannot be exchanged and delivered like merchandise, and that whoever wants to possess them against their will wants to destroy them."[24] In his article Arnim minimizes the historical conflict between Tyrol and Bavaria, which calls into question his idea of a united German front against France, by casting Bavaria as a victim rather than an ally of Napoleon. "Reconciliation in the Summer Holiday" gives further evidence of the contradictions that trouble Arnim's ideas of German and Tyrolean identity. The problem is not (or not only) that war has torn apart the social fabric of the region but rather that Arnim's vision of social harmony is contradictory to begin with. He conceives of Tyrol as both an autonomous region—"a distinct, immutable people that is grounded in itself" (603)—and part of a broader German alliance against Napoleon. He pictures Tyrolean society as both closed and open, both static and dynamic.

---

23. On Arnim's concept of crisis, see also Bruce Duncan, "Die Versöhnung in der Sommerfrische: Eine ungedruckte Erzählung Achim von Arnims," *Aurora* 40 (1980): 100–146; here 144.
24. Arnim, *Werke*, 6:422.

The narrator's development throughout the text illustrates these contradictions and gestures toward their resolution. Indeed, the narrator's integration into Tyrolean society gives the text a performative dimension. Just as Arnim's speech at the Christian-German Table Society produces the distinctions it ostensibly describes, "Reconciliation in the Summer Holiday" attempts to perform the social integration it conjures. Originally a Protestant from a big city, the narrator assimilates to the rural culture of Tyrol and later converts to Catholicism. In the end he seems fully integrated into his new environment while also completely faithful to his former life and self: "I am now Catholic and married to Antonie. I work my field like my neighbor, I dress and speak like a Tyrolean—and feel that I did not change, that I am still the same person. It is only that the external circumstances afford me the calm that I missed in our people and that is the condition for all progress in our internal betterment" (607). One may of course argue that there is no contradiction here because the narrator sees Protestantism and Catholicism as continuous, just as he deems Tyrol and Bavaria natural allies. Indeed, Raphael himself expresses this view that Christian religious differences are not truly detrimental to the "shared national spirit"—which nevertheless "expresses itself most magnificently in the creation of a new shared faith, through free choice and without external force" (559). Yet in "Reconciliation in the Summer Holiday," the emergence of a shared religion is neither spontaneous nor free from coercion. The idea of freely arising uniformity is undermined both by the biblical expulsion imagery at the text's beginning and by the necessity that propels the narrator's initial adoption of Tyrolean dress and language: he needs to replace his torn clothes and make himself understood during his erratic wanderings.

Arnim's insistence on the impossibility of Jewish assimilation has to be read in this context, as a screen that masks the tensions in the narrator's own transformation. Consider the problem of language. Raphael's smooth and beautiful language—presumably High German—is the source of his uncanny power over Therese and her alienation from her country and her family. After he reads verses to her and apparently hypnotizes her, she begins to speak High German "as she never before was able to" (548). When she reunites with Joseph, however, she quickly forgets everything she read in the books with Raphael. Therese's linguistic movement between High German and Tyrolean dialect illustrates her estrangement from and reintegration into a native environment. Forgetting is impossible for the narrator, however, who speaks the Tyrolean dialect with Therese's family but has to translate his conversations into a language understood by his readers. He explicitly states that this translation requires him to sacrifice "many an ingenousness permitted by the vernacular but not the written language" (552). In other words, writing continues to expose the narrator to others who do not belong to the community into which he seeks to integrate. Raphael comes to embody this negativity, the incompleteness of the narrator's own transformation. Through the figure of Raphael, "Reconciliation in the Summer Holiday" both expresses and disavows the contradictions inherent in German Christian identity.

The unhappy Christian-Jewish love affair takes center stage in "Reconciliation in the Summer Holiday" because love and marriage are invoked as possible means of resolving the inner German conflict. Upon their return Joseph offers Max Therese's hand in marriage as a token of his gratitude, a proposal that evokes the idea of peace established through the exogamic exchange of women. But there are two different visions of peace in the text: peace as the restoration of an original state (which is based on endogamy) and peace through the establishment of a new alliance (which requires exogamy). These two visions are mutually exclusive. In terms of the plot this means that Therese cannot marry both Max and Joseph, which is why the two men leave the decision to a roll of the dice, and the winner, Joseph, gets to marry her. This impossibility of a dual connection is, however, overlaid by the more ostensible impossibility of Christian-Jewish intermarriage. As both Joseph and the narrator acknowledge, Raphael has also the right to marry Therese, or at least to cast dice for her, since he saved her life. Raphael's death conveniently withdraws him from the circle of male contenders and preempts any attempt on his part to defend his "right." A symptom of the tensions that riddle Arnim's vision of peace is the very proliferation of potential lovers in the second half of the story. There is not only Max but also Artur (Arundel), the young officer who arouses Raphael's jealousy and whose misguided sense of military honor causes the catastrophe. In the end Artur, gone mad, still lingers around, an embodiment of competing claims to Therese—and to Tyrolean identity—that appeared to have been buried with Raphael.

Colonial Mimicry in *Gentry by Entailment*

As we have seen, Arnim's 1811 texts simultaneously demand a complete Jewish transformation (modeled on religious conversion) and posit its impossibility. These texts are haunted by the specter of superficial Jewish assimilation and conversions without true faith. The only successful transformation of Jews seems to occur at the time of their death. Calling any change short of death a deception, Arnim issues a contradictory injunction to the Jews: "Assimilate, but don't assimilate!" Another way of thinking this double imperative is in terms of what the postcolonial critic Homi Bhabha calls "colonial mimicry." Postcolonial theory can shed light on the eighteenth- and nineteenth-century program of Jewish emancipation because this program was a form of internal colonization through which a previously segregated group was absorbed into the social majority.[25] The fact that Dorothea Veit, for instance, contemplated ending her novel *Florentin* on a colonial endeavor (in which Florentin is ambiguously positioned as a colonizer rather than a colonized) is one indication that colonialism provided a model to think through

---

25. See Baumann, *Modernity and Ambivalence.* For a productive use of postcolonial theory to analyze German-Jewish relations, see Hess, *Germans, Jews, and the Claims of Modernity.*

the integration of minorities. In what follows now I will argue that, seen through the lens of postcolonial theory, the tension I identified earlier in Arnim's system of thought—between modern, or racial, antisemitism and the Enlightenment belief in Jewish transformability—turns out to be constitutive of an ideological program.

Homi Bhabha shares with Slavoj Žižek the notion that ideologies operate not only by constructing knowledge but also by manipulating affects and fantasies. Both hold that ideologies can incorporate a great deal of ambivalence without losing their effectiveness. Bhabha indeed suggests that ambivalence is a quintessential colonial gesture by which the colonized other is split into an object of desire and an object of derision. He points to texts by colonial administrators who propose a limited—and emphatically only a limited—assimilation of the colonized to the colonizers as the most effective way to keep them under control. Mimicry thus understood is a form of imitation that flaunts the parts at the expense of the whole and the surface at the expense of the interior. Bhabha's most intriguing suggestion is that the efficacy of colonial mimicry hinges upon the production of constant slippages. The administrators' demand for colonial mimicry expresses "the desire for a reformed, recognizable Other, *as a subject of a difference that is almost the same, but not* quite."[26] To maintain this sense of difference, the fact that imitation is "not quite" like the original has to remain tangible, as does the discrepancy between colonial ideology and colonial politics. The proposal of a Christian missionary to partially reform and partially accept local practices, for instance, is clearly at odds with the missionary ideal of complete conversion but for this very reason well suited to keep the natives in a subservient position. Colonial mimicry thus understood stabilizes existing power relations.[27]

In what follows now, I argue that the notion of colonial mimicry is useful for thinking through one of Arnim's aesthetically and politically most complex texts, *Gentry by Entailment*. In contrast to the previously analyzed works, this 1819 novella does not perform the future national community but tells a story of historical decline. Set in a German city just before the French Revolution, the text relates the return of the possessor of an entailed estate to his long-neglected manor and his ill-fated love for the (supposedly) Jewish girl Esther. Esther is harassed and finally murdered by her stepmother, Vashti, who is depicted in the worst antisemitic clichés as a nasty, greedy old Jewess. Through the figure of Vashti, *Gentry by Entailment* blames Jews and Judaism for the presumed ills of modernity, including industrialization, the rule of money, and the transformation of human bonds into exchange relationships. At the end of the story, the city is occupied by French troops, and Vashti emerges as a vital agent of industrialization and capitalism; she buys the entailed estate for

---

26. Homi K. Bhabha, "On Mimicry and Men: The Ambivalence of Colonial Discourse," in *The Location of Culture* (New York: Routledge, 1994), 85–92; here 86 (Bhabha's emphasis).

27. It should be noted that colonial mimicry is a power strategy that can backfire. Bhabha also uses the term to describe the subversive effects of a minority's "mimicry," whose reiteration of the majority's cultural norms can change the terms in which these norms are articulated.

a cheap price and establishes an ammonia factory on its site. The novella, which begins with a reflection on the richness of life before the French Revolution, concludes with a statement that sums up the character of the postrevolutionary epoch: "And credit came to take the place of feudal right."[28] While this plot summary captures the fusion of anticapitalism and antisemitism in later Romanticism, it obscures the degree of ambiguity that marks the text's historical narrative and its representation of Jewish difference—and that is part and parcel of colonial mimicry.

To begin with, there is a pervasive ambiguity regarding the cause and the character of historical change. On the one hand, Arnim explains the downfall of the old regime in terms of its own immanent failings. The decline of the entailed estate reflects the flaws of this legal institution, which stipulates that the entire estate is bequeathed to the oldest son at the expense of the younger children.[29] The tenant, an exponent of the old order who could be read as a representative of the Romantic artist, contributes to his own and his beloved's death through his passivity and inability to act. These inner deficiencies of the people and institutions of the ancient regime furnish proof of the narrator's initial suggestion that this regime was prone to "wanton self-destruction" (5/*107*). On the other hand, Arnim uses antisemitic projection mechanisms to explain the rise of capitalism and the attendant social malaise. The tenant, a dreamy man who is engaged in abstract studies and paralyzed by the specters of the past, is (in an allusion to the Christian fascination with the Kabbalah) immediately attracted to the books of Jewish legends he encounters in his cousin's house. This cousin, a former lieutenant who in his money-oriented pragmatism is the exact opposite of the otherworldly tenant, sends out "trained decoy pigeons" (7/*110*: *Raubtauben*) to steal other people's pigeons and learns Hebrew to outsmart the Jews in business. His house is located right next to the Jewish Alley, a metonymy that emphasizes the connection between Jews and a money-grubbing mentality. Judaism thus becomes associated with extreme spiritualism and extreme materialism alike. To the extent that it is represented as external to Christianity, both spatially and ideologically, Judaism functions as a screen onto which the failings of the old society are projected. The novella's use of Jewish symbolism to depict the ancient regime invites the conclusion that the regime's flaws were due to Jewish influence to begin with.

The novella figures the doom of the old order through the impossible love story between the manor's tenant and the beautiful Esther, who later turns out to be a Christian adopted at birth by a Jew. The tenant's inability to express his love for Esther and rescue her from her stepmother epitomizes the old regime's lack of

---

28. Achim von Arnim, *Gentry by Entailment*, trans. Alan Brown (London: Atlas Press, 1990), 42. For the original German, see Arnim, *Werke*, 4:147. Further citations from these editions will be included parenthetically in the text, with the page number in the English translation followed by the page number in the German edition in italics, as here (42/*147*).

29. On Arnim's critique of this institution, see Riedl, "'. . . das ist ein ewig Schachern und Zänken . . . .'"

vitality and its inability to reproduce itself. This is only one of many instances of failing heterosexual love in Arnim, whose work is replete with crises of marriage and procreation. He generally depicts the family as an institution of trade rather than of procreation; children are being exchanged all the time.[30] The significance of parental failure in *Gentry by Entailment* emerges most clearly when read against the backdrop of the text that first introduced this character constellation into German literature: Lessing's *Nathan the Wise*, which Arnim explicitly references in *Gentry by Entailment* and which I discussed in the first chapter of this book. A comparison between the two literary accounts of adoptive fatherhood and (presumed) interreligious love reveals the distance between Enlightenment calls for emancipation and later Romantic antisemitism. While Recha's adoption is an act of compassion that demonstrates Nathan's ability to control his emotions through reason (he receives Recha just after his own family has perished in a pogrom), Esther's adoption is an economic transaction by which her surrogate father acquires the capital that forms the basis of his successful business. And whereas *Nathan the Wise* creates hope for a better understanding between the different religions in the future, *Gentry by Entailment* ends with the bleak prospect of the total victory of an exploitative capitalism denounced as Jewish.

Arnim's representation of adoptive fatherhood reflects an essentialist conception of Jews and Judaism. While in both Arnim and Lessing the adoptive father attempts to shape the personality of the daughter according to the ideals of the time, the Jewish father in *Gentry by Entailment* has much less influence on the character formation of his adoptive daughter than does Nathan in *Nathan the Wise*. Recha, who was raised without superficial book knowledge, embodies the intuitive reason and virtue cherished by the enlightened Nathan; in that sense she remains her father's true daughter even after the revelation of her Christian origins. Esther has grown into an educated salon hostess who charms her environment with wit and beauty, yet her manners appear superficial accomplishments at best and psychopathological symptoms at worst. Each night Esther hears a pistol shot that makes her get up and sing, dance, and entertain imaginary guests as if she were a true salon hostess. In so doing she tries to make up for the loss of her active social life after her father's death, but she also acts out another kind of grief. Her fits began about a year ago, after she and a Christian soldier had fallen in love with each other and been harassed by both Jews and Christians—the imaginary shots Esther has been hearing since then echo the shot by which her Christian lover committed suicide. The fact that the reader never sees her act as a Jewish *salonnière* except during these theatrical performances born out of grief casts doubt on the transformative effect of her father's education. Whereas the adoptive father's pedagogy makes a real difference in *Nathan*, it is a mere polishing of manners in *Gentry by Entailment*,

---

30. See Volker Hoffmann, "Künstliche Zeugung und Zeugung von Kunst im Erzählwerk Achim von Arnims." *Aurora* 46 (1986): 158–67.

and a maddening one at that. The stark contrast between the humble, compassionate Esther and her heartless, greedy stepmother, Vashti, further emphasizes the adopted girl's separateness from her Jewish surroundings. The figure of Esther thus illustrates the ineffectiveness of adoptive fatherhood, as an act of artificial production that is ultimately not productive at all.

The notion of a profound psychological difference between Jews and Christians that cannot be erased by pedagogical or other "civilizing" measures marks Arnim's antisemitism as modern. However, a closer analysis of *Gentry by Entailment* reveals once more the difficulty of placing Arnim on a linear trajectory from traditional anti-Judaism to modern, or racial, antisemitism. For instance, although Arnim posits the existence of indelible mental and psychological differences between Jews and Christians, he does not unequivocally locate them on the physical body. The depiction of Vashti as "a hideous Jewess with a nose like an eagle, eyes like almandite, skin like smoked goose-breast and a belly like a burgomaster's" (19/*122*) is a caricature rather than a realistic portrait. More precisely, Arnim's depiction of Vashti combines features of the caricature, which fixates physical features by exaggerating them, and of the grotesque, which transcends the realm of reality toward the improbable.[31] In the quote above the grotesque comparisons undermine the mimetic character of Vashti's portrayal. Allegorical accessories such as Vashti's black head scarf, which the tenant mistakes for a raven, further detach physical surface from psychical interior rather than produce the alignment of physique and character so crucial in racial antisemitism.[32]

The lack of concrete and realistic physical detail is particularly conspicuous in the portrayal of Esther, who is shown to be largely a product of the tenant's projections. Initially the reader learns nothing about her looks except that she reminds the tenant "in every feature and movement" (10/*113*) of his late mother. Even when the narrator describes her in greater detail, he focuses on aspects that obscure rather than reveal the contours of her face. These details include a paleness that covers her face "like a noxious spring mist" (20/*123*) and the ways that her eyes are narrowed, "as flowers towards evening draw their petals closer about the sun of their calyx" (20/*123*). The reader is unable to get a clear picture of Esther in part because s/he perceives her mostly through the perspective of the tenant, whose impressions of Esther are predominantly aural. When he first witnesses Esther's daily "salon" performance, he listens to her without seeing her clearly. Even when he stands

---

31. On the genres of the caricature and the grotesque and their function in the novella, see Günter Oesterle, "'Illegitime Kreuzungen': Zur Ikonität und Temporalität des Grotesken in Achim von Arnim's *Die Majoratsherren*," *Études Germaniques* 43, no. 1 (March 1988): 25–51.

32. The fact that Vashti's Jewishness manifests itself primarily in her language, including her "Hebrew abuse" and "most distorted Yiddish" (20/*122*), might be taken as a sign of the culturalist understanding of "race" that controlled most German thinking about the subject during the first half of the nineteenth century. However, I argue that the vagueness of physical characteristics in *Die Majorats-Herren* has the specific narrative function of creating ambiguous identities.

next to Esther and beholds her body and face, it is her voice that attracts his attention and confirms his impression of her resemblance to his mother. The tenant in fact actively produces the image of Esther and her sphere, for instance, by visualizing her verbal fantasies. While Esther knows that she speaks "to the empty air" (23/126) and opens the door to a "Nothing" (23/127), the tenant appears to actually see the guests as soon as her voice animates them. This is so because the two are sympathetically linked through their exchange at birth, but also because the tenant is generally capable of visualizing the immaterial.[33] His fantasies are the stuff of which Esther is made.

The vagueness in the depiction of Esther's physical appearance is crucial for the story because it allows her to function both as the tenant's mother surrogate and as a stereotypical "beautiful Jewess." A well-known example of the beautiful Jewess in literature is Rebecca in Walter Scott's *Ivanhoe*, which was published in 1819, the same year as *Gentry by Entailment*.[34] The ambiguous invocation of this literary stereotype allows Arnim to explain the tenant's death as the result of either an incestuous attachment to his mother or an erotic infatuation with a beautiful stranger. Esther's double role as mother surrogate and exotic stranger is made possible by a proliferation of doubles, inversions, and permutations that undermines the clear-cut dichotomy between Jews and Christians. One instance of inversion occurs when the tenant asks his cousin about Esther's identity and learns that she is a "Schicksa" (*Schickselchen*; 10/113). The German word *Schickse* derives from the Yiddish *shikse* and originally from the Hebrew *shikutz*, or "detested thing." It referred mainly to idols before it became first the derogatory Jewish term for Christian women still known today, and then the derogatory Christian term for Jewish women used in *Gentry by Entailment*. The novella also inverts the biblical opposition between Esther and Vashti. In the biblical book of Esther, both Esther and Vashti are the wives of the Persian king Ahasuerus, but it is Esther who is Jewish, and Vashti who is non-Jewish.[35] Finally, the text includes a poem that features an actual "beautiful Jewess," thus further conflating the literary stereotype and the figure of Esther. This poem recounts the fate of the beautiful daughter of a nasty old Jewess—a relationship that recalls that between Esther and Vasthi in the novella. The poem's description of the daughter's suicide in the ocean as a form of baptism alludes to the idea implied in the literary stereotype of the "beautiful Jewess" of a special affinity of Jewish women to Christianity. Since the daughter

33. See also Heinrich Henel, "Arnims *Majoratsherren*," in *Romantikforschung seit 1945*, ed. Klaus Peter et al. (Königstein: Athenäum, Hain, Scriptor, Hanstein, 1980), 145–67; here 151.

34. For examples of this stereotype in German literature, see Florian Krobb, *Die schöne Jüdin: Jüdische Frauengestalten in der deutschsprachigen Erzählliteratur vom 17. Jahrhundert bis zum Ersten Weltkrieg* (Tübingen: Max Niemeyer, 1993).

35. Esther became the wife of the Persian king Ahasuerus after his first wife, Vashti, had refused to appear in front of him. The temporal sequence, too, is inverted in Arnim's novella, which has Vashti join Esther's adoptive father after the death of his first wife.

in the poem is for all we know her mother's biological daughter, her doubling of Esther only further confounds the reader's sense of who or what is a "real" Jew.

If Arnim's reinterpretation of the idea of adoptive fatherhood aims at establish-ing clear boundaries between Jews and Christians, his literary play with doubles, inversions, and permutations constantly blurs these boundaries. Just as in "On the Distinguishing Signs of Jewishness," this de-essentializing of identity undermines any attempt to define Jews and Judaism in racial terms. However, the ambiguity Arnim creates around the question of who is truly Jewish does not diminish the novella's antisemitism. Rather, this ambiguity becomes part and parcel of colonial mimicry, or an ideological program in which total assimilation is simultaneously demanded and declared impossible. The figure of Esther in *Gentry by Entailment* provides a salient example of the slippages produced by colonial mimicry. This figure allows Arnim to play with the tantalizing image of the "beautiful Jewess" while positing the existence of indelible differences between Jews and Christians. Whether we identify Esther as a Christian who becomes partially Jewish or, as suggested by the poem, as a Jew who attempts to become a Christian (and can do so only by dying), she is the site where the limits of assimilation are constantly being tested and reinforced—all the while the very possibility of these two differ-ent readings destabilizes the notion of a clearly defined religious-ethnic identity that gave rise to the demand for assimilation in the first place.

Reading Arnim with Žižek and Bhabha suggests that this ambiguity, which expresses a *psychical* ambivalence about the process of modernization, ultimately enhances the *political* efficacy of antisemitism. Žižek's and Bhabha's insight that ideology is bound up with affect helps explain the proliferation of Christian-Jewish love stories at this juncture in history. At a moment when Jewish acculturation and German nationalism emerge simultaneously, literary representations of inter-religious love serve to reimagine the interplay between difference and similarity. As I have shown, even the blatantly antisemitic "On the Distinguishing Signs of Jewishness" includes a fantasy of interreligious sex to gloss over the impasses in its argument about immutable Jewish difference. In "Reconciliation in the Summer Holiday" and *Gentry by Entailment*, the Christian-Jewish love story allows for an even fuller expression of ambivalence and uncertainty. In each of the cases, the love relationship reveals the internal contradictions of an ideology without weaken-ing its power. For all their ambiguities, Arnim's love stories leave little doubt that Christian-Jewish love either does not exist or leads nowhere. Arnim's dismissal of love as a means of integration forms a contrast to the open-ended love stories in Veit's *Florentin* or in Lessing's plays. As I have shown in the previous two chap-ters, *Florentin*'s hope for a fatherland founded on love is suspended rather than abrogated. In Lessing, interreligious love emerges as a possibility that is relegated to an open-ended future (in *Die Juden*) or an inaccessible past (in *Nathan der Weise*), thereby transmuting from a private affair into a metaphor for social relations. In Arnim, this process of metaphorization comes to a decided standstill.

PART II

1900

The Crisis of Jewish
Emancipation and Assimilation

In jumping to the turn of the twentieth century, I bracket the mid-nineteenth century, a period in which literary representations of interreligious romance became more numerous and more openly political. During the nineteenth century the struggle for marriage reform, especially for the introduction of civil marriage, became central to liberal efforts to secularize society. Christian-Jewish love relationships emerged as a popular literary theme because of the challenge they posed to religious norms and institutions. The literary depiction of the plight of characters who fall in love but are unable to marry across religious lines, or who are forced to give up their religious identities in order to do so, became a vehicle of social critique. Thus Fanny Lewald's 1843 novel *Jenny* indicts the prejudice encountered by, and the conversion typically required of, Jews who wanted to marry a Christian. It is not always obvious in the novel that the establishment of civil marriage would solve the problems faced by interreligious couples, but its absence is certainly shown to contribute to these problems.[1] Here and elsewhere, the literary

---

1. On *Jenny* and other prose texts that advocate civil marriage by depicting the plight of Christian-Jewish couples, see Lezzi, *"Liebe ist meine Religion!,"* 163–275. Among other things, Lezzi argues that the different representations of Christian-Jewish love and marriage in nineteenth-century literature reflect the growing differences between Reform-oriented, Conservative, and neo-Orthodox factions of Judaism. On the role of romance in nineteenth-century German Jewish middlebrow literature, see also Jonathan Hess, *Middlebrow Literature and the Making of German-Jewish Identity* (Stanford, Calif.: Stanford University Press, 2010), 111–56.

dramatization of thwarted interreligious love invites a critique of the incompleteness of Jewish emancipation.

Part II of this book focuses on a historical moment in which the debates about love, marriage, and Jewish assimilation intersect in new and pertinent ways. The Austrian-Hungarian and the German governments had granted legal equality to Jews in 1867 and 1871, respectively. Around 1900, however, the rise of racial antisemitism had called into question the promises of emancipation and created a sense of crisis for many German-speaking Jews. At the same time, the introduction of civil marriage in the German Empire had led to a gradual increase of Christian-Jewish intermarriages and turned them into a focal point of public debates about Jewish identity and belonging. In what follows, I will highlight three ideological undercurrents in these debates—the homogenization of national identity and the racialization and feminization of Jewish identity—before I explore the responses of modern German Jewish authors to these new ideological challenges.

The introduction of civil marriage in the German Empire in 1875 greatly facilitated the contraction of Christian-Jewish intermarriages, and the number of such unions began to rise slowly but steadily.[2] Since it made civil marriage mandatory, the new law brought all marriages under the purview of the state, which meant that governmental institutions became involved in the wedding process, and marriage itself became a potential means of forging a national identity. In fact, in the German Empire civil marriage was introduced soon after the 1871 unification during the so-called *Kulturkampf*, by which the government attempted to quell the power of the Catholic Church and secure Protestant-Prussian hegemony throughout the empire. While Christian-Jewish intermarriage never took center stage in the public debates—the number of such unions was quite small compared with the number of Protestant-Catholic unions—it frequently figured in discussions of the "Jewish question." The situation in Austria was more complex. The Habsburg Empire never introduced mandatory civil marriage, but an 1868 law stipulated the possibility of a *Notzivilehe* (emergency civil marriage) for couples who could not get married in a religious institution. Since Christian-Jewish couples in Austria faced additional restrictions—for example, the requirement that one of the partners convert to the other's confession or become *konfessionslos* (unaffiliated with any religion)—they began to intermarry at a somewhat slower rate than in Germany.[3]

---

2. On the debates that led to the introduction of civil marriage in Germany and Austria, see Inken Fuhrmann, *Die Diskussion über die Einführung der fakultativen Zivilehe in Deutschland und Österreich seit Mitte des 19. Jahrhunderts* (Frankfurt am Main: Peter Lang, 1998). On the social history of Christian-Jewish intermarriage in Germany, see Kerstin Meiring, *Die christlich-jüdische Mischehe in Deutschland 1840–1933* (Hamburg: Dölling and Galitz, 1998).

3. See the chapter "Intermarriage and Conversion," in Marsha L. Rozenblit, *The Jews of Vienna, 1867–1914: Assimilation and Identity* (Albany: State University of New York Press, 1983), 127–46.

Especially in the first decades of the German Empire, the discussion of Christian-Jewish intermarriage was bound up with the quest for a homogeneous national identity. Non-Jewish publicists who championed a complete absorption of Jews into German society often recommended intermarriage as an important step in that direction, and they usually imagined the integration process to be unidirectional. In advocating Christian-Jewish intermarriage, they implicitly or explicitly required Jews to relinquish their separateness. This tendency is palpable, for instance, in the book *Baptisms of Jews* (*Judentaufen*, 1912) a compilation of the responses of (mostly non-Jewish) authors to three questions, one of which asked about the consequences of Jewish-Gentile intermarriage. The writer Richard Dehmel calls therein on Jews to adopt a more positive view toward intermarriage, reasoning: "We abolished the ghetto and can therefore demand that the Jews do away with a ghetto mentality."[4] Dehmel's unwillingness to recognize claims to particularity as legitimate is typical of the dominant understanding of assimilation of the time. In Germany, the term "assimilation" came into wider usage only after full political emancipation was achieved, and was especially in the beginning bound up with nationalist attempts to define a homogeneous German identity. Whereas German Jews had been able to understand earlier terms such as *Verschmelzung* (fusion) and *Amalgamierung* (amalgamation) as a call for a religious and cultural renewal rather than a renunciation of collective identity, *Assimilation* implied a more complete effacement of differences.[5] The willingness of Jews to intermarry became a measure of assimilation thus understood, a criterion of their national belonging and sociocultural integration.

That the call for intermarriage was a double-edged sword is evident in the use that antisemites made of it. One example is Heinrich von Treitschke, a German nationalist of originally liberal orientation who, to the great disappointment of many Jews, became one of the leading agitators in the *Berliner Antisemitismusstreit* (Berlin debate on antisemitism) of the late 1870s. In an 1879 essay, Treitschke calls "blood mixing . . . the most effective means toward an equalizing of tribal differences" and chides Jews for their reluctance to convert to Christianity and marry Christians.[6] He then elaborates this thought into a paradox. Treitschke argues that legal emancipation, which occurred in the wake of the 1871 foundation of the German Empire, made it less necessary for Jews eager to integrate into German society to convert to Christianity. This in turn decreased their chances of marrying, and thereby completely merging with, non-Jews, the majority of whom still fervently adhered to the Christian faith. Treitschke calls on Jews to fulfill their part of the emancipation bargain and integrate into German society, and at the same time

---

4. Richard Dehmel, in Werner Sombart et al., *Judentaufen* (Munich: Georg Müller, 1912), 25.

5. See David Sorkin, "Emancipation and Assimilation: Two Concepts and Their Application to German-Jewish History," *Leo Baeck Institute Yearbook* 35 (1990): 17–33.

6. Heinrich von Treitschke, "Noch einige Bemerkungen zur Judenfrage," in *Der Berliner Antisemitismusstreit*, ed. Walter Boehlich (Frankfurt am Main: Insel, 1965), 77–90; here 79.

intimates that this will not happen because emancipation actually hinders integration. While advocating for Christian-Jewish intermarriage, Treitschke effectively performs the same antisemitic gesture as Archim von Arnim, who rejects intermarriage: he simultaneously demands complete Jewish assimilation and questions its feasibility. By projecting an ideal of social homogeneity to which emancipated Jews by definition cannot conform, Treitschke issues a contradictory command to Jews, something like "Be like us! Know that you cannot be like us!"

Around 1900, the racialization of Jewish identity—and, arguably, of all identity—put pressures on the Romantic love ideal and its conflation of love, sex, and marriage. The debates about Jewish-Gentile intermarriage became tied up with racial discourses about procreation, heredity, and the mutability and immutability of the Jewish body. The establishment of racial science as an academic discipline focused attention on the biological origin and destiny of the Jewish "race." Initially, Felix von Luschan's 1892 theory of the Jews as a *Rassengemisch*, a medley of the three antique races of Semites, Hittites, and Amorites, was widely accepted. The discussion soon grew more polemical, especially with the widespread reception of the works of Arthur de Gobineau and Houston Stewart Chamberlain, and turned from history to the present. Racial scientists were alternately concerned with Jewish endogamy or "inbreeding," to which they attributed negative effects such as degeneration and susceptibility to disease, and with interracial marriage, which they viewed as a source of racial destabilization and disharmony. As Veronika Lipphardt sums up, Jews were seen as being either biologically too close or biologically too distant from their spouses—in either case, incapable of a healthy marriage.[7] One corollary of the development of racial science was an increased interest in the children of interracial marriages. As we have seen, the Romantic discourse of marriage was less concerned with procreation because children pose a potential threat to the imagined harmony of the married couple. In the rare speculations about Christian-Jewish intermarriage, children were even less of a concern because, as a result of social taboos and legal restrictions, few such marriages materialized. Around 1900, however, the offspring of intermarriages became a central concern as the increased number of such unions coincided with widespread interest in eugenics and racial hygiene.

The biological sciences began to shape the debates about assimilation and intermarriage. Biologistic thought informs the views of both supporters of assimilation, who promote intermarriage as a means of biological fusion between Germans and

---

7. See Veronika Lipphardt, *Biologie der Juden: Jüdische Wissenschaftler über "Rasse" und Vererbung 1900–1935* (Göttingen: Vandenhoeck and Ruprecht, 2008), esp. 162–63. Lipphardt observes that around 1900, the discussion of Jewish inbreeding occupied center stage, while around 1915 the discussion focused mostly on intermarriage. Both inbreeding and racial mixing were occasionally credited with positive effects, such as the creation of pure racial characteristics or the opportunity for racial renewal. However, negative views of both inbreeding and racial mixing were more prevalent, especially among non-Jewish scientists.

Jews, and antisemites who attack it as a vehicle of racial contamination and degeneration. In an 1899 article in the *Fackel*, Karl Kraus recommends intermarriage as "the only serious attempt" at a union between Jews and Christians.[8] To be sure, Kraus sets out to repudiate notions of racial difference in favor of social, cultural, and religious explanations for Jewish separateness. Yet he nevertheless introduces biologistic ideas when he broaches the topic of intermarriage. His remark that in the past Jews were able to resist the "temptations of the blood to contract . . . mixed marriages" implies that the same instinctual forces propel people into intermarriages in his own times.[9] Opponents of assimilation often cite the alleged difficulties of Christian-Jewish intermarriages to claim that assimilation is impossible. The well-known sociologist Werner Sombart mentions the higher infertility and divorce rates of such unions and concludes that the "blood difference" between the Jews and "the 'Aryan' tribes" renders "a total assimilation, a total fusion" in the future improbable.[10] Whereas Sombart still envisions a peaceful if unequal coexistence of Jews and non-Jews, the more rabid antisemites of his time transform the notion of racial incompatibility into a vision of racial war conducted by sexual means. They concoct fantasies according to which male Jews seek to infiltrate and ultimately dominate the Aryan race by spreading their semen among Aryan women.[11]

The homogenization of German identity and the racialization of Jewish identity are two trends in which the debates about Jewish-Gentile intermarriage are wrapped up. A third trend is the feminization of "the Jew" that often follows from the use of love as a metaphor for interreligious rapprochement. When nineteenth-century writers compare the relationship between Jews and non-Jews to a love affair, they inevitably cast the Jew in the role of the woman. Correspondingly, they figure Jewish assimilation as the passive surrender of a minority to the majority culture, just as according to the mores of the time a wife would submit to her husband.[12] In 1892 the German Jewish journalist Maximilian Harden draws on this idea to combat the recent rise of antisemitism and carve out a space for Jews in German culture. He claims that past persecutions have in fact strengthened the Jews and endowed them with a special ability to adapt to new environments,

---

8. Karl Kraus, *Die Fackel* 11 (1899): 5.

9. Kraus, *Die Fackel* 11:4.

10. Werner Sombart, *Die Zukunft der Juden* (Leipzig: Duncker & Humblot, 1912), 52.

11. See, for instance, Hermann Ahlwardt, *Der Verzweiflungskampf der arischen Völker mit dem Judentum* (Berlin: Grobhäuser, 1890), 220–21; and Houston Stewart Chamberlain, *Die Grundlagen des 19. Jahrhunders*, 4th ed. (Munich: Bruckmann, 1903), 1:324.

12. This gendering of social roles had begun in the eighteenth century and continued during the nineteenth century. In his 1869 anthropological study *Der jüdische Stamm* (*The Jewish Tribe*), the prominent Viennese rabbi Adolf Jellinek ascribes to Jews the capacity to adapt to a great variety of different environments. He argues that they share this capacity with women, who are just as emotional, imaginative, and quick-witted but also as moody, unsystematic, and uncreative as Jews, and he compares the Jews' relationship to Gentiles and a woman's flirtatious behavior toward a man: "A woman is glad when she is pleasing to a man, and a Jew when he receives the compliment of a non-Jew." Adolf Jellinek, *Der jüdische Stamm: Ethnographische Studien* (Vienna: Herzfeld and Bauer, 1869), 95.

which he terms, with Darwin, "mimicry." Harden depicts Jews as feminine and their relationship to Germans as a marriage of sorts. This simile serves as both a warning to the antisemites to let go of their Jew hatred and a recommendation to the Jews to renounce their traditional ways of living: since divorce is impossible, the Jews would do wise to submit to the Gentiles' will just as a wife submits to her husband's will.[13]

As Ritchie Robertson has noted, the analogy between assimilation and marriage potentially undermines the argument for which it is mounted. If Jews assimilate to Gentile culture as women follow their husbands in marriage, a certain difference will persist, just like sexual difference.[14] One way to solve this incongruity is to imagine the disappearance of such difference over the course of time, as did one of the contributors to the previously mentioned book *Judentaufen*. In response to the question about the consequences of Jewish-Gentile intermarriage, L. Gurlitt quotes Bismarck's famous statement about the fine race that could emerge from the crossbreeding of a "Germanic stallion" and a "Jewish mare." Citing the experience of his own family, Gurlitt predicts that the Jewish element in a mixed family will disappear within a few generations. In other words, he translates the notion of female submission into one of genetic recession.[15] In these discussions of intermarriage, racial thinking and gender stereotyping combine to promote an idea of assimilation as the minority's total adaptation to the majority.

Part II of this book examines modern German Jewish writers who seek to wrest love away from biologist thought and reinstate it as a model of sociopolitical integration. The focus is on authors of Jewish extraction because it is at this moment, around 1900, that a critical countertradition of German Jewish authors who use the idea of love to create new models of group relations emerges more clearly. Chapter 4 explores the work of three middlebrow authors—Ludwig Jacobowski, Max Nordau, and Georg Hermann—who write Christian-Jewish love stories in order to promote a larger political project, such as Zionism and the Liberal campaign against antisemitism. I show how these authors often participate in the racial discourses they seek to repudiate, and I speculate about what it means that their "interracial" love stories all end with the death of the Jewish partner. Chapter 5 turns to a place where the rise of modern antisemitism was of even greater concern: turn-of-the-century Vienna, which was governed by an openly antisemitic mayor. It is here that Arthur Schnitzler, in a novel that explores a range of Jewish reactions to the

---

13. See Maximilian Harden, "Sem," in *Apostata: Neue Folge* (Berlin: Stilke, 1893), 155–56.

14. See Ritchie Robertson, "Historicizing Weininger: The Nineteenth-Century German Image of the Feminized Jew," in *Modernity, Culture, and "the Jew,"* ed. Bryan Cheyette and Laura Marcus (Stanford, Calif.: Stanford University Press, 1998), 23–39; here 27. Christina von Braun has argued that the feminization of the Jew in racial antisemitism served to turn religious difference into biological (and immutable) difference. See von Braun, "Antisemitismus und Misogynie: Vom Zusammenhang zweier Erscheinungen," in *Von einer Welt in die andere: Jüdinnen im 19. und 20. Jahrhundert*, ed. Jutta Dick and Barbara Hahn (Vienna: Christian Brandstätter, 1993), 179–96.

15. See Gurlitt, in Sombart et al., *Judentaufen*, 49–50.

crisis of modern Jewish identity, affirms the power of Eros in Jewish-Gentile inter-action. In so doing he suggests an alternative to both Sigmund Freud's conspicu-ous silence about Jewish-Gentile love and Otto Weininger's definition of Jewish "self-overcoming" as self-annihilation. I end with a chapter on Franz Rosenzweig and Else Lasker-Schüler, two modernists who around the First World War offer emphatic visions of interreligious encounters in and through love. Yet in so doing, they redefine love as a force of disjunction rather than unification.

4

Refiguring the Language of Race

Ludwig Jacobowski, Max Nordau, Georg Hermann

At a time when intermarriage became a trope in the debates about Jewish emancipation and assimilation, literary representations of Christian-Jewish love affairs—now often considered "interracial"—could not help but offer socio-political commentary. Together with political debates, literary texts constituted a discursive network in which love and marriage were privileged metaphors for Jewish-Gentile relations. In this chapter, I will demonstrate this through an examination of three literary works that are plotted around Jewish-Gentile love affairs: Ludwig Jacobowski's *Werther the Jew* (*Werther, der Jude*, 1892), Max Nordau's *Doctor Kohn* (1898), and Georg Hermann's *Jettchen Gebert* (1906 and 1908). Although no longer widely known today, these works had a significant public impact at the time of their publication. Jacobowski's and Hermann's novels met with great popular success, and Nordau's play, though largely ignored by theater houses, was an important political statement by a rising leader of Zionism. The public impact of the works is one reason to begin our inquiry into modernist usages of tropes of love with these texts. Another one is the structural similarity of their plots. All three works dramatize a love affair that ends tragically with the (direct or indirect) suicide of the Jewish partner. What do these tragic endings imply about the position of Jews within German society? Should we read them allegorically, as expressions of pessimism regarding the project of Jewish emancipation and acculturation?

This chapter explores the ways in which love stories intervene in the turn-of-the-century debates about the "Jewish question." By reading literary texts in conjunction with journalistic and political writings produced by their authors, or by someone in their environment, I reconstruct their larger political projects. Both Jacobowski and Nordau confront racial antisemitism, the former as a member of the Verein zur Abwehr des Antisemitismus (Society for the Defense against Antisemitism) and the latter through his engagement with the Zionist movement. Although Jacobowski and Nordau opt for different political solutions, their literary love stories similarly highlight the obstacles faced by assimilated Jews in times of crisis. Hermann was much less concerned about antisemitism, at least during the time when he wrote *Jettchen Gebert*. Yet his novel, too, has a political dimension, as it partakes in the inner-Jewish debates about the effects of intermarriage on Jewish communities. By reconstructing these connections, I do not suggest that the literary texts "reflect" the issues brought up in nonliterary texts. Rather, I identify points of intersection between literary and political discourse and ask what the love story allows a writer to do that other modes of discourse may not do. How do literary love stories reference, recast, and rethink the problems left unresolved in political and theoretical writings?

The authors discussed in this chapter hold diverse political commitments, ranging from radical assimilationism (Jacobowski) to political Zionism (Nordau) to mainstream liberalism (Hermann). Yet their literary love stories share certain features that allow us to gauge the limits and the possibilities of love as a model of integration around 1900. On the one hand, the works analyzed in this chapter show just how ideologically fraught love at the time had become as a metaphor for group relations. As I have argued, the model of heterosexual love leading to marriage and procreation favors some visions of integration over others. Among other things, it tends to go hand in hand with an understanding of assimilation as a minority's complete adaptation to a majority culture. Other ideological strictures imposed by tropes of love include the racialization and feminization of Jewish identity, both of which are noticeable in the works analyzed in this chapter. Overall, however, these works show how tropes of love potentially escape the ideological constraints of increasingly homogenized and racialized models of identity. The authors of all three works evoke but do not fully embrace racial or other essentialist notions of Jews and Judaism. Instead, the love plot generates a host of equivocations between the social and the biological, the particular and the universal, the individual and the collective, creating a metaphorical surplus that opens up new venues to rethink the project of Jewish assimilation. The fact that the love stories all end tragically takes nothing away from this potential. As I will argue, it may be precisely the failure of love on the level of the literary plot that enables its success as fuel for the social imagination.

Ludwig Jacobowski and the Sexual Myths of Modern Antisemitism

Jacobowski's 1892 *Werther the Jew* takes its cues from the most famous German love novel to depict the struggles of an assimilated young Jew in an increasingly anti-semitic Germany. Though largely forgotten today, *Werther the Jew* was a major success at the time of its publication. It received favorable reviews in a number of journals, was translated into six languages, and went through seven editions by 1920. Jacobowski, who at the age of six had moved with his family from the East Prussian province Posen to Berlin and later studied literature, philosophy, and history, wrote the novel when he was only twenty-three years old. Around the same time, he joined the Verein zur Abwehr des Antisemitismus, a largely non-Jewish organization founded in 1891 to educate the public about the dangers of political antisemitism.[1] The Verein espoused an ideology of emancipation that aimed at the effacement of differences between Jews and Christians. At one point it promoted intermarriage as a strategy of integration, as "one of the most practical and significant means to draw the different religious denominations closer to one another."[2] The Verein also addressed what it perceived to be Jewish weaknesses, implying that antisemitic prejudice had some basis in reality. Such arguments recall the apologetic discourse of Jewish "betterment" that accompanied Jewish emancipation in Germany from the Enlightenment on.[3]

Jacobowski, who was actively involved with the Verein and employed as its substitute treasurer, seems to have concurred that Jews were at least partially responsible for antisemitism. In one of three political interventions he published between 1891 and 1894, he debunks the antisemitic myth that Jews committed a disproportionate number of crimes. But he believes that, because of their over-representation in the trading profession, Jews were indeed disproportionally involved in professional crimes such as fraud, extortion, and bankruptcy. He demands a Jewish ethical self-reformation: "Here is the place where the old Jew-ish generation is mortal [*sterblich*]. Here is where the young generation has to begin its ethical reform so that this stain, too, can be washed off. Here it is neces-sary for the young generation to invalidate this important and accurate argument for antisemitism as well."[4] Jacobowski was much more adamant in his rejection of the stereotype of Jewish moral depravity. In a response to Hermann Ahlwardt, a

---

1. On Jacobowski's biographical background and political engagement, see Fred B. Stern, *Ludwig Jacobowski: Persönlichkeit und Werk eines Dichters* (Darmstadt: Joseph Melzer, 1966).
2. *Mitteilungen aus dem Verein zur Abwehr des Antisemitismus* 4 (1894): 355; quoted in Meiring, *Die christlich-jüdische Mischehe*, 35.
3. See Barbara Suchy, "The Verein zur Abwehr des Antisemitismus: From Its Beginnings to the First World War," *Leo Baeck Institute Yearbook* 28 (1983): 205–39, esp. 224–25.
4. Ludwig Jacobowski, "Der Juden Anteil am Verbrechen: Nach amtlichen Quellen dargestellt" (1892), in Jacobowski, *Gesammelte Werke in einem Band: Jubiläumsausgabe zum 100. Todestag*, ed. Alexander Müller and Michael Matthias Schardt (Oldenburg: Igel Verlag Literatur, 2000), 1074–1112; here 1104.

notorious antisemitic agitator who a short time later was elected to the Reichstag, he vehemently attacks Ahlwardt's use of sexual imagery. He calls Ahlwardt's remarks about adulterous Jewish women and Jewish seducers of Gentile women false and propagandistic.[5] While this response betrays an Enlightenment belief in the power of rational argument, it was a qualitatively new form of protest against antisemitism. As other scholars have noted, compared to the apologetic tone of previous official Jewish reactions, Jacobowski's response was "suffused with a degree of righteous indignation and anger heretofore unusual in polemical works by Jewish liberals."[6]

This dual response to anti-Jewish prejudice—qualified acceptance of some and decided rejection of other stereotypes—also informs Jacobowski's novel *Werther the Jew*. The protagonist, Leo Wolff, is a philosophy student in Berlin and member of a new generation of young Jews "who grew up in an environment permeated by hatred."[7] He encounters antisemitic sneers at every corner, from a stranger on the street, a member of his fraternity, even his Gentile girlfriend. In response he espouses a program of Jewish self-reformation reminiscent of the strategies recommended by the Verein and in Jacobowski's own political writings. Leo hopes to defeat antisemitism by embracing the highest ethical standards and leading an exemplary life. He likes to think that his father's righteous business practices will help reduce the stigma surrounding Jewish bankers (35). Personally, he seeks to implement the program of self-improvement in his relationship with his Gentile girlfriend Helene, a shop assistant who is deeply in love with him. While his fellow fraternity students boast about their sexual conquests, Leo pledges to behave chastely toward Helene, "for he had to remain true to himself if he wanted to be a Jew, pure to the world and to himself" (46). However, Leo's plan to refute the antisemitic stereotype of the morally depraved Jew utterly fails, and the novel ends with Helene's and his successive suicides. In the years following the novel's first publication, some Zionists read Leo's tragic downfall as evidence of the futility of Jewish assimilation. Jacobowski rejected this interpretation and, in the foreword to the third edition, of 1898, made his proassimilation stance explicit. The solution to the "Jewish question," he wrote, is a "complete absorption in German spirit and German ethos [*Gesittung*]" (12). How can a love story that ends tragically be a call to social and cultural integration?

Werther the Jew takes center stage in the literary history of the "German-Jewish love affair" because the text separates, to a previously unseen degree, sexual desire

---

5. Ludwig Jacobowski, "Offene Antwort eines Juden auf Herrn Ahlwardts 'Der Eid eines Juden'" (1891), in *Gesammelte Werke*, 937–56.

6. Sanford Ragins, *Jewish Responses to Anti-Semitism in Germany, 1870–1914: A Study in the History of Ideas* (Cincinnati: Hebrew Union College Press, 1980), 43–44.

7. Ludwig Jacobowski, *Werther, der Jude*, in *Gesammelte Werke*, 9–215; here 101. All further citations of *Werther the Jew* refer to this edition and will be included parenthetically in the text and notes.

from love, marriage, and procreation.[8] One effect of this separation is that desire appears to motivate the social process of assimilation; Leo is indeed "in love" with German culture and society. The splitting of the love object into several partial objects reinforces this impression. Rather than forming one-half of a Jewish-Gentile couple, Leo is attracted to a range of people, each of whom embodies an aspect of his relationship to German society. Helene represents the ideal type of the society into which he wishes to assimilate. In contrast to his Gentile friends, who prefer Jewish girls because of their reputedly greater passion and refinement, Leo is drawn to the Germanic archetype of female innocence: "He, however, was drawn to the blond Margaret-type with incomprehensible force. And especially to his girlfriend" (47). What separates Leo and Helene are class differences—as the future heir of his father's large fortune, he is not expected to marry a girl from the lower middle classes—and the antisemitism of Helene's family. Leo's attitude toward Helene vacillates between love and vanity, compassion and cruelty. He frequently uses her as an outlet for his frustration with the antisemitism of his environment. As Mark Anderson argues, Helene "represents a kind of inaccessible and idealised other that parallels the Lotte figure in Goethe's *Werther*. That Leo treats her sadistically . . . is only a consequence of his essentially masochistic relation to the social group she represents."[9]

Different people among his friends and acquaintances fulfill different roles in Leo's program of Jewish self-reformation. He enjoys the flirtatious overtures of Erna, the beautiful and youthful wife of his former principal who recently moved to Berlin, and develops a devotion to her strongly tinged with masochism. Because an affair with Erna would be a betrayal of both Helene and his beloved former teacher, the mere thought of her launches Leo into a cycle of transgression, remorse, and renewed efforts at self-improvement. Then there is Grete, Erna's proud and enigmatic stepdaughter, for whom Leo harbors ambivalent feelings. It is never quite clear whether Leo and Grete hate each other—or rather, the Jew and the antisemite in each other—or are secretly attracted to each other.[10] Finally,

---

8. See also Eva Lezzi, *"Liebe ist meine Religion!,"* 345. *Werther the Jew* participates here in a more general trend to decouple sexual desire from marriage and procreation. A symptom of this trend is the establishment of the science of sexuality as an independent field of inquiry. See Volkmar Sigusch, *Geschichte der Sexualwissenschaft* (Frankfurt am Main: Campus, 2008); and Tracie Matysik, *Reforming the Moral Subject: Ethics and Sexuality in Central Europe, 1890–1930* (Ithaca, N.Y.: Cornell University Press, 2008).

9. Mark M. Anderson, "'Jewish' Mimesis? Imitation and Assimilation in Thomas Mann's 'Wälsungenblut' and Ludwig Jacobwoki's *Werther, der Jude*," *German Life and Letters* 49, no. 2 (April 1996): 193–204; here 199. According to Anderson, Jacobowski combines in Helene the figure of Gretchen, the archetypal victim who embodies Faust's guilt, and of Lotte, the unattainable woman who highlights Werther's social ostracism. Leo's entry into German society is a form of Faustian striving that is ironically undercut by his identification with Werther.

10. During Leo's long monologue on Jews and antisemitism, Grete and Leo pretend indifference to each other (100–104). Leo is convinced that she has "antisemitic tendencies" (105), yet Grete might just as well feel secretly attracted to him and offended by his coldness. When Leo is devastated about

throughout the novel Leo thinks of Richard Manzow, his best friend from child-hood on. Richard takes on the role of William in Goethe's *Werther*, the absent male interlocutor to whom Leo can reveal his innermost thoughts and feelings in letters and imagined conversations. Their relationship is highly affectionate—Leo thinks of "his big, strong, faithful Richard" (190)—and distinctly gendered: Richard is a very manly man, previously the best dueler in Leo's fraternity, and generously accepting of Leo's "womanly weakness" (56). The very thought of Richard puts Leo at ease, because it counterbalances the antisemitic slander he experiences in daily life.

The erotic charge of Leo's program of ethical self-reformation is also evident in the figure of the "ideal Jew" to whom he repeatedly addresses his self-depreciations. Examples of this ideal Jew, who at the same time embodies the ideal human, are Spinoza and Jesus. Jonathan Hess has linked this train of thought to the tendency among nineteenth-century German Jews to appropriate Jesus as a Jew, an attempt to locate the resources for Jewish transformation in Judaism rather than in German culture.[11] Indeed, Leo's ideal Jew invokes the idea of a special ethical mandate carried by Jews, a secularized version of the biblical idea of chosenness that had become popular among assimilated Jews in the nineteenth century. In *Werther the Jew*, this idea takes on a strong affective charge. One crucial passage depicts the *jouissance* Leo experiences in his manic search for defects in himself and other Jews. His moral masochism culminates in an imagined confession to the superego-like figure of the "ideal Jew":

> He searched for defects and deficiencies where there were none and he conducted this search with a pleasure [*Wollust*] of sorts, with the pleasure of pain [*Wollust des Schmerzes*]. For whenever he unleashed in front of himself, in himself, with himself a furious speech against the Jews, he felt as if he were striking himself slowly and unfailingly in the heart. He felt then as if he were confessing his own defects in front of an ideal figure, who was with him and went, stood, and sat next to him, in front of the figure of the ideal Jew, as he imagined him.
>
> (43; my emphasis)

Werther the Jew ultimately traces Leo's moral masochism back to a hostile environment the prejudice of which he has internalized. A member of a social minority that is held up to particularly strict moral standards, Leo strives to live up to these standards without questioning their ideological presuppositions. This becomes

---

her family's financial ruin and kisses her hand, she is gripped by "a rare feeling, which she could not account for" (185). As for Leo, it is the loss of Grete's fortune that torments him most about his father's speculations.

11. See Jonathan Hess, "Fictions of a German-Jewish Public: Ludwig Jacobowski's *Werther, the Jew* and Its Readers," *Jewish Social Studies* 11, no. 2 (Winter 2005): 202–30, esp. 215.

increasingly clear as his program of Jewish self-reformation more and more fails. Taunted by his Gentile friends, he pressures Helene into sleeping with him. When Erna and her husband arrive in Berlin, Leo spends more and more time with them and begins to neglect Helene. In the novel's tragic denouement, Leo hastily leaves Berlin after he learns about the bankruptcy of the joint-stock company in which his father and, at his father's recommendation, many Gentiles of his hometown had invested money. Back home he understands that his father and his despised cousin, an *Ostjude* with a thick Yiddish accent, pulled out their own shares just in time to profit from the financial ruin of their Gentile friends. Deeply ashamed of his relatives, Leo falls ill for several weeks and misses the pleading letters of Helene, who is pregnant and commits suicide after receiving no response from him. Leo learns about her death in a letter from his fraternity, which includes a request for his resignation and the clip of a newspaper article, signed by Max von Horst, an openly antisemitic member of the fraternity. The article draws an analogy between Leo's seduction of Helene and the questionable business practices of his father, calling upon readers to join the antisemitic movement: "The old ones defraud the honest and upright Michel, and the young ones seduce his daughters! Are you still sleeping, dear Michel? Wake up!" (214). After reading the article, Leo, who had just decided to cut off all relations with his past and begin a new life together with Helene, despairs and shoots himself with a pistol, just as Werther did.

The ending of the novel combines two stock images of modern antisemitism: the Jew as sexual predator and as fraudulent speculator. This connection raises the question of whether Jacobowski participates in the antisemitism he seeks to combat. Ritchie Robertson, for instance, argues that Leo's seduction and abandonment of Helene does indeed come across as a sexual sin equivalent to his father's unethical business practices.[12] Even Leo himself perceives his sexual desire for Erna as symptom of a moral corruption that seems to lend credence to antisemitic prejudice: "Then he felt like a mean fellow who mouthed high words about the ethical reformation of the Jews and in reality was only a vulgar Jew, each inch a scoundrel, a scoundrel" (107).[13] However, Jacobowski exposes rather than reproduces the sexual myths of modern antisemitism. Whereas he uses the cliché of the fraudulent Jewish speculator rather unreflectively, leaving little doubt that Leo's father and cousin knowingly contributed to the financial ruin of their Gentile friends, he subjects Leo's love life to a sociopsychological analysis in literary

---

12. Robertson, *The "Jewish Question" in German Literature*, 279. From a contemporary point of view, Jacobowski's critique of the sexual stereotypes of antisemitism indeed seems narrow and apologetic, especially since it goes hand in hand with his acceptance of other stereotypes. By highlighting the "Jewish" physiognomies of Leo's fraudulent cousin and father and their Yiddish-sounding language, Jacobowski even participates in racial discourse. However, my argument is that his critique of the sexual stereotypes of antisemitism is more successful, and the focus on sexual imagery indeed productive.

13. For example, the ability to resist the temptation of the principal's wife becomes a measure of the success of Leo's self-transformation (109).

form. The novel makes clear that the newspaper article sent by Max von Horst utterly and malevolently misconstrues the course of events. For rather than acting upon anti-Gentile impulses, Leo is all too eager to obey the imperatives of German society. He persuades Helene to have sex with him because the other fraternity students taunt him about his chastity and because he wants to refute the stereotype of the effeminate Jew (64–69). Not knowing that Helene is pregnant, he leaves Berlin in order to save his Gentile friends from the financial ruin caused by his father's economic transactions. Ironically, his attempt to refute the stereotype of the deceitful Jew ends up confirming, in the eyes of the antisemites, that of the sexually depraved Jew.

Werther the Jew renders Leo's wretched psychical condition, his tendency to torment himself and others, legible as a response to the impasses of Jewish assimilation. To be sure, the novel is aesthetically neither particularly complex nor particularly innovative. Its use of free indirect speech to give a richer texture to the inner life of literary characters, for instance, is rather schematic. Yet the book is important for highlighting the social dimension of Leo's erotic desires, for tracing an individual pathology back to a social pathology. Leo is attracted to Erna because she potentially raises his status in the eyes of others; he savors the fact that other men admire Erna, and initially praises her only to make Grete and Helene jealous. When he invokes the erotic license of students to justify his infatuation with a married woman (125), he indeed has a point, for the fraternity code informs his passions on all levels. Ultimately, the novel shows how a Jewish student who seeks acceptance in German society gets caught between two different codes of behavior. In order to assimilate, Leo has to obey two utterly contradictory social imperatives: he must be sexually licentious to be a true German (fraternity student) and sexually pure to be a true German (rather than the morally depraved Jew of the antisemitic imagination). *Werther the Jew* uses the literary devices of the psychological novel to dramatize Leo's tormented response to this contradiction. In so doing, the novel dismantles the antisemitic myth of the pernicious "Jewish seducer" of "Aryan" women.

Sexual imagery was crucial to the racial antisemites Jacobowski sought to combat. Hermann Ahlwardt, for instance, alleged that male Jews, spurred on by selectively permissive Talmudic laws, pursue non-Jewish women in order to seduce them (but never marry them). He portrayed the Berlin clothing stores as places where Jewish bosses sexually exploited Christian salesgirls. In so doing, Ahlwartdt helped launch the pornographic antisemitism that would become virulent in National Socialism, in which Jews were depicted as seducers and rapists of non-Jewish girls, death-bringing demons who crucified their victims in acts of *Rassenschande* (racial defilement).[14] Read against the backdrop of such imagery,

---

14. See Ahlwardt, *Der Verzweiflungskampf der arischen Völker mit dem Judentum*, 220–27. It has been argued that such sexual fantasies reflect the inversion of gender roles in the secularization of sacrifice. Whereas sacrificial death was traditionally a male prerogative—Jesus being its prime model—in the

Jacobowski's intervention becomes significant. *Werther the Jew* not only traces the social etiology of Leo's erotic desires but also validates them as sources of political protest. The novel adapts Goethe's critique of eighteenth-century society to an era that has rationalized and instrumentalized antisemitism. In Goethe, the protagonist's impossible love for a woman who is engaged to another man intensifies his sense of his self as well as his social ostracism. Werther's overflowing emotionality is a protest against the rationalism and utilitarianism of those around him, especially the eventual husband of his beloved Lotte. Jacobowski suggests that in an age of calculated hatred it falls upon the Jews, who in their upward mobility and social vulnerability resemble the eighteenth-century bourgeois male, to incarnate sensitivity and sensibility. In a programmatic passage, Leo pictures the opposition between himself and Max von Horst as an opposition between (Jewish) emotional sensibility and (German) instrumental reason:

> Here the German and the Jew had opposed each other, both from the young generation of those who were supposed to build the future. Here they had exchanged roles, here Horst was no longer Werther, but it was he who represented with his whole heart the power of feeling. It was he who had to play Werther's role with his heart-blood [*Herzblut*] while Horst was the *sober* German nationalist and *careerist*, who felt Jew hatred from instinct and from *cold calculation*.
>
> (190; my emphasis)

How might the end of the novel—the depiction of Leo's suicide—have advanced the goal Jacobowski states in the foreword to the third edition, to promote the "complete absorption" of Jews into German society? As several critics have noted, the novel's tragic ending may have been intended to produce a cathartic effect in German Jewish readers, who in the process of reading might overcome their own anxieties about assimilation. Moreover, *Werther the Jew* ends on two utopian visions: the love between Leo and Helene, which now seems true and mutual, and the friendship between Leo and Richard, which transcends even death.[15] In the novel's very last scene, Richard, who has been physically absent throughout the novel, finally makes his appearance. He finds the dying Leo, kisses him, and lifts up his body: "Then the young German knew that he held a dead man in his arm, his old friend, the young Jew" (215). This sentence forms a stark contrast to the famous last sentence of Goethe's novel, which describes Werther's funeral in

---

modern imagination women tend to assume the role of the redeemer. See Christina von Braun, "Zur Bedeutung der Sexualbilder im rassistischen Antisemitismus," in *Jüdische Kultur und Weiblichkeit in der Moderne*, ed. Inge Stephan, Sabine Schilling, and Sigrid Weigel (Cologne: Böhlau, 1994), 23–49, esp. 48.

15. In *"Liebe ist meine Religion!,"* Lezzi points out that the suicides of Leo and Helene mirror each other (349).

the most laconic manner: "No clergyman attended."[16] Whereas Werther's funeral drains death of all transcendence, the loving attention Richard, the minister's son, lavishes on Leo bestows some meaning on Leo's death and suggests that he will not be forgotten. It should be noted, however, that this redemptive ending reinstates the hierarchy implied in the marriage model of assimilation. The final scene in which the "young German" holds the "young Jew" in his arms highlights the imbalanced character of their relationship, the fact that the German has been the active and the Jew the passive partner all along.

Max Nordau and the Zionist Project of Remasculinization

In his 1898 play, *Doctor Kohn*, Max Nordau, an aspiring leader of the emerging Zionist movement, has one of the characters exclaim: "What hopes did our generation place on mixed marriage! We truly expected it to bring about the reconciliation of the races!"[17] Convinced that antisemitism was inextirpable, Nordau ostensibly wrote the play to prove these hopes wrong. *Doctor Kohn* tells the story of Julius Christian Moser, a converted Jew married to a Christian woman, and their children, all of whom struggle with identity problems of one kind or another. When the acclaimed Jewish mathematician Leo Kohn wishes to marry Moser's daughter Christine and runs into the vehement opposition of her family, Moser recognizes that the program of assimilation he pursued all his life has failed. His antisemitic brother-in-law proclaims: "Mixed marriages are a misfortune and a disaster. We do not want them! Every time a Jew forces himself into a Christian home, crass materialism and moral insensitivity follow him, and the atmosphere of the family, as well as that of the children, becomes thoroughly unhealthy" (137–38). The brother-in-law refers here to the potential marriage between Christine and Leo, but his words apply of course just as much to Moser's own marriage, a fact that is not lost on Moser. He is outraged by his brother-in-law's words, yet in the end has to conclude that he remained a guest in his own house and a stranger to his wife; their marriage continues only with a sense of insuperable alienation between the spouses. The second Christian-Jewish love affair and potential intermarriage ends even more tragically, as Leo dies in a duel to which Christine's brother provoked him. Does this tragic ending signify, as has been suggested, the "immutability of Jewish identity and the impossibility of interracial marriage"?[18] In what follows, I will argue that Nordau's stance toward intermarriage, like that of the

---

16. Johann Wolfgang von Goethe, *The Sufferings of Young Werther*, trans. Stanley Corngold (New York: W. W. Norton, 2012), 150.

17. Max Nordau, *Doktor Kohn: Bürgerliches Trauerspiel aus der Gegenwart, in vier Aufzügen*, 2nd ed. (Berlin: Ernst Hofmann, 1899), 185. All further citations of *Doctor Kohn* refer to this edition and will be included parenthetically in the text.

18. Sander Gilman, *Love + Marriage = Death: And Other Essays on Representing Difference* (Stanford, Calif.: Stanford University Press, 1998), 51.

Zionist movement in general, is more fraught and complex. Around the turn of the twentieth century, Zionists began to ponder the significance of endogamous marriage for the national reconstitution of the Jews, but their conclusions, including Nordau's, were far from clear. As I will show, *Doctor Kohn* is a Zionist call for Jewish remasculinization rather than an indictment of intermarriage. It is also part of Nordau's ongoing search for new forms of Jewish communality, for the sake of which he creatively adapts the language of race.

Nordau wrote *Doctor Kohn* in 1897 during a time of personal and political transition. Born and raised in the Hungarian city of Pest, Nordau lived in Paris for most of his life. For decades he identified as a cosmopolitan German intellectual and considered his Jewish background a contingency with negligible impact on his life. In the early and mid-1890s, however, he experienced a number of personal and political disappointments—among other things, he received antisemitic letters on the German island of Borkum and witnessed the beginnings of the Dreyfus affair in France—that focused his attention on the situation of the Jews in Europe. In 1895 Herzl won him over to the idea of a Jewish state; he soon got involved in the newly forming Zionist movement and became one of its most important leaders.[19] Around the same time, Nordau began a love relationship with Anna Kaufmann, a Danish Protestant and the widow of his friend Richard Kaufmann. The couple had a daughter in January 1897 and got married a year later, even though Nordau worried that this step would compromise his position as a Zionist leader.

As a Zionist thinker, Nordau rejected love as a model or metaphor for Jewish-Gentile rapprochement. In his celebrated speech at the first Zionist Congress in 1897—written while he vacationed together with Anna, their daughter, and her four children from her first marriage—Nordau describes Jewish emancipation and assimilation as an excessive and self-destructive love for the social majority. It is the Jew's misfortune, Nordau writes, "that upon hearing emancipation's first call to love [*Liebeswort der Emanzipation*], he tore every trace of Jewish solidarity out of his heart in order to make room for the sole rule of love for his fellow countrymen."[20] In an 1898 speech delivered in Berlin, Nordau compares the Jews' relationship to Germany to a child's bond with his mother as well as a lover's nostalgic memories of his lost beloved.[21] Love in this view is an inappropriate model for group relations, permissible only as a memory of the past or as an expression of pain caused by a necessary separation. It is thus not difficult to imagine why Nordau insisted that his

---

19. For a detailed and nonteleological account of Nordau's development into a Zionist, see Michael Stanislawski, *Zionism and the Fin-de-Siècle: Cosmopolitianism and Nationalism from Nordau to Jabotinsky* (Berkeley: University of California Press, 2001). On Nordau's life and work, see also Christoph Schulte, *Psychopathologie des Fin de siècle: Der Kulturkritiker, Arzt und Zionist Max Nordau* (Frankfurt am Main: Fischer Taschenbuch, 1987); and Petra Zudrell, *Der Kulturkritiker und Schriftsteller Max Nordau: Zwischen Zionismus, Deutschtum und Judentum* (Würzburg: Könighausen and Neumann, 2003).

20. Max Nordau, *Zionistische Schriften*, 2nd expanded ed. (Berlin: Jüdischer Verlag, 1923), 54.

21. See Nordau, *Zionistische Schriften*, 249–50.

own marriage was a purely personal decision and devoid of political significance. He tried to resolve the contradiction between his theoretical rejection and practical contraction of intermarriage by attributing the difficulties of such unions to rampant antisemitism in Germany.[22] Perhaps he was able to imagine Paris—despite the raging Dreyfus affair—as a more neutral space in which a German-speaking Jew and a Danish Protestant could meet on equal footing.

Nordau's worries about possible political reverberations of his marriage to Anna Kaufmann turned out to be well founded, as some opponents of Zionism tried to use his marriage to discredit the movement. Reacting to these accusations in the periodical *Zion*, Willy Bambus emphasizes that the overwhelming majority of Zionists are opposed to intermarriage, but he also concedes that personal circumstances allow for exceptions from the rule and that anyone's family life deserves protection from public slander.[23] The Zionist stance toward intermarriage was anything but uniform, especially in the early days of the movement. Theodor Herzl had never been opposed to intermarriage. In fact, his remarks on the subject in *The Jewish State* uncomfortably echo Treitschke's: intermarriage is the only vehicle of true assimilation, since it brings about an "identity of feeling and manner" rather than a mere "external conformity in dress, habits, customs, and language."[24] However, Herzl thought intermarriage unlikely to provide a solution to the "Jewish question" because he expected abiding antisemitism in Europe to prevent such unions from occurring on a larger scale. From a Zionist perspective, Herzl explained when congratulating Nordau on his marriage to Anna Kaufmann, intermarriage posed no problem whatsoever, because a citizen of the future Jewish state would surely be able to marry a foreign woman and bring her to his country.[25] The stance of other Zionists toward intermarriage depended on the degree to which they espoused the racial theories of the time. Some Zionists cited racial arguments to promote Jewish endogamy, while others agreed with Herzl that the spouses and children of intermarried Jews would be welcome citizens of the future Jewish state.[26] Tellingly, Zionists who held positive views about intermarriage often focused on unions between Jewish men and Gentile women. In a 1904 article in *Die jüdische Rundschau*, an anonymous author signing as "Simplicissimus" writes that Gentile women could infuse the Jewish people with the positive

---

22. See Max Nordau, *Erinnerungen*, trans. S. O. Fangor (Leipzig: Renaissance, 1928), 186.

23. Willy Bambus, "Die Mischehe," *Zion: Monatsschrift für die nationalen Interessen des jüdischen Volkes* 4, no. 5 (May 1898): 19–21.

24. Theodor Herzl, *The Jewish State*, based on a revised translation published by Scopus Publishing; further rev. and ed. by Jacob M. Alkow (New York: Dover Publications, 1988), 77.

25. See Herzl's letter to Nordau: "If our work were already completed today, then it would not be prohibited to a Jewish citizen, that is to the citizen of the existing State of Jews, to marry a woman from another country. In this way she would become a Jewess, irrespective of confession, . . . If I am not mistaken, Moses was married to a Midianite." Quoted in Mark H. Gelber, *Melancholy Pride: Nation, Race, and Gender in the German Literature of Cultural Zionism* (Tübingen: Max Niemeyer, 2000), 79.

26. For a survey of Zionist stances toward intermarriage, see Alan T. Levenson, "Jewish Reactions to Intermarriage in Nineteenth-Century Germany" (PhD diss., Ohio State University, 1990), 175–207.

qualities of their peoples, including excellence in warfare and statesmanship.[27] This gendering circumvents one of the implications of the intermarriage model outlined above—namely, the feminization of Jews and Judaism. By dropping certain kinds of intermarriages from consideration, Zionists (like many of their liberal counterparts) put the Jews into the safe position of a male joining his female partner to his family and his people.

Doctor Kohn can be read as part and parcel of the Zionist program of Jewish remasculinization. The play attempts to refute the antisemitic argument against intermarriage by making it clear that the family's misery results from the emasculation of the Jewish husband rather than from racial incompatibility, a corrosive Jewish spirit, or anything along these lines. In order to gain acceptance, Moser has assumed a completely subordinate position in his wife's family and given up much of his paternal authority in his own family. Too weak to punish his children, he secretly pays off his younger son's debts rather than confront him with his financial irresponsibility; and in allowing his sons to grow up antisemites, he has committed what he now considers to be his greatest mistake. If Nordau reproduces the antisemitic stereotype of the effeminate Jew in the figure of Moser, he attempts to refute this stereotype in his depiction of Leo Kohn, a proto-Zionist whose own interreligious love affair appears to be based on a more equal footing. Leo Kohn and Christine Moser are obviously in love with each other and respectful of each other's religious background. Yet their love, too, ends tragically. After he suffers a grave insult from one of Moser's sons, Leo challenges his prospective brother-in-law to a duel, thus displaying the pride and honor he postulates as necessary for all Jews. But because he does not want to hurt the brother of his beloved, he shoots in the air and dies tragically.

Leo's passion for Christine and his duel with her brother instantiate a program of Jewish remasculinization meant to correct precisely the kind of mistakes committed by Moser. Leo, a highly gifted mathematician who has been awarded an international research prize yet denied a professorship at the local university, is clearly the hero of the play. His call for a revitalization of the Jewish people through a cultural revolution resonates with Nordau's own developing Zionist views. Leo's courtship of Christine provides him with ample opportunity to display the pride and honor he seeks to bestow on all Jews. He will shed blood for Christine but not suffer any ridicule (40); the tragedy of his situation only reinforces his sense of heroism (96). He makes it clear that he will claim the strong position in the family that Moser so obviously lacks: "I will not put myself in the position of thanking a Christian family with subservience for having admitted me into their clan" (94). Announcing that he will take his wife into his world rather than the other way around, he promises to

---

27. Simplicissimus, "Ueber Mischehen und jüdisch-nationale Gesinnung," *Jüdische Rundschau* 18 (May 1904): 189–90; here 190. The author speculates that the offspring from Jewish-Gentile marriages may help fight for Jewish independence and thus put an end to the misery of Eastern European Jews.

correct the "skewed" gender balance—the effeminacy of the Jewish man—he finds in Moser's home.

Leo's death in a duel carries a special symbolic significance because the duel was so crucial to the turn-of-the-century redefinition of male Jewish identity. Nordau wrote the play shortly after the antisemitic Deutsch-österreichische Studenten-schaft (German Austrian Student Union) in their notorious *Waidhofener Beschluß* declared Jews *satisfaktionsunfähig* (unqualified to give satisfaction), because they lacked any sense of honor. On their part, assimilated Jews used military meta-phors to denounce converts to Christianity and to assert their Jewishness in the face of growing antisemitism. In the 1890s numerous Jewish-national fraternities that practiced dueling came into being. While Nordau initially did not share this enthusiasm—he once called the duel "an irruption of primal human barbarism into our highly developed political and social institutions"[28]—his depiction of the duel in *Doctor Kohn* is quite positive. As Mark Gelber has suggested, Nordau may have paid homage to Theodor Herzl, who had always supported dueling as a way of reestablishing male Jewish pride and honor. Herzl's *The New Ghetto* (*Das neue Ghetto*, 1894) depicts the death of the Jewish protagonist in a duel with an anti-semite as a worthwhile sacrifice. Yet Nordau describes the duel with a somewhat different accent. In contrast to Herzl, he recounts the grueling details of the duel on stage and, even more important, he grants significant space to the pain of Leo's parents, Orthodox Jews who detest duels but tragically lose their only son in one.[29] Nordau's nuanced representation of the duel in *Doctor Kohn* tempers his effort to counter the antisemitic stereotype of the effeminate Jew through an equally ideo-logical program of Jewish remasculinization.

At stake in Leo's love affair with Christine is the question of how to balance the quest for community with the claims of individuality. In *Doctor Kohn*, Nordau uses the language of race to think through the nature of Jewish communality. The play, which begins with two Gentiles exchanging anti-Jewish views, reflects a dilemma that characterizes many of his Zionist writings: racial antisemitism appears to set the discursive bounds within which any definition of Jewishness has to stay, wit-tingly or unwittingly, approvingly or disapprovingly. Before his conversion to Zionism Nordau embraced a voluntarist, language-based definition of nationality that allowed him to identify staunchly as German. In his Zionist writings he faces the problem of how to define a Jewish nationality without assuming a shared reli-gion, language, or biology. Nordau questions the racial definition of Jews and Juda-ism but seems unable to do entirely without it. One way of solving the dilemma is

---

28. Max Nordau, *Die conventionellen Lügen der Kulturmenschheit* (Leipzig: B. Elischer Nachfol-ger, 1883), 327.

29. See Gelber, *Melancholy Pride*, 75. Gelber emphasizes the fact that Kohn is dueling with his pro-spective brother-in-law, which turns the duel into a no-win situation, since he will lose no matter what happens. Kohn's shooting in the air also recalls a famous 1841 duel between Salomon Strauß and Hein-rich Heine, after which Heine commented that a duel could never give satisfaction anyway.

an orientation toward the future. Nordau argues that the Jews may not have much in common in the present but that this can change quickly if antisemitism continues to oppress them. Just like the Pilgrims, who were good Englishmen who founded the American nation, and the Spanish, who gave birth to new peoples in South America, Jews from various European nations can and must become a distinct nation in the future.[30] Nordau further temporalizes the grounds of Jewish communality when he posits the existence of a Jewish character (*Wesen*) that remains, however, curiously undefined.[31] He refers to this character only in passing, as that which is lacking or repressed in assimilated Jews, a memory of a shared past or the potential for a shared future. His notion of a Jewish character takes on a function similar to the idea of Jewish blood in Martin Buber in that it constitutes a ground of communality that is either no longer or not yet fully realized.[32]

In *Doctor Kohn*, Nordau's wrestling with the language of race plays out in Leo's views about the nature of Jews and Judaism. When Leo speaks about the Jewish "race," he usually refers to the beliefs of antisemites, whose notion of an indelible racial difference between Germans and Jews he rejects. Yet at times he, too, characterizes Jewishness as an inborn quality, a "soul" or "character," just as Nordau himself did. The play figures such an essence, for instance, through gestures. Leo suggests that even if he tried to hide his Jewishness from the Gentile family, he would inevitably betray himself through an inflection of his voice or a movement of his hands or shoulders (93–94). This is exactly what Moser does when he appears on stage "with a Jewish gesture, ducking his head, drawing his arms up, both hands opened and facing forward" (26). In another passage, Leo's oscillation between the vocabularies of interiority and exteriority raises the question of how receptive the Jewish soul is to education and historical change: "They take our Jewish soul away through education and instruction and do not allow us to realize fully the German soul they *breathe into us*. That is the great crime committed against us. They make us renounce our own natural character, they *dress us up* in a foreign one, and then let us feel that it is a *disguise* by which we make a fool of ourselves" (86–87; my emphasis). The shift in this passage from a notion of breathing to one of disguise retracts the idea that the transformation of the Jewish soul is possible or desirable; instead Leo demands the recovery of the true Jewish soul.

Leo is aware of the contradiction between his affirmation of Jewishness and his wish to marry Christine. He tries to resolve this contradiction by positing a human

---

30. See Nordau, *Zionistische Schriften*, 8–9. Nordau's article was originally published in *Die Welt* 2 (1897).

31. See, for instance, Nordau's speech at the first Zionist Congress on August 29, 1897, in Nordau, *Zionistische Schriften*, 51.

32. On the future-orientation of Nordau's conception of Jewish communality, see also Caspar Battegay, *Das andere Blut: Gemeinschaft im deutsch-jüdischen Schreiben 1830–1930* (Cologne: Böhlau, 2011), 162–73. Battegay shows how Nordau shunned the racial discourse of blood—which reduces the individual to the group of his origin—and preferred the metaphor of muscles, with its implications that the individual Jew can strengthen himself, and in turn his people.

right to individualism, the free choice of a love object: "My apparent contradictions find a higher resolution in the purely human. I love Fräulein Christine. My love is a most personal affair with which neither my forefathers nor my race have any connection. Here I am an individual and nothing else, an individual who loves and who fights for the happiness of his life" (96).

Leo touches here upon a problem that also occupied Nordau in his pre-Zionist writings—namely, the relationship between the feelings of the individual and the demands of society.[33] In his *The Conventional Lies of Our Civilization* (*Die conventionellen Lügen der Kulturmenschheit*, 1883), Nordau reconciles the individual's right to love and society's right to control its population by recasting romantic love in evolutionary-biological terms. He deplores the decline of marriage to a union based on economic calculation and advocates the contraction of love marriages. He argues that marriages of convenience threaten the harmony of family life, the biological health of the offspring, and the evolution of the human race, whereas love marriages ensure individual and group happiness and the perpetuation of a healthy race. His emphasis on the collective good distinguishes Nordau from earlier proponents of love marriages. In a distinctly Social Darwinist idiom he argues that the attraction to a genetically compatible member of the opposite sex serves the purposes of selective breeding: "Love is a being's instinctive recognition that he has to form a pair with a particular being of the opposite sex so that his good qualities will be increased and his bad will be leveled, and his type will be preserved in his offspring in an at least unstunted and, possibly, in a more ideal form."[34] Nordau goes on to explain why love-based marriage is historically a relatively new phenomenon. Since people from "primitive" cultures or lower social classes are less psychologically differentiated and compatible with most people of their environment, they do not need love to produce strong and healthy offspring. The need for love arises from the mental and psychological differentiation of educated people in modern civilization, in which romantic love promotes the rights of both the individual and the species. Based on this theory, Nordau throughout *The Conventional Lies* valorizes the kind of individualism displayed by Leo.

To be sure, in *Doctor Kohn* individual desires and social demands are much more at odds with each other. As his fate shows, Leo never manages to reconcile his Zionist search for Jewish communality with his Romantic longing for individuation in and through love.[35] What enables Nordau to mediate between Romantic individualism and Zionist collectivism is the construction of Christine, the child

---

33. On the continuities between Nordau's pre-Zionist and his Zionist writings, see also Jay Geller, "The Conventional Lies and Paradoxes of Jewish Assimilation: Max Nordau's Pre-Zionist Answer to the Jewish Question," *Jewish Social Studies* 1, no. 3 (Spring 1995): 129–60.

34. Nordau, *Die conventionellen Lügen der Kulturmenschheit*, 265.

35. This may reflect a widespread sense among Zionists that the reconstitution of the Jewish people requires sacrifices on the part of the individual. Nordau himself said that he would not have entered an interreligious love affair if he had already been a Zionist.

of an interfaith marriage and the embodiment of the "purely human" (96) the existence of which Leo postulates so emphatically. Christine is the mouthpiece of a humanism never entirely discredited in the play. As such she gets the play's final line: "Oh Daddy, why do humans hurt each other so much?" (200). She is aware of her own mixed background and hopes that it will facilitate her cross-ing of the religious divide. The fact that she is a hybrid who looks like both her Christian mother and her father's Jewish mother (107) makes Christine the most versatile element in the play's plot. Because she is both Jewish (and thus compat-ible with her Jewish lover) and non-Jewish (and thus proof of love's transcendence of ethno-religious boundaries), the figure of Christine allows Nordau to posit Jew-ish distinctiveness while repudiating racial antisemitism. More precisely, this fig-ure allows him to hover ambiguously between acceptance and rejection of racial theories. For throughout the play it remains unclear to what extent the affection between Leo and Christine springs from shared Jewishness. Christine describes herself as a typical faithful "German girl" (55) but also mentions that her love for Leo has made her aware of the Jew within her (69). She gladly accepts the pejora-tive epithet "Jew girl" (131) when she faces her family's vehement resistance to her union with Leo. In so doing she confirms the suspicions of her antisemitic uncle, who has always thought her quite recalcitrant to Christian religious teachings and surmises that her demeanor encouraged Leo to begin with (119). The play never entirely dismisses the possibility that the antisemite has a point here: that the girl Leo loves is a Jew at heart.

In *Doctor Kohn*, the succession of two Christian-Jewish love affairs, the second of which amends some of the problems caused by the first, has an effect akin to the temporalization of Jewishness in Nordau's Zionist writings. The play leaves open the question of whether the relationship between Leo and Christine repre-sents a return to origins or a departure into the future: Does love bring out the Jew in Christine or create a new mélange between Judaism and Christianity? Does love further Leo's attempt to recover a Jewish essence or persuade him to seek new arrangements between personal life and religious affiliation? The tragic ending helps sustain the play's fundamental ambiguity, for Leo's death saves Nordau from having to reveal much about the strength and the nature of the second Christian-Jewish love relationship. Rather than making a conclu-sive statement about "interracial" love and marriage, the ending of *Doctor Kohn* turns to the past in order to open up a future. In the final scene, Moser concludes that he has remained and will always remain a stranger in his conjugal family. The reason for this estrangement, however, is not the purported incompatibility between the races but Moser's failure to educate his sons properly. Moser realizes that although he cannot return to the Orthodox Jewish world of Leo's parents, he nevertheless has the obligation to transmit his knowledge of this world to his children: "But it is still my flesh and blood, though no longer my soul, and this I ought to have taught my children" (200). By dissociating his changeable "soul" from the quintessential ciphers of racial discourse, "flesh and blood," Moser refers the question of Jewish belonging once again to the future.

Georg Hermann and the Inner-Jewish Debates on Intermarriage

Political antisemitism was on a temporary decline in Germany when Georg Hermann, in his time one of the most popular German Jewish writers, seized upon the theme of interfaith love. Hermann was born in 1871 as the youngest child of a Jewish family long established in Berlin. After studying art and literature, he began writing articles for about forty different newspapers and journals. When his novel *Jettchen Gebert* appeared in two parts in 1906 and 1908, it quickly became a best seller and its author a mainstay of the German literary establishment. In 1909 Hermann cofounded the Schutzverband Deutscher Schriftsteller (Association of German Authors), and most of Germany's leading literary authors joined within a few years. As for Hermann's relationship to Jews and Judaism, throughout his life he embraced liberalism and rejected political Zionism. According to Hermann, he did not experience any anti-Jewish discrimination before the First World War. It was only afterward that rising antisemitism—first evident in the notorious 1916 *Judenzählung* (Jew count) in the German military—was brought to his attention. But later in life he said that his writing had always been informed by Judaism and his literary characters were overwhelmingly Jewish, even if he had worn his Judaism like a vest, "beneath the coat of a reputable European."[36]

Jettchen Gebert, one of the most detailed accounts of Jewish family life in German literature, appears to advocate Jewish endogamy. The novel leaves little doubt that its Jewish heroine belongs with her Jewish uncle despite her infatuation with a Gentile writer. Set in the Biedermeier period, in 1839–40, a historical period that was fashionable at the time and that Hermann reconstructs with great care, the novel takes place among the acculturated Jewish bourgeoisie of Berlin. In contrast to the works of Jacobowski and Nordau, antisemitism plays practically no role in Hermann's novel, which rather presents Jews as quintessential members of the German middle class. This social mainstreaming may explain why *Jettchen Gebert* enjoyed enormous popular success among Jewish and non-Jewish audiences alike. Yet the balancing act it accomplishes is still striking. Given the ideological stakes in the intermarriage debates, how could a novel simultaneously promote Jewish assimilation and Jewish endogamy— and meet with such widespread approval? In what follows I argue that this

---

36. Quoted in Cornelius Geerard van Liere, *Georg Hermann: Materialien zur Kenntnis seines Lebens und seines Werkes* (Amsterdam: Rodopi, 1974), 180. On Hermann's relationship to Judaism, see also Hans-Otto Horch, "Über Georg Hermann: Plädoyer zur Wiederentdeckung eines bedeutenden deutsch-jüdischen Schriftstellers," *Bulletin des Leo Baeck Instituts* 77 (1987): 73–94.

feat hinges upon the novel's creative reworking of the semantics of family. As *Jettchen Gebert* depicts the victory of family affection over romantic love, "family" functions as both a cipher of racial endogamy and a common denominator between middle-class Jews and Gentiles.

The slow but steady rise in the number of Christian-Jewish marriages after the introduction of civil marriage led to intense inner-Jewish debates between 1890 and 1914. Next to conversion and communal secession, intermarriage was one of three forms of "defection" passionately discussed by a growing sector of the German Jewish public. While some advocated intermarriage as a vehicle of assimilation, others, including many liberals and Zionists, expressed concerns about the detrimental effect of intermarriage on Jewish communities.[37] The debates began with the publication of serial stories and novels in leading German Jewish periodicals and continued with the appearance of several academic studies, including Arthur Ruppin's *The Jews in the Modern World* (*Die Juden der Gegenwart*, 1904) and Felix Theilhaber's *The Demise of the German Jews* (*Der Untergang der deutschen Juden*, 1911), that drew on the new discipline of demographic statistics. These academic works deplored the losses the Jewish communities suffered through intermarriage, largely because the offspring of such unions tended to be raised Christian, and asked how Jews could survive as a distinct group without relying upon religion as a cohesive factor. While social and political commentators of the liberal Jewish mainstream were largely critical of intermarriage during the first decade of the twentieth century, the literary stories and serial novels published in their periodicals slightly earlier convey a more complex message.[38] Typically, the Jewish partner feels genuine love for her (sometimes his) Gentile partner but finds herself (sometimes himself) betrayed. While romantic love is capable of transcending ethno-religious boundaries, social constraints, in particular the abiding antisemitism of the Christian environment, ultimately prove stronger than love.

---

37. On the inner-Jewish debates about Christian-Jewish intermarriage, see Levenson, "Jewish Reactions to Intermarriage." As for the actual marriage behavior of Jews, most social historians agree that the trend toward endogamy persisted throughout the German Empire. Endogamous marriages had always been important to the preservation of Jewish group identity and became even more so during the nineteenth-century processes of secularization and acculturation. If endogamy had traditionally created a diasporic network of affiliations and alliances, the relegation of Judaism to the domestic sphere further increased its significance. The home became the very site of Jewishness, a place in which Judaism was still practiced to some degree and which offered a refuge from antisemitism. The Jewish home was often reserved for family life and gatherings with other Jews, while social interaction between Jews and non-Jews occurred largely outside the home. As the family became the principal site where Jewish values were inculcated and Jewish identities created, the liberal Jewish mainstream sought to defend Jewish endogamy despite its general support of acculturation. For an overview of the demographic trends, see Monika Richarz, "Demographic Developments," in *German-Jewish History in Modern Times*, ed. Michael A. Meyer, with the assistance of Michael Brenner (New York: Columbia University Press, 1996-98), 3:7–34, esp. 13–17; and Steven M. Lowenstein, "Jewish Intermarriage and Conversion in Germany and Austria," *Modern Judaism* 25, no. 1 (2005): 23–61.

38. See Meiring, *Die christlich-jüdische Mischehe in Deutschland*, 50–70. For examples of stories and serial novels, see 166–67, nn. 94, 96.

Hermann's message regarding the power of family ties resonated with the views of the Jewish liberal mainstream in turn-of-the-century Germany. In two reviews of the novel in the *Allgemeine Zeitung des Judentums*, at the time the most important German Jewish periodical, Ludwig Geiger applauds *Jettchen Gebert* as an exemplary Jewish novel. He ponders the obstacles in the way of Jewish-Gentile intermarriage: "Where does the *inner* detachment of Henriette from Kößling come from? It comes—if you want to express it in lofty language—from the insight into the disparity between Judaism and Germanism [*Germanentume*]."[39] Geiger goes on to contrast the Gentile's individualism and future orientation with the Jew's faithfulness to family and tradition, which survived the decline of formal religiosity. Around the time of his review, the *Allgemeine Zeitung des Judentums* also featured a number of stories and serial novels about Jewish-Gentile love affairs and marriages. In fact, these feuilletons began to appear several years before intermarriage became a subject of social and political debates, indicating, perhaps, that literary texts are more capable of achieving the balancing act the topic required. As Alan Levenson has noted, liberally minded Jews who were interested in the continuation of Judaism, such as the typical reader of the *Allgemeine Zeitung des Judentums*, faced a certain dilemma. How could they lay claim to a German identity while defending the practice of Jewish endogamy—especially at a time when willingness to intermarry became a criterion of their social integration?[40]

One way of avoiding the dilemma was to distinguish between love and marriage. One of the feuilletons that appeared in *Allgemeine Zeitung des Judentums*, Clara Baumbach's "Faith and Love" ("Glaube und Liebe" 1904) provides a salient example of how to caution against Christian-Jewish intermarriage while promoting love as a means of improving interreligious relations.[41] The serial novella relates the story of Melitta and Grittano, a German Jewish woman and an Italian officer, who meet at a resort and become powerfully attracted to each other. Although Grittano is free of antisemitism and willing to antagonize his family and his superiors by marrying a Jew, Melitta decides against their connection and departs earlier than planned, breaking into tears as the train leaves the station. The text prepares the reader for the unhappy ending by cautioning against Grittano's readiness to ignore social conventions and against a passion that is powerful enough to rob Melissa of her free will. "Faith and Love" also plays on widespread anti-Catholic sentiments in the German Empire to convey the unlikelihood of happiness in intermarriage. It is in a Catholic church that Melitta realizes that she does not want to abandon her God and that she will remain a stranger in Grittano's environment: she could just

---

39. Ludwig Geiger, "Henriette Jacoby," *Allgemeine Zeitung des Judentums* 72, no. 23 (1908): 271–73; here 272. See also Geiger's earlier review, "Jettchen Gebert," *AZdJ* 70, no. 49 (1906): 585–87.

40. See Levenson, "Jewish Reactions to Intermarriage," 81–110.

41. See Clara Baumbach, "Glaube und Liebe," *Allgemeine Zeitung des Judentums* 68, nos. 20–24 (1904): 239–40, 248–50, 261–63, 272–75, 286–88.

as well be a Protestant unwilling to marry a Catholic. Yet the story leaves no doubt that Melitta and Grittano have genuine feelings for each other and that these feelings foster a better understanding between Jews and Christians. Like other feuilletons published in *Allgemeine Zeitung des Judentums*, "Faith and Love" intimates that interfaith love can cure the social ills caused by prejudice, as when Melitta's charms win over an antisemitic baron. The serial novella sends a double message: love between Jews and Gentiles is possible, but marriage is not advisable.

Hermann's *Jettchen Gebert*, which appeared in two parts in 1906 and 1908, resembles these feuilletons in its depiction of the love between a Jewish woman and a Gentile man who are not destined to marry.[42] The relationship between Jettchen Gebert and Fritz Kößling, a friend of Jettchen's intellectual and freethinking uncle Jason, is a classic case of romantic love, marked by fatefulness, uniqueness, and idealization. It is never quite clear whether the obstacles to their union are more socioeconomic (Kößling is poor, and Jettchen used to a lavish lifestyle) or religious (the Geberts do not practice Judaism but take pride in never having given up their religion despite the pressures of the Christian environment). In any case, the relatives with whom the orphan Jettchen grew up vehemently oppose the marriage, and Jettchen marries a cousin of hers, an *Ostjude* of stocky stature and questionable morals whom Herrmann portrays in the most stereotypical manner. Convinced that she can never love her husband, Jettchen secretly departs from her own wedding banquet.

If the first part of the novel dramatizes the opposition between Jettchen and Kößling's affection for each other and the stuffy atmosphere, philistine minds, and constant quarreling in the Gebert family, the second part inverts this opposition. After her departure from the wedding, Jettchen moves to the home of her uncle Jason and gradually discovers her love for him. Jettchen continues to meet Kößling and ostensibly harbors hopes to marry him, but their relationship is marred by all kinds of misgivings and misunderstandings. Just as Kößling is finally about to gain acceptance in Jettchen's family, Jettchen sleeps with him once and shortly afterward commits suicide by thrusting a needle into her heart. In her farewell letter, which is addressed to Kößling but read by Jason, she explains that she cannot marry Kößling because she belongs to someone else (i.e., Jason), whom she cannot marry because she has already belonged to (i.e., slept with) Kößling. The tragedy unravels not because the family thwarts Jettchen's happiness or because Jettchen cannot sustain the courage she displayed at her wedding banquet, but because she realizes that she will never enjoy with Kößling the emotional intimacy she experienced with Jason.

---

42. The two parts of the novel are *Jettchen Gebert* (1906) and *Henriette Jacoby* (1908). In what follows, I will cite from the following edition by Gert and Gundel Mattenklott: Georg Hermann, *Werke und Briefe*, vol. 2, *Jettchen Gebert*; and *Werke und Briefe*, vol. 3, *Henriette Jacoby* (Berlin: Das Neue Berlin, 1998). Further citations from this edition will be included parenthetically in the text with the abbreviations *JG* and *HJ*.

The narrator conveys the changing meaning of family primarily through Jason's eyes and mind. If Jason initially maintains an ironic distance from his family's shallowness and conventionality, he gradually comes to appreciate the warmth and stability afforded by family bonds. Among the events that intensify the sense of family connection are Jason's contraction of typhus, the death of his nephew, and Jettchen's move back to her aunt and uncle, which inspires in her a sense of responsibility for the family's reputation. While family ties emerge as the most reliable basis of human relations, elusive yet indelible psychological differences cause a gradual alienation between Jettchen and Kößling. When Kößling despairs over his bleak prospects in work and love and rediscovers Christianity, Jason begins to fear for the happiness of Kößling and Jettchen: "He, Jason Gebert, suddenly felt that it really caused deep differences in character and feeling, which one could perhaps conceal but hardly reconcile" (*HJ* 163). Tellingly, these differences do not transpire in specific religious traditions but in the affective response to such traditions whatever their origin. Thus Jason and Jettchen take Christmas much more seriously than Kößling because they cherish the opportunity to express affection toward their loved ones. It is a sour point in the relationship between Kößling and Jettchen that he forgets to buy her a Christmas present (*HJ* 166). Jason and Jettchen, in contrast, have successfully transformed the Christian holiday into a celebration of family bonds.

Jason's belief in temperamental differences between Jews and Gentiles echoes the reflections on Jews as a race in Hermann's art criticism. After attending art-historical lectures as a student of the University of Berlin, Hermann published several articles on Jewish artists in *Ost und West*, a journal committed to the renaissance of Jewish culture in Germany. Although Hermann always distanced himself from political Zionism and, according to his own testimony, felt at best latently Jewish before the First World War, his articles employ the rhetoric of race typical of cultural Zionism. Hermann argues that even though no overt thematic or stylistic features distinguish them from the works of non-Jewish artists, the paintings of Max Liebermann and Camille Pisarro are in an elusive yet essential way Jewish.[43] In a 1903 article, he describes the differences between German and Jewish art as one between muscles, coldness, and idealism on the one hand, and nerves, warmth, and esprit on the other. The vagueness of this depiction is characteristic of cultural Zionism, whose rhetoric of race could attach itself to almost any feature of a given artwork.[44] In *Jettchen Gebert*,

---

43. See Georg Hermann, "Camille Pisarro," *Ost und West* 4, no. 1 (1904): 16; and "Max Liebermann," *Ost und West* 3, no. 6 (1903): 377–80.

44. See Georg Hermann, "Max Liebermann," in *Juedische Kuenstler*, ed. Martin Buber (Berlin: Juedischer Verlag, 1903), 107–35, esp. 110–14. See also Arpe Caspary, "Usumes Maske: Vom gesichterten und ungesichterten Schreiben," in *Aber ihr Ruf verhallt ins Leere hinein: Der Schriftsteller Georg Hermann (1871 Berlin–1943 Auschwitz)*, ed. Kerstin Schoor (Berlin: Weidler, 1999), 57–86; here 62; and Gelber, *Melancholy Pride,* 155–56.

family becomes just such a racial marker of Jewishness when Jason and Jettchen emphasize the importance of family ties for Jews (*JG* 145, 275). The incestuous character of their relationship, both real and symbolic, establishes another, more elusive link to racial thought. Jason is not only Jettchen's uncle but also a father substitute; he taught her most of what she knows and instilled his dreams in her. His symbolic fatherhood culminates in a Pygmalion vision that casts Jettchen, who finally returns his love, as Jason's creation awakening to life (*HJ* 266). It has been argued that the proliferation of incest motifs in modern literature reflects a growing concern with race and racial purity, and that sibling incest in particular comes to signify intraracial desire and harmony.[45] *Jettchen Gebert* participates in this revaluation of incest in suggesting that a shared family origin produces the psychical attunement required for lasting love.

While the invocation of family serves to delineate boundaries between racial groups, it also fosters a constant flux and exchange between Jews and Gentiles and the categories habitually employed to distinguish them. The narrative focus on the members of one Jewish family creates the impression that Jews are the norm and Gentiles the exception. Furthermore, the valorization of family life that here comes to justify Jewish endogamy has been a centerpiece of bourgeois morality since the eighteenth century. With the shift from arranged to love-based marriage, the intimate sphere of the family became the idealized site of bourgeois subjectivity, at least in the literary imagination. The eighteenth-century bourgeois tragedy contrasts familial intimacy with the representative character of courtly life, pitting bourgeois privacy, authenticity, and morality against aristocratic publicity, artificiality, and licentiousness. *Jettchen Gebert* redeploys elements of this literary tradition in detailed descriptions of Jason's and Jettchen's domestic life in the face of public adversity. A series of displacements and inversions further propels the novel's Jewish figures into the center of German society. Most important, Kößling, the only Gentile portrayed in some detail, is structurally positioned as a Jew whose social ostracism and existential worries reflect a constant struggle for recognition. While the Geberts embody tradition and establishment, Kößling is poor and depends on his intelligence for social advancement. His restlessness and homelessness contrast with Jettchen's sense of belonging, as does his alienation from nature with her enjoyment of nature. Hermann's representation of urban space as both static and dynamic, both closed and open, aids this inversion of social roles typically associated with Jews and Gentiles. Jettchen, who moves almost exclusively in the old town center, is securely located in Berlin, whereas

---

45. See Christina von Braun, "*Blutschande*: From the Incest Taboo to the Nuremberg Racial Laws," in *Encountering the Other(s): Studies in Literature, History, and Culture*, ed. Gisela Brinker-Gabler (Albany: State University of New York Press, 1995), 127–48. One would have to add that the marriage between uncle and niece was legally permitted at the time. See Max Marcuse, *Vom Inzest* (Halle: Carl Marhold Verlagsbuchhandlung, 1915), 66. In fact, such marriages were at some point quite customary in Jewish circles. See Lezzi, "*Liebe ist meine Religion!*," 87–88.

Kößling, who likes to explore Berlin's outer districts, never loses the stigma of the newcomer.[46]

Love and Death

These three case studies show how the love story around 1900 functions as a medium of political intervention. The authors' literary texts work in tandem with the political writings produced by them and by other participants in the public debate: Jacobowski analyzes the social psychology behind erotic attachments and dismantles the sexual stereotypes of racial antisemitism. Nordau espouses the program of Jewish remasculinization, which was central to political Zionism. Hermann aids the cause of liberal Judaism, which seeks to repudiate racial antisemitism while preserving Jewish distinctiveness. Their works demonstrate a very interesting potential for love while precluding the intermarriage to which love seems directed. The combined message of the three is one of familial segregation within even an integrationist political model. As such they continue the political vision of Enlightenment thinkers such as Moses Mendelssohn.

What do we make of the fact that all three works end with the (quasi) suicide of the Jewish partner of the love affair? Are these endings further evidence that modern German Jewish authors are caught up in racial discourses, including ideas about racial incompatibility? There is something to be said for this argument. Death is associated with the mode of the tragic and a sense of inevitability, the poetic equivalent of biological destiny. The works discussed in this chapter are indeed tragic in the sense that they culminate in a catastrophe caused by a fundamental flaw or an irresolvable conflict. In *Werther the Jew*, Leo Wolff's efforts to combat antisemitic stereotypes entangle him only more deeply in what he perceives to be the guilt of the older Jewish generation. In *Doctor Kohn*, Leo Kohn's irreconcilable conflicts between Romantic individualism and Zionist collectivism make catastrophe appear inevitable. The same is true of Jettchen Gebert's inner conflicts between romantic love and family affection.

As a plot element, however, death may well enable love to function as a model or metaphor of the social bond. To offer a concrete observation, in all three works discussed in this chapter, the literary staging of death creates new interconnections between Jews and Gentiles or renders existing ones visible. In Jacobowski, death

---

46. It has often been noted that Kößling is an alter ego of Georg Hermann, who also came from a poor background. Kößling in fact bears the name of one branch of Hermann's family. Another allusion to Kößling's (metaphorical) Jewishness can be found in Jettchen's suicide. The suicide is modeled on the 1834 death of Charlotte Stieglitz, a famous woman of the Vormärz era of whom Jettchen learns from a book of Jason's. In her farewell letter, Charlotte Stieglitz expressed the hope that her death would empower her husband, the frequently depressed writer Heinrich Stieglitz, who was born Jewish and converted to Christianity at the age of thirteen. Like Kößling, Stieglitz earned his living as a librarian and tutor. See Charlotte Stieglitz, *Geschichte eines Denkmals*, ed. Susanne Ledanff (Frankfurt am Main: Ullstein, 1986).

reunites Leo Wolff with his beloved Richard and Helene. In Nordau, death finally bestows on Leo Kohn the status of equality with Gentiles for which he fought. *Jettchen Gebert* ends with a scene in which Jason reads Jettchen's suicide note, which Kößling was meant to receive but did not—he apparently committed suicide when he heard about Jettchen's death. The story of the letter's writing and reception continues the love triangle between Jason, Jettchen, and Kößling that structures the novel as a whole. The three main characters harbor strong affections for each other, and even as the narrative focus is on the Jewish-Gentile couple, Jason is always present, whether in reality or in Jettchen's thought. The final scene once again emphasizes this interconnectedness. Even if the Gentile writer is but an intermediary between the Jewish lovers, he is still necessary, for it is to his imagined presence that Jettchen can finally voice her love for Jason.

To offer a more speculative thought, death potentially disrupts the teleological force of love stories. The death of one partner is the surest way to have the interreligious love affair fail and in that process be raised to a model. In general, failure in one specific case does not invalidate a model, because the failure can always be blamed on the particular circumstances of that situation. In addition, the failure of love usually forestalls reproduction, and it is in reproduction that biology most easily ushers in teleology. Only the children of intermarriages can prove or disprove claims about the purported effects of "blood mixing," whether these claims are lodged in biologistic ideas about miscegenation or in the antisemitic injunction to the Jews "Be like us! Know that you cannot be like us!" As I have argued, Treitschke and others conjure the idea of biological fusion only to posit its impossibility, thereby foreclosing the imagination of less totalizing models of social integration. Literary representations of "interracial" love affairs that fail before they produce children avoid, at the very least, the trap of this double bind.

5

Eros and Thanatos in Fin-de-Siècle Vienna

Sigmund Freud, Otto Weininger, Arthur Schnitzler

The crisis of Jewish emancipation and assimilation was felt with particular acuity in turn-of-the-century Vienna. In 1895, political antisemitism attained its biggest electoral success when Karl Lueger, leader of the Christian Socialists, was elected mayor of Vienna. Although Emperor Franz Joseph, who was opposed to antisemitism, initially refused to confirm Lueger as mayor, he did confirm him in 1897, ushering in more than a decade of antiliberal rule in the city. Lueger's election had been preceded by a decline of political liberalism, with which Jews had historically identified, and the rise of the Austrian Pan-German movement, which under the leadership of Georg von Schoenerer had embraced racial antisemitism in its program in 1885. To be sure, in comparison to Schoenerer's racist fanaticism, Lueger's views were eclectic and opportunistic. His notorious remark "I decide who is a Jew" indicates his selective and cynical use of racial ideology. Lueger was also known for having several Jewish friends, and as a mayor he refrained from implementing anti-Jewish policies or retracting Jewish civil rights. His political ascent and eventual election were nevertheless a shock for many Jews in Vienna, and for good reasons. In 1897, they witnessed an openly antisemitic politician taking over the government of a city that had been a paragon of integration.

There was a higher concentration of Jews in turn-of-the-century Vienna than in the major German cities, with the result that artists, writers, and performers of

Jewish background played a prominent role in Viennese cultural life. Jakob Wassermann reveled at the omnipresence of Jews upon his arrival in the city in 1898: Jews
were active in "the banks, the press, the theatre, literature, social organizations. . . .
The court, the lower class and the Jews gave the city its stamp. And that the Jews,
as the most mobile group, kept all the others in continuous motion is, on the whole,
not surprising. Yet I was amazed at the hosts of Jewish physicians, attorneys, club-
men, snobs, dandies, proletarians, actors, newspapermen and poets."[1] There are
several explanations for the prominence of Jews in Viennese public life. During
the second half of the nineteenth century, Vienna had seen an influx of Jewish
immigrants from other parts of the Habsburg Empire. The Habsburg Empire was
home to a variety of ethnic, religious, and cultural groups among which tensions
increased in the course of the nineteenth century. Jews were often forced to choose
between competing linguistic and political allegiances. Many opted for assimilation
to German-language culture, and the Germanness of Vienna was part of its attraction for Jewish immigrants. Yet their own German identity remained precarious
and ambiguous, predisposing Jews to become agents of cultural renewal. Vienna
was a mecca for immigrants of all sorts, and the multiethnic and multicultural
character of the city left its mark on Viennese Jewish identity: "The Germanness
of Viennese Jews, who had for the most part arrived recently in the city, often
from non-German speaking areas, was even more beset with ambiguity—and
hence with creative potential—than that of Viennese Christians."[2] While the rise
of political antisemitism in Vienna did not pose an immediate physical threat to the
Jews, it called into question their tenuous yet highly productive identification with
German culture.

Vienna around 1900 also was a locale famously fraught with questions of sex and
love. It was the birthplace of psychoanalysis, the place where Sigmund Freud and
others formulated their revolutionary insights about the power of Eros in individual and communal life. In particular in his later work, in books such as *The Future
of an Illusion* (1927) and *Civilization and Its Discontents* (1930), Freud analyzes the
role of erotic and aggressive drives in human culture and society. In *Group Psychology and the Analysis of the Ego* (1921), for instance, he argues that the same libidinal
energy that propels individuals into love relationships helps constitute social bodies
such as the church and the military. If deflected from the goal (intercourse) and the
object (an individual of the opposite sex) of mature sexuality, libidinal energy can
create lasting social bonds and become a glue of society. Freud's theory of the social
role of aim-inhibited or sublimated eroticism potentially supports an idea discussed
throughout this book: that erotic love may spark social or political renewal. For if

1. Quoted in Robert S. Wistrich, *The Jews of Vienna in the Age of Franz Joseph* (New York: Oxford
University Press, 1989), 172–73.
2. Steven M. Lowenstein, "Jewish Participation in German Culture," in Meyer, ed., *German-
Jewish History in Modern Times,* 3:313.

the sexual drive propels people into larger social units, it also remains stubbornly resistant to dominant social formations and thus a force of social change. The natural fate of the sexual drive is to become fixated on an individual and transformed into love, thereby promoting the formation of a couple, which according to Freud is inherently antisocial. The more passionately two people are in love with each other, the more indifferent they become to the larger social context in which they live. Since the dyad of the lovers is at odds with the demands of the group, erotic love potentially destabilizes society and forces it to reorganize itself along new lines.

In this chapter, I argue Freud himself did not pursue the implication of his own theory for Christian-Jewish love, about which he maintained a conspicuous silence. My examples will be drawn from *On the Psychopathology of Everyday Life* (1901), which Freud completed just around the turn of the century and which belongs to the "cultural" books mentioned above. Freud blurs therein the line between the normal and the neurotic by showing that the principles active in neuroses also govern everyday parapraxes such as slips of the tongue and lapses of memory. I will briefly discuss the book's allusions to religious difference in love relationships and argue that they surface only in the form of symptomatic leftovers. The focus of this chapter is on two Viennese writers—Otto Weininger and Arthur Schnitzler—who rethink the connection between Jewishness and eroticism in ways that Freud's work eschews. As in previous chapters, I am less concerned with conscious collaboration, reaction, or opposition than with discursive overlaps, intersections, and divergences. Although there are some known connections between these Viennese writers, these remain rather tenuous and difficult to ascertain.[3] What I wish to show is that all three writers think through the crisis of Jewish assimilation in their reflections on sex, love, and death—and that it is Schnitzler, the literary author, who reinstates love as a model of Jewish-Gentile rapprochement.

Otto Weininger's *Sex and Character* (*Geschlecht und Charakter*, 1903) is generally considered the first philosophical treatise on sexuality. Born Jewish, Weininger converted to Protestantism shortly after defending the dissertation on which *Sex and Character* is based. To today's reader, the work reads like a compilation of misogynist and antisemitic stereotypes, a pseudoscientific speculation about the nature of sexual difference. Yet at the time of its publication, *Sex and Character* quickly became enormously influential, especially after its author in October 1903

---

3. Freud had read a draft of the dissertation on which *Sex and Character* was based before Weininger submitted it to the University of Vienna. Although Freud's reaction was decidedly mixed—he would not recommend the dissertation for publication—the work's affinities to his own are unmistakable; he later complained that Weininger had lifted the theory of bisexuality from him and his friend Wilhelm Fliess. As for Freud and Schnitzler, they read each other's work and occasionally acknowledged the impact it had on their own, but they refrained from seeking each other's personal acquaintance. Freud famously confided in a letter of 1922—written on the occasion of Schnitzler's sixtieth birthday—that he had avoided a meeting out of fear of facing his double (*Doppelgängerscheu*). The relationship between Schnitzler and Weininger is the most difficult to grasp, since we have no record of encounters or interactions between them.

committed suicide in the room where Beethoven had died. Among the many modernist artists, writers, and philosophers who were influenced by Weininger are Ludwig Wittgenstein, Franz Kafka, Karl Kraus, Elias Canetti, and James Joyce. My reading of *Sex and Character* focuses on the chapter on Judaism, which Weininger added after he submitted his dissertation and which grotesquely inflates the connection between Jewishness and sexuality. Weininger declares hypersexuality the quintessential Jewish (and female) trait and postulates that mankind needs to overcome sexuality and procreation to become truly liberated. As we shall see, this idea has dire implications for the project of Jewish emancipation.

The second half of this chapter is focused on a leading exponent of Viennese modernism, Arthur Schnitzler. The son of a Jewish laryngologist, Schnitzler studied and practiced medicine before he devoted himself exclusively to writing literature. Like Freud, Schnitzler was concerned with the duality of life and death, the hidden truth of dreams, and the psychological mechanisms of denial and repression. In different ways than Freud, Schnitzler explored the workings of the unconscious (or, as he called it, the "middle consciousness") for the sake of social analysis and critique. He was a keen observer of the crisis of liberalism and the spread of antisemitism in turn-of-the-century Vienna. In his novel *The Road into the Open* (*Der Weg ins Freie*, 1908), he depicts the many ways in which Viennese Jews responded to this crisis. The novel combines this social analysis with a love story between an aristocratic man and a woman from the lower middle classes, performing a crisscrossing of literary genres that reinstates Eros as a positive social force. As I will argue, Schnitzler's recuperation of love as a model for Jewish-Gentile rapprochement has to be read against Freud's resonant silence about and Weininger's decided rejection of this model.[4]

Freud's Resonant Silence

Jay Geller has tracked down the few yet significant references to Jewish-Gentile love in Freud's *On the Psychopathology of Everyday Life*, a book that reveals the hidden truth behind seemingly random slips of the tongue and other parapraxes.[5] Almost all of the scenes in which Freud explicitly identifies individuals as Jewish involve intimate contact between Jews and Gentiles. These scenes show misgivings, fears, and other negative reactions to Jewish-Gentile love affairs: A woman has a dream about a child committing suicide by means of a snakebite. At the end of the dream analysis, she expresses apprehension that her brother might enter into

---

4. As mentioned earlier, the Habsburg Empire never mandated civil marriage, and the number of Jewish-Gentile intermarriages rose more slowly in Austria than in Germany. This is one of the reasons the topic of marriage did not become as central to the Austrian debates about Jewish assimilation—however, sex and love did, if in an indirect manner.

5. See Jay Geller, *On Freud's Jewish Body: Mitigating Circumcisions* (New York: Fordham University Press, 2007), 52–62.

a *"mésalliance"* with a *"non-Aryan"* woman.[6] A converted Jew inadvertently calls his sons *Juden* (Jews) instead of *Jungen* (youngsters) in front of his antisemitic hosts (93). He evidently has regrets about his conversion, which was necessary to marry a Christian woman. A Gentile schoolteacher sends a letter meant for his brother to the Jewish girl he has been courting. In the letter he expresses his misgivings about the potential marriage, which therefore never takes place (223). Geller concludes that these scenes indicate how fraught and complicated Jewish-Gentile relations have become, and that Freud gestures at these complications in his depictions of Jewish-Gentile love.

Overall, however, Freud maintained a resonant silence about the subject of Jewish-Gentile sex and love. Even in the passage from *The Psychopathology of Everyday Life* in which he most explicitly discusses the disadvantages of being Jewish in Austria, Freud remains evasive. He recounts his conversation with a male acquaintance who complains about the bleak prospects of his generation of the "race [*Volkstamm*] to which we both belonged" (9). The man expresses his hope for future recompense by citing, haltingly and incompletely, a line from Virgil's *Aeneid*: he says (in Latin), "Let an avenger arise from my bones," instead of "Let someone [*aliquis*] arise as an avenger from my bones" (9). In reconstructing the reasons for the misquotation, Freud finds out that the man fears that his female companion might be pregnant. Freud concludes that the man's lapse expresses his conflicting desires to have progeny (who will avenge his generation of Jews) and to *not* have progeny (with this particular woman in this particular situation). However, Freud makes no attempt to learn more about the woman's identity—we know only that she is Italian—or about the reasons for the man's apparent hesitation to marry her. Freud's account of the man's story contains its own significant omissions and evasions. Tellingly, in the next example, which involves a man forgetting lines from a famous Goethe ballad, Freud (wrongly) surmises that the religious difference between the man and the woman he is courting might have caused his memory to lapse. Freud's reference to religious difference as a potential marriage obstacle seems to be a symptomatic leftover, a displaced reminder of a problem left unspoken in his previous example.

In a different context, Eva Lezzi has suggested that Freud remained evasive about erotic attraction between Jews and Gentiles because the topic had become so overdetermined. Since the mid-nineteenth century, discourses about sexuality had become increasingly important and decoupled from questions of love, marriage, and procreation, especially with the development of the modern science of sexuality. At the same time, antisemitic discourses deployed more and more sexual imagery, for instance, by associating Jews with deviant sexuality and denouncing the

---

6. Sigmund Freud, *The Psychopathology of Everyday Life*, in *The Standard Edition of the Complete Psychological Works of Sigmund Freud,* ed. and trans. James Strachey (London: Hogarth Press, 1953–74), 6:67 (Freud's emphasis). All further citations of *The Psychopathology* refer to this edition and will be included parenthetically in the text.

new science of sexuality as Jewish. Against this backdrop, Freud's relative silence about Jewish-Gentile love affairs becomes significant. Freud intentionally shunned the (usually antisemitic) equation between Jewishness and sexuality in favor of a universal theory of Eros.[7]

Weininger's Rejection of Eros

Otto Weininger's *Sex and Character* cements the image of the effeminate Jew that had developed over the course of the nineteenth century.[8] The book is notorious for portraying both women and Jews as hypersexual, materialistic, uncreative, slavish, and in every way the opposite of the rational, autonomous subject of Kantian philosophy. Weininger draws the analogy between Jews and women, which he bases upon their purported lack of an intelligible self and their susceptibility to external influence, in the thirteenth chapter of *Sex and Character*. As with many ideas of the book, the great popularity of this analogy does not reflect its truth or originality but the degree to which it was already entrenched in fin-de-siècle Viennese culture. Weininger's portrayal of Jews as infinitely malleable and devoid of essence spelled out what many thought—and wrote—after the process of Jewish emancipation and assimilation had created a new set of anti-Jewish stereotypes. Modern antisemitism replaced the traditional Christian image of the Jews as stubborn disbelievers who refuse to recognize Jesus as the Messiah with new images that targeted assimilated Jews. The swiftness with which Jews adapted, or were said to adapt, to their non-Jewish surroundings came to symbolize the perceived threats of modern life, such as superficiality, abstraction, and instability.

There are two different arguments running through *Sex and Character*, corresponding roughly to its two parts. On the one hand, Weininger advances an innovative definition of a person's sex as relative—someone might be 40 percent feminine and 60 percent masculine—and as malleable—anyone can work to increase his or her own percentage of masculinity. Part 1 of the book, which draws on the empirical biology and psychology of the time, sets out to demonstrate this relativity in a variety of examples, including human bisexuality and intermediate sexual types. On the other hand, Weininger posits the existence of ideal types of masculinity and femininity, abbreviated M and W, which individual men and women may approximate to varying degrees but which they rarely if ever fully embody.[9] Part 2 of *Sex*

7. See Lezzi, *Liebe ist meine Religion!*," 365–86. On connections between the science of sexuality and Jewishness, see also Christina von Braun, "Ist die Sexualwissenschaft eine 'jüdische Wissenschaft'? Säkularisierung und die Entstehung der Sexualwissenschaft," in *Preußens Himmel breitet seine Sterne . . . : Beiträge zur Kultur-, Politik- und Geistesgeschichte der Neuzeit*, ed. Willi Jasper and Joachim H. Knoll (New York: Georg Olms Verlag, 2002), 2:697–714.

8. On the history of this image, see also Ritchie Robertson, "Historicizing Weininger," 23–39.

9. On the different phases of Weininger's composition of the book and the works that influenced him, see Hannelore Rodlauer, "Fragments from Weininger's Education (1895–1902)," in *Jews & Gender:*

and Character provides an extensive taxonomy of the traits appertaining to *M* and *W*: *M* is conscious, active, logical, and capable of genius and morality; *W* is unconscious, passive, illogical, and talented and conformist at best. To be sure, the two parts of Weininger's argument, which he himself characterizes as "biological and psychological" and "psychological and philosophical," respectively, do not necessarily contradict each other.[10] Yet there is an undeniable tension between the Platonic notion of ideal types and Weininger's actual theory of sexuality. Indeed, Weininger's insistence on the absolute opposition between *M* and *W* can be read as a mode of defense, an attempt to restore the clear distinction between men and women—and, by implication, between Jews and Aryans—that his own theory elides.

According to Weininger, the single most important feature of the woman and the Jew is their tendency toward matchmaking (*Kuppelei*). Matchmaking expresses a desire for fusion that manifests itself in a range of female behaviors, including sexual desire but also interest in romance novels and a general disposition toward impressionability and suggestibility. Matchmaking results in the creation of a community (*Gemeinschaft*) that subordinates the individual to the group, first and foremost the family, but also other types of communities that Weininger deems disorderly, anarchic, and formless. The only form of collectivity he valorizes is the state, which he defines like Rousseau as a voluntary association of free individuals who choose their own legislation (277). The Jewish and female propensity to conflate and connect what does not belong together, in contrast, threatens the boundaries that separate one individual from the other. In his chapter on Judaism, Weininger cites the alleged Jewish propensity to marry for money rather than love as one example of such arbitrary connectivity (281).[11]

If Weininger at times seems to suggest that romantic love leads to better connections than money or sex, a closer look at his theory of love dispels this impression. In the chapter "Eroticism and Aesthetics," Weininger initially distinguishes between love, which he defines as male, and sexuality, which he associates with women. What happens in love is that a man projects his own values on something external, thereby proving his very capacity to posit values and act autonomously. Aesthetics, or the apperception of beauty, is proof of the human, that is, male, propensity to project self-ideals outward. After this valorization of love, however, Weininger begins to discover several affinities between love and sexuality, both of which are irrevocably tainted by their dependence on something material and particular. Love is an imperfect medium of human freedom because it reduces women to a means

Responses to Otto Weininger, ed. Nancy A. Harrowitz and Barbara Hyams (Philadelphia: Temple University Press, 1995), 35–58.

10. Otto Weininger, *Sex and Character: An Investigation of Fundamental Principles*, trans. Ladislaub Löb (Bloomington: Indiana University Press, 2005), 5. All further citations of *Sex and Character* refer to this edition and will be included parenthetically in the text.

11. Lezzi points out that the opposition between Jewish arranged marriage and Christian love matches had become a stereotype by then. See Lezzi, *"Liebe ist meine Religion!,"* 363.

to an end, a screen onto which men project their own ideals. This argument is less protofeminist than it sounds.[12] For Weininger does not so much criticize the projection mechanism but its dependence on women, whom he deems unworthy of such a projection of value, or on anything material for that matter. In other words, he is less concerned with woman's reduction to an object than with man's dependence on such an object: "Instead of actively realizing the idea of perfection, love tries to show the idea as if it had already been realized. By the most subtle ruse, it pretends that the miracle has happened in the other person, but the fact remains that the lover hopes to achieve his own liberation from evil *without a struggle*" (221; Weininger's emphasis).

If love points to the possibility of human freedom, any concrete form of love necessarily betrays this possibility. This is why Weininger ultimately retracts his initial distinction between love and sexuality: "Both the sexual drive and love are attempts to realize the self. The former seeks to perpetuate the individual through a physical likeness, and the latter to perpetuate individuality through its mental image. But only a man of genius knows a love that is entirely devoid of sensuality, and he alone seeks to beget timeless children in whom the most profound essence of his mind expresses itself" (222–23). I would argue that the "love that is entirely devoid of sensuality" is an ideal that remains unrealizable even in Weininger's mind. Weininger wants to detach love so radically from an object that it becomes impossible. It is thus only consistent that he in the end recommends understanding—rather than love or sex—as the basis of the ethical male-female relationship, although he never develops this idea in any detail (307). Instead, he ends the book with an appeal to humankind to overcome sexuality in order to achieve true emancipation, fully cognizant of the fact that this would end the human species. Weininger is so opposed to sex and love because they sabotage the possibility of human self-creation and self-perpetuation; neither in biological procreation nor in mental reproduction do we determine our origin and destination. Weininger in effect equates spiritual immortality with biological death.

Weininger can be said to anticipate here the distinction between life and death drives Freud made in his later life—or more precisely, he creates a gendered and racialized version of this distinction. Weininger defines sexuality as the urge to conjoin individual elements into greater entities—what Freud will call Eros or the life drive—and freedom as the ability to reduce such entities once again to separate elements—what Freud will call Thanatos or the death drive. Throughout *Sex and Character*, Weininger associates freedom and morality with the drive to isolate, distinguish, and disentangle. The figure of the great loner who disavows all affective ties to others and who looms so large in *Sex and Character* is evidence of Weininger's obsession with monadic individuality. So is the celebration of the prostitute, who is the opposite of the mother and the embodiment of the life-denying principle

---

12. David Luft, for instance, reads Weininger as a protofeminist who critiques man's reduction of woman to an object. See his *Eros and Inwardness in Vienna: Weininger, Musil, Doderer* (Chicago: University of Chicago Press, 2003), esp. 59–65.

(208), as the only lover appropriate for the genius. What Weininger calls freedom is the ability to sever all emotional bonds and to disrupt the chain of procreation. In his mind reproduction and parenting are a form of fusion with other human beings that prevents the self-perpetuation of the individual monad. Physical procreation does not transcend mortality, because instead of producing individuals it reproduces the species, which is doomed to perish over time and therefore does not truly transcend time (197–99). The same is true of mental procreation insofar as it depends on a physical object or medium. Weininger's ideal type of man, the autonomous, self-legislating human being postulated in Kant's moral philosophy, renounces Eros and embraces Thanatos.

What are the implications of these ideas for the project of Jewish emancipation and assimilation? As Steven Beller has argued, Weininger's views on Jews and Judaism belong in the tradition of "intolerant liberalism," a political outlook that favored a quid-pro-quo model of Jewish emancipation.[13] According to this model, the granting of civil and political rights to Jews depended upon their integration into the social majority and, ultimately, the disappearance of Jewish difference. Weininger's call for the Jews to "overcome" their Jewishness evinces a belief in the individual's right to and capacity for self-determination that is liberal at its core. His demand that Jews who have successfully "overcome" their Judaism should receive full recognition by the Christian majority is consistent with liberal tenets: "On the other hand, a Jew who would have overcome, a Jew who would have become a Christian, would have every right to be taken by the Aryan for an individual and no longer to be judged as a member of a race that he has long since transcended through his moral efforts" (282). If Weininger subordinates the claims of race to the transformative power of morality, this understanding is once again well within the parameters of his time. Around 1900 the liberal model of Jewish emancipation had become infused with racial ideas that blended rather uneasily with liberalism's Enlightenment heritage. The prominent Viennese Jewish liberal Theodor Gomperz, for instance, believed in the existence of inherited racial characteristics while insisting on the individual's capacity for self-transformation.[14]

Weininger's idea of Jewish self-overcoming certainly resonates with this tradition of "intolerant liberalism." However, it is important to note that he clearly distinguishes such self-overcoming from the historical phenomenon of Jewish assimilation. In the one instance in which he actually uses the verb "to assimilate" (*assimilieren*), Weininger draws on the then-popular image of the parasite to denounce

---

13. Steven Beller, "Otto Weininger as Liberal?," in Harrowitz and Hyams, *Jews & Gender*, 91–101. Allan Janik similarly views Weininger as an advocate of Jewish emancipation in "Weininger's Vienna: The Sex-Ridden Society," in *Vienna: The World of Yesterday, 1889–1914*, ed. Stephen Eric Bronner and F. Peter Wagner (New Jersey: Humanities Press, 1997), 43–62; here 47.

14. As Beller sums up, "In his belief that individuals could overcome even their racial heritage and that political liberalism should defend their right to do so, Gomperz was typical of liberal thought in the Vienna of 1900" ("Otto Weininger as Liberal?," 96).

assimilation as a passive-aggressive behavior that subdues others and thwarts their desire for freedom. This assertion is meant to differentiate Jews from women, in whose pure passivity Weininger still sees a rudimentary redemptive potential:

> Woman is matter, which *passively* assumes any form. In the Jew there is undeniably a certain *aggressiveness*. . . . He actively adapts to different circumstances and requirements, to any environment and any race, like a parasite that changes and assumes a completely different appearance with any given host, so that it is constantly taken for a new animal, even though it always remains the same. The Jew assimilates to everything and thereby assimilates everything to himself. In so doing he is not subjected by the other, but subjects the other to himself.
>
> (289; Weininger's emphasis)

Jewish self-overcoming thus has little to do with the historical experience for which the term *assimilation* had by then become established—namely, the process by which Jews adopted the language, appearance, and customs of their non-Jewish surroundings. Weininger's rejection of Jewish assimilation as commonly understood explains the surprising turn at the end of the chapter on Judaism. There he suggests that the Jew, whom he deems fundamentally lacking in genius, might become the greatest genius of all, the religious genius. That is, to overcome Jewishness means to surpass and renew the majority culture rather than merely adapt to it. The founder of a new religion, who traverses the abyss of skepticism and nihilism before he arrives at religious belief, embodies this idea of self-overcoming. Rather than the gradual replacement of one tradition by another one, Jewish self-overcoming is a radical departure from all existing traditions and beliefs. It is a leap into newness—or into death. For from Weininger's views on freedom it follows that the only way for Jews to truly overcome Jewishness is to embrace death. Without speculating too much about the reasons for his own suicide, of which we have very little documentation, I wish to point out that suicide is a logical consequence of the ideas developed in his book. Weininger, who in a footnote in *Sex and Character* mentions that he is of Jewish descent, might have imagined becoming a true Aryan and a true man by killing himself. His suicide might have been an attempt to realize his own ideal of freedom as a form of thanatotic striving.[15]

Schnitzler's Affirmation of Eros

Arthur Schnitzler's literary oeuvre explores the many ways of Eros, often with an eye toward social contexts. Schnitzler achieved his breakthrough in 1895 with

---

15. On the notion of Weininger's "philosopher's suicide," see also Peter Kampits, "Otto Weininger und das Sein zum Tode," in *Otto Weininger: Werk und Wirkung*, ed. Jacques Le Rider and Norbert Leser (Vienna: Österreichischer Bundesverlag, 1984), 167–77.

Flirtations (*Liebelei*), a play about love, betrayal, social class, and gender roles. *Flirtations* features a prototypical "sweet girl," a young woman from the lower middle classes, involved in a relationship with an aristocratic man. Schnitzler's most controversial play, *La Ronde* (*Reigen*, written 1895–96), consists of ten dialogues between two lovers, one of whom will be shown with a new sexual partner in the next dialogue. Linking members from different social classes in a sexual chain, the play exposes the power asymmetries between them. Schnitzler's emphasis on the social contexts in which sex and love take place allows him to compare different forms of social ostracism. One of the few works in which he explicitly addresses the situation of the Jews, *Professor Bernhardi* (1912), links the discrimination against Jews and the sexual victimization of women. The play recounts the verbal attacks and legal incriminations suffered by a Jewish doctor after he prevents a Catholic priest from entering the hospital room of a dying girl. The "crime" of Professor Bernhardi is his compassion for a girl who has been abandoned by her lover and suffers medical complications after a back-alley abortion.

Four years earlier, Schnitzler had published a novel widely regarded as a key literary document of Jewish life in turn-of-the-century Vienna, *The Road into the Open*. Gershom Scholem called it the first novel of aesthetic merit "that described and put up for general discussion the crisis of German-speaking Jews in its Viennese form, and it did so with astonishing acuteness and freedom from prejudice."[16] Yet from its first publication, critics have chided the work for falling into two different parts that represent two distinct literary genres: a romance and a social novel. The protagonist Georg von Wergenthin, a Gentile baron and dilettante composer, mostly socializes with Viennese Jews of various backgrounds and worldviews. Georg's conversations with his Jewish friends and acquaintances provide a detailed picture of the Jewish reactions to the decline of liberalism and the rise of political antisemitism around 1900. We meet Zionists, socialists, overassimilated parvenus, and old-fashioned liberals, none of whom are openly privileged by the narrative. For instance, Leo Golowski, a proud Zionist likely modeled on Theodor Herzl, appears just as authentic and likable as his sister Therese, a radical socialist who rejects the idea of separate Jewish politics. Overall, *The Road into the Open* shows the impasses of assimilation without suggesting a genuine alternative. The writer Heinrich Bermann, often thought to be the author's double, speaks perhaps the most authoritative words on the matter when he disparages Jewish hopes for full integration into Austrian society while rejecting Zionism as a "purely extraneous solution to a highly internal problem."[17]

---

16. Gershom Scholem, *Von Berlin nach Jerusalem: Jugenderinnerungen* (Frankfurt am Main: Suhrkamp, 1977), 61.
17. Arthur Schnitzler, *The Road into the Open*, trans. Roger Byers (Berkeley: University of California Press, 1992), 182. For the original German, see Arthur Schnitzler, *Der Weg ins Freie* (Frankfurt am Main: Fischer Taschenbuch, 1990), 235. Further citations from these editions will be included

What do the novel's reflections on Jewish identity in times of crisis have to do with its major story line, Georg's love affair with Anna Rosner, a young Catholic woman from a lower middle class family? Many critics have answered, "Very little," and this is why the novel is ultimately a failure. Although the love affair structures the plot—Anna and Georg meet at a social gathering and fall in love, they travel to Italy when Anna gets pregnant and separate after their child dies shortly after delivery—these events seem to have little bearing on the sociopolitical issues discussed in the book. In what follows I offer a new interpretation of the novel's bifurcation by reading it with and against Weininger's *Sex and Character*. I do not claim that Schnitzler consciously responded to Weininger. Schnitzler does not mention *Sex and Character* in his diaries at all before the publication of *The Road into the Open*, and refers to Weininger's work only rarely and cursorily after that.[18] This is quite striking, given that Weininger's work became a *succès de scandale* almost immediately upon its publication in 1903. Yet even if Schnitzler had not read *Sex and Character* when he was writing *The Road into the Open*, he almost certainly had heard it referred to by friends and acquaintances. As I will argue, Schnitzler and Weininger to some extent agree in their construction of Jews and women as nonautonomous and unable to determine their own fate. However, Schnitzler exposes the corresponding idea of the male Gentile as free and self-determined as the product of wishful thinking and, even more important, he uncovers the reality of a quasierotic exchange between Jews and Gentiles.

One important parallel between Schnitzler and Weininger is the connection they establish between death and freedom. The title of Schnitzler's novel, *The Road into the Open*, has rich connotations, including the project of Jewish emancipation: on some level, every character in the book longs to be free. However, only the Christian, aristocratic Georg actually achieves a sense of freedom. The view of the open road on which the novel ends, and which stands for the many possibilities Georg sees before him, is the result of two deaths that, taken together, tear him out of the chain of procreation. On the first pages, we learn that the recent death of his father instilled a sense of freedom in Georg. The period of mourning has alienated him from his friends but also freed him from burdensome social obligations. The novel's beginning also hints that the dead father will not, as in the Freudian narrative, survive as a symbol and enable Georg to become himself a father or in another way usher in a new epoch in his life. Rather, there is a sense of circularity and repetition that undermines any idea of progression. For

---

parenthetically in the text, with the page number in the English translation followed by the page number in the German edition in italics, as here (182/*235*).

18. Schnitzler mentions Weininger four times in his diaries. On each of these occasions, he briefly reports either that he discussed Weininger with someone else or that someone else was reading Weininger. See Arthur Schnitzler, *Tagebuch*, ed. Werner Welzig et al. (Vienna: Verlag der Österreichischen Akademie der Wissenschaften, 1981–), 1:124 (January 31, 1910); 2:57 (August 18, 1913); 3:15 (January 31, 1917); 7:21 (February 13, 1920).

instance, when Georg reminisces about his father, he thinks first about an episode during which he, Georg, "had not really worked again for a half year or longer" (3–4/7). The word "again" intimates that unproductive periods are nothing new in Georg's life and will probably recur in the future. At the end of the novel, Georg recuperates a similar sense of freedom after accepting the death of his newborn son. Interestingly, it was never death itself that posed a threat to Georg but rather the contingency of this particular death; he is haunted by the physician's remark about the low probability of the complication his son suffered during delivery. The pure accident that is his son's death calls into question the purpose of individual existence and the possibility of self-determination. Significantly, the child's death ceases to trouble Georg when he learns to reinterpret contingency as necessity, and statistical probability as personal fate.

Another important parallel between Schnitzler and Weininger is that they associate freedom with men and Gentiles, and the lack thereof with women and Jews. This is where the two different genres of the novel—the romance and the social novel—come together. *The Road into the Open* construes an analogy between Georg's love affair with Anna Rosner and his friendship with Heinrich Bermann, the Jewish writer whose keen-witted self-analyses and observations about Austrian society help sharpen Georg's views and, as some critics claim, gradually lead him to a better understanding of the Viennese Jews. Heinrich is connected with Georg's love life both in Georg's mind and in the narrative sequence.[19] These seemingly accidental connections, which are skillfully woven into the textual mix of dialogue, free indirect speech, and third-person narration, point to a deeper analogy between the novel's two most important subsidiary characters, as well as between two types of relationships. At the end of the book, neither relationship seems to have a future. Georg and Anna's child is dead, and the plans for the opera on which Georg and Heinrich had begun to collaborate—an obvious allusion to the German Jewish cultural "symbiosis"—have gone nowhere. Both relationships are further marked by a distinct power differential between the partners. They initially create new connections between different classes or religions, but ultimately fail and leave the weaker partner in a state of helpless dejection. In the last pages of the novel, Anna and Heinrich are depicted in strikingly similar terms as incarnations of passivity and paralysis: Anna "remained behind, standing with limp arms, her eyes closed" (291/374), and Heinrich "just stood there, stiff, motionless, pale, as if extinguished" (296/381).[20]

---

19. For instance, Heinrich is first mentioned as the purported fiancé of Else Ehrenberg, with whom Georg has had a flirtatious friendship ever since they were teenagers. And when Georg reminisces about the party where he first got to know Anna better and lets the guests pass before his inner eye, he thinks of Heinrich just before he thinks of Anna. A moment later, this mental association materializes when Georg runs into Heinrich just after he has left Anna's house.

20. Norbert Abels perceives the analogy between Heinrich and Anna, both of whom suffer from Georg's lack of responsibility toward them. See Abels, *Sicherheit ist nirgends: Judentum und*

These representations of Anna and Heinrich—the woman and the Jew—as lacking selfhood, agency, and freedom could be directly out of Weininger. However, in contrast to Weininger, Schnitzler exposes these images as the products of a particular—and profoundly biased—mind. *The Road into the Open* shows how Georg obtains a sense of freedom by distancing himself from his female lover and his Jewish friend. Throughout the novel Georg is happiest when realizing that he is not fully committed to any woman, including Anna. And at several important junctures, Georg experiences sudden feelings of freedom and self-assurance when faced with Heinrich's dejection. When we see them together for the first time, in a conversation about Heinrich's obsession with his father and his ex-lover, Heinrich's departure inspires a sense of elation in Georg: "Georg watched him with sympathy and revulsion at the same time, and a sudden, free, almost jubilant mood came over him in which he saw himself as young, carefree, and destined for the happiest future" (43/59).[21] It remains unclear what exactly causes Georg's rather abrupt mood change; he simply seems to feel free once he realizes that Heinrich is not free. Similarly, Georg can accept the death of his child once he is confronted with Heinrich's pronounced inability to come to terms with death. Heinrich fears that his lover, an actress with whom he had a falling-out because he suspected her to be unfaithful, may have committed suicide, and he distracts himself with long tirades against philosophy, religion, and morality. It is over and against Heinrich's critique of any attempt to categorize human experience that Georg recuperates a sense of inner and outer coherence:

> Georg had the feeling that Heinrich was only trying to achieve one thing with all his talking: to shake off any responsibility for himself toward a higher law, by recognizing none. And he felt, as though in a growing opposition to Heinrich's astonishingly drivelling behavior, how in his own soul the picture of the world, which had threatened to crumble to pieces for him a few hours ago, began gradually to come together again. Until now he had rebelled against the senselessness of the fate that had struck him today, but now he began vaguely to suspect that even that which seemed to him a tragic accident, had not descended on his head from out of nowhere, but that it had

---

Aufklärung bei Arthur Schnitzler (Königstein im Taunus: Athenäum, 1982), 137. Yet like most other critics, Abels ultimately puts more emphasis on the analogy between Georg and Heinrich rather than on that between Anna and Heinrich. Jacques Le Rider argues that the closeness between Georg and Heinrich indicates the concomitance of the crisis of masculinity and the crisis of Jewish identity, and the lack of adequate responses to these. See Le Rider, *Modernity and Crises of Identity: Culture and Society in Fin-de-Siècle Vienna*, trans. Rosemary Morris (New York: Continuum, 1993), 180–83. On the crisis of the ethical self in Vienna, see also Steven Beller, *Vienna and the Jews, 1867–1938: A Cultural History* (New York: Cambridge University Press, 1989), 207–37.

21. Imke Meyer, one of few critics who have explored the connections between Schnitzler and Weininger, points out that both thinkers focus on the indefinable, malleable, "contagious" aspects of Judaism, which lead to paranoid projection mechanisms. Schnitzler analyzes such projection mechanisms, for instance, in *Leutnant Gustl*. See Imke Meyer, *Männlichkeit und Melodram: Arthur Schnitzlers erzählende Schriften* (Würzburg: Königshausen and Neumann, 2010), 158–60.

come to him from a predetermined, but dark path, like something remotely visible that approached him from far down the road, and which he was accustomed to calling necessity.

(236/302–3)

Georg's characterization of Heinrich recalls Weininger's comments on the Jewish "'free thinker'" (283) whose secular, materialist worldview is said to manifest the same lack of autonomy as Jewish religious orthodoxy. In Georg's mind, Heinrich's denial of the existence of higher laws shows only that he cannot come to terms with his lover's suicide, that he remains dependent on her. Against Heinrich's lack of self-determination, Georg sets an understanding of his child's death as a necessary and meaningful event in his life. This acceptance of death is not an act of mourning, which would enable the mourner to reinvest his libidinal energies and thereby overcome loss. Georg does not work through the death of his child by fashioning appropriate substitutes; rather, he affirms this death as the precondition of his own freedom. If anticipation of the birth of his child has previously inspired in Georg a vision of an endless genealogical chain encompassing himself, he now experiences his severance from such a chain as liberating. He remembers "the vague consciousness of standing in the continuous chain that stretched from ancestor to offspring, held fast by both hands, to have a part in the universal human destiny. Now he suddenly stood detached again, alone. . . . Now he would be able to go into the world freely again, like before" (238/305). Georg ultimately finds freedom in solitude and a sense of finitude.

Georg's distantiation from Heinrich culminates in the final passages of the novel, in which he imagines how Heinrich will commit suicide by plunging from a tower at the top of a carousel winding up in spirals. The image of the carousel leading to a tower serves throughout the novel as a metaphor for freedom in the negative sense, that is, a limitless and debilitating freedom. As the cemetery wall and the house in which Anna gave birth—the last reminders of Georg's ties to her—give way to a panoramic view of the landscape, Georg contemplates the advantages he has over Heinrich:

> He knew that [Heinrich] could not be helped. At some time he was surely destined to throw himself from a tower he had ascended in winding spirals; and that would be his end. But Georg was well, and quite satisfied. He made the decision to use the three days that remained to him as intelligently as possible. The best thing would be to spend them alone somewhere in a beautiful, quiet landscape, to rest up and collect himself for new work. He had brought the manuscript of the violin sonata with him to Vienna. He wanted to finish this before anything else.
>
> [Heinrich and Georg] went through the gate and stood out on the street. Georg turned around, but the cemetery wall blocked his view. In a few steps he again had an open view of the valley. Now he could only guess where the little house with the

grey gable stood; it was no longer visible from here. Over the red and yellow hills which enclosed the scene the sky descended in a faint autumn glow. In Georg's soul there was a soft farewell to many joys and pains, which he could hear, as it were, dying away in the valley he was now leaving; and at the same time, a greeting from unknown days which sounded toward his youth from the far-off expanses of the world.

(297/240)

The reader, however, has reason to distrust Georg's confidence in himself and his future. Georg's conviction that he will soon complete his new violin sonata, for instance, seems overly optimistic in view of the fact that he has not completed a single piece of music throughout the novel. As many critics have noted, *The Road into the Open* disrupts the logic of progression that characterizes the *Bildungsroman*. There is in the end no indication that Georg has undergone any kind of moral or spiritual development. If he has secured a position as a conductor in a provincial orchestra, this is only proof of his adaptation to the institutions of bourgeois art, not of a deeper correspondence between society's demands and his own artistic aspirations. Schnitzler, who famously introduced the interior monologue into German literature in his 1900 novella *Lieutenant Gustl*, marshals modernist literary techniques to alert the reader to the possibility of Georg's self-delusion. Georg is privileged by the narration in that he is present most of the time and able to articulate his thoughts in interior monologue and free indirect speech, yet he is also the only character criticized by the narrator, at least indirectly. While the narrator does not comment on the Jewish characters and lets them express their social anxieties and existential uncertainties in an almost unmediated fashion, he evaluates Georg's behavior by presenting it from both internal and external perspectives.[22] This technique helps expose Georg's sense of freedom as an idea, a fantasy perhaps, which Georg can sustain only by distancing himself from Jewish and female others.

This reading goes beyond the widely shared view that Schnitzler supplements individual with social psychology. Of course, this aspect is also present in *The Road into the Open*: Schnitzler suggests that in a society characterized by misogyny and antisemitism, women and Jews face greater obstacles on their paths toward self-determination. But his critique of the ideology of freedom is even more provocative. By drawing an analogy between a Gentile's uneven friendship with a Jewish writer and his love affair with a woman from a lower social class, Schnitzler advances a critique of Weininger's biased concept of freedom. Whereas Weininger hypostatizes social stereotypes in his conception of moral autonomy as male and

---

22. An outside judgment of Georg occurs, for instance, through the sudden intrusion of an external perspective. The passage on the disrupted chain of procreation, for instance, concludes with a certain hesitation, likely spoken by the narrator, about Georg's self-proclaimed sense of freedom: "Could he really?" (238/*305*).

Aryan, Schnitzler exposes a similar idea of freedom as the product—and possibly a delusion—of a particular, socially situated mind.

Even more important, Schnitzler's interweaving of a love story and a social novel allows for a conception of Jewish assimilation in which Eros has a place. *The Road into the Open* construes Jewish-Gentile interaction as a quasierotic exchange, an alternative to Weininger's model of radical Jewish self-transformation or self-annihilation. Against Weininger, Schnitzler rehabilitates the idea of love as a model of social interaction in general and Jewish-Gentile rapprochement in particular. While Weininger wants to sever all emotional ties between individuals, Schitzler suggests that such ties are effective even where they are disavowed. The love story told in *The Road into the Open* spills over into the social novel and, among other things, charges Jewish-Gentile relations with affect. As one of the characters puts it, Jews are prone to fall in love with Georg: "An unequalled conqueror of hearts. Even Therese is infatuated with him. And recently Heinrich Bermann; he was almost comical. . . . Well yes, a handsome, slender, blond young man; Baron, Christian, German,—what Jew could resist this magic" (253/*323–24*). This comment is of course meant sarcastically, but it also contains some truth. Georg's interactions with his Jewish friends, both male and female, frequently have an erotic tinge. He flirts with a number of Jewish women, and there are distinctly homoerotic overtones in his encounters with Leo in particular.

This returns us to the question of why Schnitzler chose for his novel such a hybrid form, a combination of two literary genres. As Abigail Gillman has argued, the formal hybridity that characterizes Viennese Jewish modernism at large has a special function *In the Road into the Open*. It is part and parcel of an "aesthetics of detachment" by which Schnitzler avoids taking a clear political stance or offering a "solution" to the "Jewish question."[23] In a letter to the Danish critic Georg Brandes, Schnitzler explained his decision to give Georg a non-Jewish mistress: "I finally had no intention of proving anything, neither that Christians and Jews don't get along, nor that they are able to get along—I wanted rather to represent, without bias, people and relationships I have observed (whether in the outside world or in fantasy makes no difference)."[24] Schnitzler's wariness of facile allegorization is well justified. As we saw in the previous chapter, in the racialized discourses of the turn of the century, literary representations of Jewish-Gentile love stories are prone to become commentaries on the compatibility or incompatibility of the "races." Schnitzler avoids this by analogizing Georg's faltering love affair with Anna and his uneven friendship with Heinrich without collapsing the one into the other. He

---

23. Abigail Gillman, *Viennese Jewish Modernism: Freud, Hofmannsthal, Beer-Hofmann, and Schnitzler* (University Park: Pennsylvania State University Press, 2009), 107–19. According to Gillman, Viennese Jewish modernism constitutes "a coherent Jewish countertradition" (178), marked by a preference for hybrid forms and for genres of memory.

24. Quoted in Gillman, *Viennese Jewish Modernism*, 113.

chooses a bifurcated structure that allows for a cross-pollination of literary genres and other kinds of boundary crossings. Georg constantly moves between public and private spheres, between romantic tête-à-têtes with his Catholic mistress and political discussions with his Jewish friends.

The Road into the Open construes connections between the social and the erotic throughout. If differences in social power define love relationships, love also energizes social interaction, and in particular Georg's interaction with his Jewish friends and acquaintances. Schnitzler pictures Georg's mind as a porous structure that is infiltrated by the thoughts and feelings of others. Images flow freely from one mind to another, and in the process change Georg's perception and understanding of the world. In fact, nothing characterizes Georg more than the trait Weininger explicitly labels Jewish and female: susceptibility to the influence of others. At one point Heinrich says of Georg: "Nothing like that would ever have occurred to you in your life, if you hadn't been associating with a character like me, and if it weren't sometimes your way, not to think your own thoughts, but rather those of someone else who was stronger—or weaker than yourself" (296/380). One of the novel's central images, the carousel (*Ringelspiel*) that spirals up to a tower, shows that Heinrich has a point here. In the Prater amusement park, where Heinrich and Georg see a giant Ferris wheel and take a ride on the roller coaster, Heinrich concocts the image of the carousel rising up to a tower (40/55), an image that Georg picks up and elaborates throughout the novel. At the end of *The Road into the Open*, Georg pictures what he believes to be Heinrich's certain future demise as a fall from just such a tower while rejoicing in what he imagines to be his own open and happy future (297/381). A related image helps Georg recuperate a sense of meaning and coherence after his child's death. As Georg compares his own experience of death with Heinrich's, he pits the purposeful movement along a path, which signifies necessity, against the movement of a fall "out of nowhere," which signifies the *Zufall* or contingency of death (236/302–3.). In other words, Georg borrows from Heinrich the terms in which he articulates his own sense of freedom. He is indebted to his Jewish friend for the very image by which he distances himself from him.

Georg's subconscious exchange with others is also erotic in that it is a source of his creativity. Something happens along Georg's path, something he has not planned or premeditated. The few moments of his artistic productivity we witness spring from scenes of love or friendship, such as when Georg composes a song during his flirtation with another (possibly Jewish) woman. This is why the two dominant readings of Georg as either an incorrigible antisemite or a Gentile who gradually comes to understand his Jewish friends equally miss the point. More than exposing Georg's ideological biases or depicting his inner development, *The Road into the Open* shows that he has always already been interacting with Jews in a manner he cannot fully acknowledge. This is the most important effect of the novel's bifurcation and the point in which Schnitzler most clearly differs from Weininger. By incorporating a love story into his social commentary, Schnitzler rehabilitates

Eros as a mode of interpersonal connection, with implications for Jewish-Gentile rapprochement. While Weininger can accept Jewish assimilation (or what he terms "self-overcoming") only as a form of suicidal striving, Schnitzler depicts assimilation as a mutual, quasierotic exchange across open boundaries. In so doing, Schnitzler brings two central concerns of turn-of-the-century Vienna together: the crisis of Jewish assimilation and the contemplation of the role of Eros in individual and social life. His suggestion that the Gentile man is most dependent on his female lover and his Jewish friend when he declares his independence is an ingenious response to Viennese antisemitism (and misogyny).

6

Revelatory Love, or the Dynamics of Dissimilation

Franz Rosenzweig and Else Lasker-Schüler

In this final chapter, I turn to two German Jewish modernists who at first sight may not seem to have much in common: Franz Rosenzweig and Else Lasker-Schüler. Rosenzweig was a philosopher who, after writing a dissertation on Hegel and a classic of modern Jewish thought, *The Star of Redemption* (*Der Stern der Erlö-sung*, written in 1918–19, published in 1921), went on to reform and revitalize Jew-ish adult education in Weimar Germany. Lasker-Schüler was a bohemian artist who mixed elements of high and low culture and played with conventions of gen-der and religious identity. What these two writers share, however, is a rather em-phatic vision of interfaith encounters in and through love. They are notably less concerned with the racial discourses with which other modernists were contend-ing. In the previous chapter we saw how Arthur Schnitzler rehabilitates Eros as a mode of Christian-Jewish rapprochement only indirectly, by juxtaposing a love story and a social plot. In this chapter, I show how Rosenzweig and Lasker-Schüler more unequivocally valorize love as a model of Christian-Jewish relations as they turn toward religious conceptions of love. They are post-secular thinkers who re-visit Jewish religious traditions after secularization has taken hold, both in the Jew-ish families in which they were raised and in the German society in which they lived and wrote.

Rosenzweig himself called the return of many of his Jewish contemporaries to Jewish religious traditions "dissimilation."[1] More precisely, he considered dissimilation a transhistorical phenomenon, an enduring and productive tension between Jews and the people among whom they lived. The term has since come to refer more specifically to the process of Jewish self-reflection and self-renewal at the beginning of the twentieth century. As such, dissimilation is often understood to be a reaction to the rise of racial antisemitism during the late nineteenth century and its exacerbation during the First World War, developments that called into question earlier ideals of emancipation and assimilation.[2] It is noteworthy, however, that Rosenzweig himself rarely addressed antisemitism but was more broadly concerned with the destructive effects of nationalism. He famously began writing *The Star of Redemption* in the trenches of the First World War, which he believed was caused by an excessive nationalism that had perverted the biblical notion of divine election. His project in *The Star of Redemption* was to restore the true meaning of Jewish separateness—namely, the idea that Jews live withdrawn from history and symbolically anticipate redemption.[3]

In this chapter, I read *The Star of Redemption* in the light of the letters Rosenzweig wrote around the same time to his Christian lover Margrit Rosenstock-Huessy. Their love affair occurred during a period of transition for Rosenzweig, the time when he decided to leave academia for good and devote himself entirely to Jewish adult education. The correspondence with Rosenstock-Huessy shows that his emphatic decision for a Jewish life—which included marriage to a Jewish woman and establishment of a Jewish household—developed in a close dialogue with his Christian friends and his Christian lover. Reading *The Star of Redemption* in conjunction with these letters does not reduce philosophy to autobiography. Rather, it brings out the sociopolitical dimension of Rosenzweig's thinking. In the first part of this chapter, I show how Rosenzweig develops a concept of revelatory love—which can be experienced in the encounter with God or with the human-as-stranger—as the foundation of a new kind of universality. In the second part, I read Lasker-Schüler's bold reinterpretation of biblical stories in *Hebrew Ballads* (*Hebräische Balladen*, 1913) as a poetic performance of such love. Both Rosenzweig

---

1. See the diary entry from April 3, 1922, in Franz Rosenzweig, *Der Mensch und sein Werk: Gesammelte Schriften* I, *Briefe und Tagebücher*, vol. 2, *1918–1929*, ed. Rachel Rosenzweig and Edith Rosenzweig-Scheinmann, with the cooperation of Bernhard Casper (The Hague: Martinus Nijhoff, 1979), 770.

2. On the concept of dissimilation, see Shulamit Volkov, *Germans, Jews, and Antisemites: Trials in Emancipation* (New York: Cambridge University Press, 2006), 256–75; and Jonathan Skolnik, *Jewish Pasts, German Fictions: History, Memory, and Minority Culture in Germany, 1824–1955* (Stanford, Calif.: Stanford University Press, 2014), esp. 7–9. Taking his cue from Rosenzweig, Skolnik expands "dissimilation" into a concept suited to analyze German Jewish culture at large.

3. On Rosenzweig's philosophy of history and its reflection on the First World War, see Paul Mendes-Flohr, "Franz Rosenzweig and the Crisis of Historicism," in *The Philosophy of Franz Rosenzweig*, ed. Paul Mendes-Flohr (Hanover, N.H.: University Press of New England, 1988), 138–61; and Stéphane Mosès, *The Angel of History: Rosenzweig, Benjamin, Scholem*, trans. Barbara Harshaw (Stanford, Calif.: Stanford University Press, 2009), 17–61.

and Lasker-Schüler depict love as a force that proliferates differences rather than creates a union, and, in so doing, offer new models for living together in an inescapably pluralist world. Finally, I turn toward the darker vision of Lasker-Schüler's "The Wonder-Working Rabbi of Barcelona" ("Der Wunderrabbiner von Barcelona," 1921). This short, cryptic text, which juxtaposes a Christian-Jewish love story and the depiction of a brutal pogrom, suggests that antisemitic violence is a *failed response* to revelatory love.

Rosenzweig on Singularity and Universality: *The Star of Redemption*

Franz Rosenzweig's major work, *The Star of Redemption*, is many things: a critique of German Idealism, a founding document of modern existentialism, a revival of the concept of revelation, and a vision of how Jewish particularity can be realized within modern, secular German culture. But it is also a book about love, both divine and human, and the role of love in the constitution of human communities. In two of the middle chapters of the book, Rosenzweig defines revelation as an outpouring of divine love, and redemption as an infinite series of acts of neighbor-love. Together these chapters articulate a paradox that also occupies contemporary theorists who seek to reinstate love as a model of social and political relations: that love, which is focused on an object in its singularity, may become the foundation of a new kind of universality.

Revelation in Rosenzweig is an act of divine love in which God addresses a human being and thereby ensouls her and makes her a subject. Although conceived as a personal experience, it is modeled on the historical revelation at Sinai, where God gave the Decalogue to the people of Israel, a small and powerless group of ex-slaves undistinguished by special talents or virtues. This lack of distinction is crucial, for divine love is groundless. It enigmatically seizes upon an object to confer on it a radical singularity. Divine love "transfixes [*ergreift*] individuals—men, nations, epochs, things—in an enigmatic transfixion [*Ergreifen*]. It is incalculable in its transfixion except for the one certainty that it will yet transfix also what has not yet been transfixed. This would seem to imply a constriction of the concept of divine love, yet this apparent narrow-mindedness first turns this love into veritable love."[4] This is why the sounding of the proper name is the signature linguistic event of revelation. When God calls upon man by this name, he tears him out of the generic context of a social group: "That which has a name of its own can no longer be a thing, no longer everyman's affair. It is incapable of utter absorption

<hr />

4. Franz Rosenzweig, *The Star of Redemption*, trans. William Hallo (Notre Dame, Ind.: University of Notre Dame Press, 1985), 164–65. All further citations of *The Star of Redemption* refer to this edition and will be included parenthetically in the text.

into the category [*Gattung*] for there can be no category for it to belong to; it is its own category" (186–87).

Rosenzweig's conception of divine love as an act of singularization resonates with several contemporary theories of love. According to Roland Barthes's *A Lover's Discourse*, the beloved's uniqueness defies linguistic predication. Predication specifies but also abstracts an object by subsuming it under a class of objects with similar properties. The beloved, in contrast, cannot be described through any attributes, except for "adorable," which captures the excessive quality of his or her being: "The other makes language indecisive: one cannot speak *of* the other, *about* the other; every attribute is false, painful, erroneous, awkward: the other is *unqualifiable*."[5] In his book *The Coming Community*, Giorgio Agamben similarly views love as an expression of singularity and takes note of the ways that the beloved eludes categorization. We may love someone else *for* being smart, petite, brunette, and so on, but not *because of* these characteristics—which can therefore never be entirely abstracted from *this* person who is in *this* place. Because love neither hinges upon nor glosses over the other's concrete qualities, it can enter the particular into a new relation with the universal.[6]

Like Agamben, Rosenzweig does not settle on a notion of pure particularity but rather envisions new modes of connecting particulars. Love in all its registers provides this mode. Divine love is intensely focused on one object yet capable of moving from one object to the next one. God shifts his attention from one place to the next until, in an infinitely distant future, he will love everything. Rosenzweig is eager to distinguish this kind of progressive love from universal love: "Love is no all-love. Revelation knows of no 'all-loving' father; God's love is ever wholly of the moment and to the point at which it is directed, and only in the infinity of time does it reach one point after another, step by step, and inform the All [*das All*]" (164).

Rosenzweig elaborates the idea of an infinite connectivity between particulars in his discussion of neighbor-love, which is the main subject of the chapter on redemption in *The Star of Redemption*. Neighbor-love, which carries divine love into the world, is the foundation of human communities and the principal path to redemption. Neighbor-love ushers in a process in which a circle of people expands and contracts again. Rosenzweig pictures the emergence of community as a succession of individual voices uniting in a chorus. Acts of neighbor-love are calls that elicit incalculable responses from others: "It is quite indefinite, however, which sequence this global migration will observe. The reveille is always answered by the nighest voice; but it is not for the bugler to choose which it will be. He never sees more than the next [*das Nächste*], the neighbor [*den Nächsten*]" (235). This process continues until the different voices join together into the redemptive We. The description of

---

5. Barthes, *A Lover's Discourse,* 35; Barthes's emphasis.
6. See Agamben, *The Coming Community*, 1–2; see also my introduction, above, pp. 10–11.

how this We defines itself by alternately reaching out to and excluding others is one of the most frequently cited and hotly debated passages of *The Star of Redemption*:

> The We encompasses everything it can grasp and reach or at least sight. But what it can no longer reach nor sight, that it must eject from its bright, melodious circle into the dread cold of the Nought: for the sake of its own exclusive-inclusive unity, it must say to it: Ye ... Yes, the Ye is dreadful. It is the judgment. The We cannot avoid this sitting in judgment, for only with this judgment does it give a definite content to the totality of its We. This content nevertheless is not distinctive; it subtracts nothing from the totality of the We. For the judgment does not distinguish a distinct content as against the We, no other content, that is, than the Nought.
>
> (237)

This passage is at the heart of an ongoing controversy about whether Rosen-zweig is a communitarian thinker or a theorist of alterity, whether he advances a holistic theory of community or opens up new venues to think about ethical encounters with others. Peter Gordon, the main proponent of the first view, argues that the passage is indebted to conservative political theories, including commu-nitarian doctrines that posit the necessity of a community's inner uniformity, and the work of Carl Schmitt, who stresses the importance of an ultimately arbitrary distinction between friend and enemy.[7] In contrast, scholars who seek to enlist Rosenzweig for an ethics of alterity, such as Eric Santner and Kenneth Reinhard, point out that the community he envisions shares neither an essence nor a nameable enemy; that the distinction between the We and the Ye is devoid of positive con-tent.[8] I believe there is a lot to be said for this second view. Consider the question of who or what is a neighbor. The neighbor is neither a family member nor a blood relative; she does not possess any talents or virtues of interest to me; she does not need to be like me. As Rosenzweig writes, the neighbor is the "Anyone" (236) who happens to be next to me at this very moment. Communities based on neighbor-love could never take the form of, for instance, a group of white Christians distanc-ing itself from a group of black Muslims. Yet neither does the We dissolve such predicates into an all-encompassing category such as human being. What keeps the community together is the shared fidelity to the event of neighbor-love, which can infinitely recur and propagate in new directions. Precisely because the We poten-tially includes everyone, it needs to temporarily demarcate its boundaries to remain tangible. The momentary contraction of the community prevents it from lapsing into empty generality.

---

7. See Peter Eli Gordon, *Rosenzweig and Heidegger: Between Judaism and German Philosophy* (Berke-ley: University of California Press, 2003), esp. 11–12, 199, 215.

8. See Eric Santner's critique of Gordon's definitions of neighbor and community in Žižek, Sant-ner, and Reinhard, *The Neighbor*, 106–10.

The scholarly debate about the nature of community in *The Star of Redemption* reflects a real tension in the work that merits further attention. In the chapter on redemption, Rosenzweig describes the community based on neighbor-love as a spontaneous and unpredictable development. He does not characterize this community in more specific terms because it potentially includes everyone. Neighbor-love is the basis of a social bond that dissolves fixed social identities. In subsequent chapters of *The Star of Redemption*, however, Rosenzweig offers detailed analyses of two religious communities, Jews and Christians, and their different roles within the divine economy. Briefly summarized, the Jews are already with God and serve as a messianic reminder on earth; the Christians are perpetually on the way to God and capable of spreading his word. Rosenzweig deems religious ritual and social cohesiveness central to the fulfillment of the Jewish mission in particular. Only because the Jews live separate from the other nations as a "blood community" can they anticipate the redemption of everyone.[9] How can these two very different notions of community—the infinitely open neighborhood and the unchanging religious community—go together?[10]

The Personal and the Political in the "Gritli" Letters

The correspondence between Franz Rosenzweig and Margrit Rosenstock-Huessy, which was first published in 2002, offers new answers to this question.[11] Margrit

---

9. See, for instance, the following: "Christianity must proselytize. This is just as essential to it as self-preservation through shutting the pure spring of blood off from foreign admixture is to the eternal people" (341). It is important to note that the notion of a "blood community" in Rosenzweig is not a racial concept. Rather, blood signifies a specific temporality that is also realized in the liturgical tradition of Judaism and that enables Jews to anticipate eternity within historical time. On the discourse of blood in Rosenzweig and other modern German Jewish writers, see also Battegay, *Das andere Blut*; and Katja Garloff, "Kafka's Racial Melancholy," in *Kafka for the Twenty-First Century*, ed. Stanley Corngold and Ruth Gross (New York: Camden House, 2011), 89–104.

10. Leonora Banitzky resolves this tension by pointing to the structure of *The Star of Redemption*, which does not present a series of progressive arguments but rather a sequence in reverse order: part 1 (on logic) is predicated on part 2 (on love and experience), which is predicated on part 3 (on community). The possibility of a modern (pluralistic) neighborhood arises from the existence of a traditional (Jewish) community. However, Banitzky does not explain how exactly the closed religious community leads to a broader, inclusive neighborhood. See Leora Batnitzky, *Idolatry and Representation: The Philosophy of Franz Rosenzweig Reconsidered* (Princeton, N.J.: Princeton University Press, 2000), 62–79.

11. Rosenzweig's letters were first published in Franz Rosenzweig, *Die "Gritli"-Briefe: Briefe an Margrit Rosenstock-Huessy*, ed. Inken Rühle and Reinhold Mayer (Tübingen: Bilam, 2002). This edition is incomplete, and some scholars have argued that its many omissions and abridgments amount to censorship. For an even-handed critique of the edition, see Michael Zank, "The Rosenzweig-Rosenstock Triangle, or, What Can We Learn from *Letters to Gritli*? A Review Essay," *Modern Judaism* 23, no. 1 (2003): 74–98. Zank's main point of critique is that the Rühle/Mayer edition downplays the importance of Eugen Rosenstock-Huessy in both the relationship and the correspondence. Shortly after the appearance of the Rühle/Mayer edition, the Eugen Rosenstock-Huessy Society issued a complete electronic edition, *The Gritli Letters (Grili Briefe)*, transcr. Ulrike von Moltke, ed. Michael Gormann-Thelen and Elfriede Büchsel, http://www.argobooks.org/gritli/. All quotations from the letters I use in this chapter can be found in both the print and the electronic versions; in what follows, I provide the date of the letter in parentheses. It should also be mentioned that only one

Rosenstock-Huessy—whom Rosenzweig affectionately called "Gritli"—was a Christian and the wife of his best friend, Eugen. A born Jew who converted to Christianity as a young man, Eugen Rosenstock-Huessy in the summer of 1913 attempted, and almost succeeded, to persuade Rosenzweig to follow his path and become a Christian. The conversation created a grave crisis for Rosenzweig, ultimately leading to his decision to remain Jewish and live a more consciously Jewish life. In June 1917, Rosenzweig met Eugen Rosenstock-Huessy's wife and in the following year began a passionate love affair with her. (Eugen Rosenstock-Huessy knew about the affair between his wife and his best friend and, after initial bouts of jealousy, seems to have approved and in some sense felt a part of it.) Rosenzweig completed *The Star of Redemption* between August 1918 and February 1919 while writing to Margrit Rosenstock-Huessy on an almost daily basis. He later called the book, and in particular the chapter on revelation, his and Rosenstock-Huessy's "child" (01/17/20) and the "seal" (12/04/20) that would have to substitute for their wedding ring. In what follows now, I read his correspondence with Rosenstock-Huessy not as an autobiographical document but as a thought experiment that complements *The Star of Redemption*. In other words, I do not argue that the book reflects his impossible love for Rosenstock-Huessy, but that his letters to her instantiate the theory of love developed in *The Star of Redemption*.[12]

Rosenzweig's letters to Rosenstock-Huessy exhibit the same tension between established and spontaneous communities as *The Star of Redemption*. He insists on the separation between Jews and Christians and believes that Jewish endogamy is crucial to this end.[13] At the same time he depicts modes of interreligious contact through love and believes that the triangle of himself and the Rosenstock-Huessys exemplifies such love. He calls their bond a "revelation" and a "miracle" occurring between individuals (09/06/19 and 08/03/19), and distinguishes it from the institutionalized communality that binds him to other Jews. Yet he considers both necessary. If his love for Margrit and Eugen Rosenstock-Huessy testifies to the possibility of "new names" in life, the "old names," including established religious institutions, are God's testament in the world (09/06/19). While *revelation* (love) ushers the lovers into a world of possibility, these established institutions anticipate *redemption* in the actual world. Rosenzweig's belief in the necessity of religious institutions explains his indignation at any attempt, on the part of Eugen Rosenstock-Huessy and others, to alienate him from the new Jewish life he was trying to build for himself. He explains to Margrit Rosenstock-Huessy his dual commitment to the Jewish

---

side of the correspondence still exists, since Rosenzweig's wife, Edith, destroyed Margrit Rosenstock-Huessy's letters after his death.

12. The most extensive reading of the Gritli letters thus far has been undertaken by Ephraim Meir, *Letters of Love: Franz Rosenzweig's Spiritual Biography and Oeuvre in Light of the Gritli Letters* (New York: Peter Lang, 2006). Meir reads the correspondence as an intercultural dialogue that respects the other's alterity.

13. He speaks, for instance, of the "danger of mixed marriage" (10/02/19).

community and his Christian friends and lover(s): "I adhere in the world to that which God *has* rendered *real* here, to the institutions that have been put onto the earth as sources of divine inspiration, visible to all. They are testimonies of God on our to-be-redeemed and redeemed earth, testimonies just as real and as much part of this world as the miracle of revelation in the narrow magic circle of our hearts" (09/06/19; Rosenzweig's emphasis).

What is striking about Rosenzweig's letters is how they project his lover into the place of revelation. He describes Margrit Rosenstock-Huessy as the major force behind the composition of the revelation chapter of *The Star of Redemption*: "This book II 2 that I am now writing belongs to you. . . . It is not 'for you' but—yours. Yours—as I am. Sometimes I feel as if I were a child who cannot write but wants to very much, and you are guiding my pen" (11/02/18). From his letters it appears that Rosenzweig in his personal life tried to follow the path from revelation to redemption laid out in *The Star of Redemption*. After Rosenstock-Huessy's love has opened up his soul, he searches for a female "neighbor" with whom he can contract a marriage and create a Jewish home—and finds her in Edith Hahn. The power of this construction also explains what may otherwise seem psychologically quite implausible: Rosenzweig hopes that his love for Rosenstock-Huessy, whom he cannot marry, both because she is married to someone else and because she is a Christian, will inspire his affection for his soon-to-be Jewish wife. He describes his love for Rosenstock-Huessy in various metaphors as a "stormproof tree" that protects the "tender shoot" of his love for Hahn (01/06/20) and as a live-giving juice that sustains his relationship with Hahn (01/18/20). He also claims that Rosenstock-Huessy's letters restore to him the possibility of language, enabling him to read Hahn's letters on one occasion (3/13/20) and to speak with her after a deadening day of silence on another (6/26/20). Again, I do not suggest that the letters offer an accurate psychological analysis of Rosenzweig's feelings, but that they construe his Christian lover as a human source of revelation: as the force that opens him up to language, to the world, and to others.

I call the experience of an overpowering address from an Other that inspires all future relations to others "revelatory love." To be sure, for Rosenzweig, all love ultimately flows from the same source, which is why he also speaks of Rosenstock-Huessy as his "next one" or neighbor (05/06/19). Yet his encounter with Rosenstock-Huessy is revelatory in that it is said to spark in him the very ability to love. The idea of revelatory love is part and parcel of what Eric Santner has called Rosenzweig's "*postsecular* thinking."[14] Like other recent commentators, Santner views Rosenzweig as a post-Nietzschean thinker for whom redemption leads *into* life rather than beyond it. Yet redemption in Rosenzweig still depends upon a force extraneous to the subject, a notion Santner compares to the psychoanalytic understanding of

---

14. Žižek, Santner, and Reinhard, *The Neighbor*, 133; Santner's emphasis. See also Eric L. Santner, *On the Psychotheology of Everyday Life: Reflections on Freud and Rosenzweig* (Chicago: University of Chicago Press, 2001).

the cure: "There is really no such thing as self-analysis; one cannot give to one-self the possibility of new possibilities. Something must *happen*, something beyond one's own control, calculations, and labor, something that comes from the locus of the Other."[15] Santner's comparison between Freud and Rosenzweig hinges upon a materialist conception of desire according to which human drives are formed through social interpellation. Social and political laws structure the desire of individuals, creating "deep individual and social patterns of servitude" that help sustain the existing sociopolitical order.[16] What Rosenzweig calls revelation, and Freud calls the psychoanalytic cure, allows us to break such patterns by making us conscious of them and opening us up to an encounter with our neighbor. Revelation enables us to attend to what is agitating, strange, and unresolved in others rather than reducing them to a set of attributes or making up fantasies about them. In Santner's reading, Rosenzweig the postsecular thinker invokes God in order to reimagine the social bond.

The work of modern German Jewish writers shows that cultural difference is a privileged source of such Otherness that straddles the lines between religious and secular thought. Witness Freud's bold construction, in *Moses and Monotheism* (his final published work), of the biblical Moses as an Egyptian, a "great stranger" who imposes a new and demanding religion on the Hebrews. Like Rosenzweig, Freud could not imagine that a new and superior truth—namely, monotheism and the instinctual renunciation it requires—can emerge from within a people. Such a truth has to come from the outside. The construction of Moses as an Egyptian allows Freud to suggest an external force without recourse to a notion of divine intervention. Rosenstock-Huessy's Christianity and Swiss nationality are another example of religious and cultural otherness taking the place of God's otherness. This kind of otherness cannot be expressed in a series of predicates but rather disrupts the very processes of linguistic predication and social identification. When Rosenzweig states that Rosenstock-Huessy's Christianity and Swiss nationality were never truly important to him (10/06/19) this is consistent with his view that revelatory love propels people out of their social identities. In love, markers of social, cultural, or religious identity matter only insofar as they are integral and inalienable aspects of the other's being. Lovers cannot reduce each other to representatives of another religion. As Rosenzweig writes to Rosenstock-Huessy, "You see *my* Jewishness, but I am not, for you, 'the' Jew" (08/19/19; Rosenzweig's emphasis). In other words, the religious difference between the lovers matters, but it cannot be reified and abstracted from the context of their lives. Religious difference becomes a question of place rather than identity.[17]

---

15. Žižek, Santner, and Reinhard, *The Neighbor*, 123.

16. Žižek, Santner, and Reinhard, *The Neighbor*, 132.

17. Stéphane Mosès notes that Rosenzweig's emphasis on place reflects his belief in the plurality of religious truth. Already in his 1916 correspondence with Eugen Rosenstock-Huessy, Rosenzweig attempts "to show that Judaism and Christianity are equally *true*, or at the very least that they have equal rights in their relation to truth. Two years later, in *The Star of Redemption*, Rosenzweig would show

The emphasis on place is an important feature of Rosenzweig's thought and a reason, I suggest, why his work is a rich resource in the contemporary search for a conception of the universal that does not eliminate the particular. Throughout the correspondence it is clear that Rosenzweig's love for Rosenstock-Huessy does not diminish his sense of religious difference or bring Jews and Christians closer together as a group. Theirs is an encounter that momentarily suspends differences but ultimately makes each of them more aware of their particular place in life. Rosenzweig's various attempts to explain Judaism to Rosenstock-Huessy, for instance, are not hermeneutical exercises meant to reduce differences in and through interpretation. Thus he warns her that a Christian's understanding of Jewish Bible commentaries must remain limited because Judaism is to be lived rather than understood. What she nevertheless comprehends, she owes to the fact that she lives part of his life with him—and this togetherness is of course limited in all sorts of ways: "One is not *supposed* to understand the Bible, one is supposed to become more alive. But because this life is now a Jewish life, the Christian reader is barred from the commentary. What you do still understand, you can understand only because you live my life with me" (11/07/19; Rosenzweig's emphasis). Over the course of the correspondence, the irreducible distance between the lovers becomes the hallmark of revelatory love, and in fact of all love.

Revelatory love, whether experienced in the encounter with God or with the human-as-stranger, becomes Rosenzweig's model for social relations. A striking passage from the "Gritli" letters sums up Rosenzweig's theory of love. At the time he considered publishing *The Star of Redemption* with a publisher specializing in Christian works, which made him think intensely about Christian-Jewish relations and his own position vis-à-vis the Christian world. In this context Rosenzweig describes love as a mode of rapprochement that enhances a sense of separateness, that does not create a union but sustains a dualism. As the end of the letter shows, this model of distance-in-proximity also applies to his relationship with Rosenstock-Huessy. I suggest reading the "Yours," which here and in other letters replaces the proper name as a signature, as a sign of devotion rather than possession. This "Yours" shows how love reorients the self toward the other without collapsing the difference between the two:

> "Rapprochement" exists only if there is no *fusion*. If an I and a You become *one*; if the I does not remain I, and the You, You; if the little word "and" is disavowed—that is Tristan and Isolde—"thus we die now inseparable, eternally one without end etc."— and thus not love. Love recognizes the separateness of places, it presupposes this

---

that no 'objective discourse of truth is possible, but rather that all knowledge refers to truth from the perspective of a particular point in space and time. Truth is not present in an absolute sense but is rather revealed *hic et nunc*, forever varied, to the experience of subjects already placed in one point or another in the world." Stéphane Mosès, "On the Correspondence between Franz Rosenzweig and Eugen-Rosenstock-Huessy," in *The German-Jewish Dialogue Reconsidered: A Symposium in Honor of George L. Mosse*, ed. Klaus L. Berghahn (New York: Peter Lang, 1996), 109–23; here 113.

separateness, or perhaps even establishes it for the first time. (For what would prevent, in the world of loveless things, one thing from occupying the place of another!) Love does *not* say I am You *but*—and now you have to understand me completely and agree with me—: I am

Yours.

(07/01/19; Rosenzweig's emphasis)

Revelatory Love in Else Lasker-Schüler's *Hebrew Ballads*

Else Lasker-Schüler's turn to Jewish culture and religion is another instance of Jewish dissimilation, if an idiosyncratic one. Born into an acculturated German Jewish family, in 1894 Lasker-Schüler married a Jewish physician and moved with him to Berlin, where the couple divorced a few years later. In Berlin she joined a bohemian circle of artists and writers, published her first volume of poetry in 1902, and became affiliated with the Expressionist movement. She also made the acquaintance of several thinkers dedicated to the renaissance of Jewish culture, including the philosopher Martin Buber and the Hebrew writer Shmuel Josef Agnon. Lasker-Schüler's understanding of Judaism remained eclectic, and her writing an example of what Paul Mendes-Flohr has termed the "aesthetic affirmation of Judaism" fashionable among Western European Jews of the time.[18] Her affirmation involved playful masquerades, both in literature and in real life, that reversed gender roles and combined different cultural and religious traditions. She accompanied her literary portrayals of "wild" and "Oriental" Jews with a flamboyant self-stylization as a Jewish-Muslim Oriental, often appearing in the coffeehouses of Berlin in caftan, wide trousers, and with gold rings around her ankles. She also claimed a special affinity to Semitic languages. On one occasion she wrote proudly: "Theologians often tell me that I am writing German like Hebrew or Aramaic";[19] and on another she told Ari Zvi Greenberg, an acclaimed Hebrew poet who wanted to translate some of her poems: "But I am writing in Hebrew."[20]

In what follows, I argue that Rosenzweig's theory of revelatory love sheds light on the work in which Lasker-Schüler most clearly embraces the Hebrew tradition, her *Hebrew Ballads*. Interfaith romance features prominently in this poetry cycle, which originally comprised fifteen poems, though Lasker-Schüler repeatedly expanded and rearranged it.[21] Some of the poems build on existing biblical

---

18. Paul Mendes-Flohr, *Divided Passions: Jewish Intellectuals and the Experience of Modernity* (Detroit: Wayne State University Press, 1991), 77–132; here 100.

19. Else Lasker-Schüler, *Gesichte: Essays und andere Geschichten* (Berlin: Cassirer, 1913), 20.

20. Quoted in Michael Brenner, *The Renaissance of Jewish Culture in Weimar Germany* (New Haven, Conn.: Yale University Press, 1996), 137.

21. In what follows, I cite from the second, augmented edition of *Hebräische Balladen* as reprinted in Else Lasker-Schüler, *Werke und Briefe: Kritische Ausgabe*, ed. Norbert Oellers, Heinz Rölleke, and Itta Shedletzky (Frankfurt am Main: Jüdischer Verlag im Suhrkamp Verlag, 1996–2010), 1.1:155–67.

models, such as those of Esther and Ruth. Others boldly retell biblical stories to turn them into visions of a love that crosses religious, national, and other boundaries. Even the poems that do not explicitly refer to biblical stories are shot through with religious vocabulary. Lasker-Schüler not only works from a religious text, however idiosyncratically, but recounts instances of divine love throughout the cycle, couching her visions of erotic love in allusions to divine love and vice versa. Thus the poem "Reconciliation" ("Versöhnung") conflates the religious service on Yom Kippur, the high Jewish holiday devoted to fasting and repentance, with a scene of reconciling lovers who attempt kisses and redden each other's cheeks. The poem simultaneously secularizes the religious holiday and renders erotic love religious. The title of another poem, "Sabaoth" ("Zebaot"), refers to the divine attribute commonly translated as "heavenly hosts." This poem both cites and disrupts the Romantic tradition of conferring the divine powers of creation on the poet. As the speaker addresses God first as "you godlike youth" and then as "you poet," these apostrophes recall the Romantic image of the poet-prophet.[22] However, the speaker's inability to reach her addressee preserves a sense of radical alterity. The term *postsecular* captures this kind of stalled secularization and the potential for sociopolitical renewal it harbors.

Christanne Miller has argued that Lasker-Schüler's emphasis on love rather than politics is itself a political gesture. Writing on the eve of the First World War, Lasker-Schüler rejects the masculinist, militarist culture of her time, which also influenced some sectors of the Jewish public sphere. Her portrayals of unions between people of different religions or social classes conjure alternative modes of bonding and alternative models of community. Love in this view can, if not overturn, at least diminish social differences and hierarchies.[23] I believe that Miller is right about the political impetus behind Lasker-Schüler's work but wrong in her conception of love as a form of social leveling. The poems in *Hebrew Ballads* are far from creating seamless fusions between people from different backgrounds. The recurrent themes of exile, departure, and abandonment indicate that the unity of the biblical figures conjoined in the poems remains incomplete. The two poems about Ruth and Boas provide one example. Lasker-Schüler turns the biblical story

---

22. In the German original, "du Gottjüngling" and "Du Dichter." Lasker-Schüler, *Werke und Briefe*, 1.1:162. All further citations of *The Hebrew Ballads* refer to this edition and will be included parenthetically in the text. I have drawn on the following existing translations, which I have, however, frequently combined and/or changed: Else Lasker-Schüler, *Hebrew Ballads and Other Poems*, trans. Audri Durchslag and Jeanette Litman-Demeestère (Philadelphia: Jewish Publication Society of America, 1980); and Else Lasker-Schüler, *Star in My Forehead: Selected Poems*, trans. Janine Canan (Duluth, Minn.: Holy Cow! Press, 2000).

23. See Cristanne Miller, "Reading the Politics of Else Lasker-Schüler's 1914 *Hebrew Ballads*," *Modernism/Modernity* 6, no. 2 (April 1999): 135–59. Miller sums up: "Lasker-Schüler . . . models an ideal of tenderness between people of different nations and unequal power where the ostensibly less powerful is more honored" (150). Miller seems unaware of the Christian biases of her argument. For instance, when she remarks that "legalistic judgment bows to affection and mercy in 'Abraham and Issac,'" (150), she forgets that legalism and lack of love are stock images of the antisemitic repertoire.

of Ruth, which is primarily about loyalty, economic security, and communal recognition, into one of unfulfilled yearning for love and nostalgic longing for home.
Ruth's integration into the new community remains conspicuously incomplete.[24] In
what follows, I will show that this is true of the *Hebrew Ballads* in general: if love
reconciles people separated along social and religious lines, it also introduces new
divisions along new lines. As in Rosenzweig, love in Lasker-Schüler leads to the
proliferation of differences rather than the creation of unity.[25]

The poem "Jacob and Esau" ("Jakob und Esau") draws on a particularly rich
trope for interreligious relations. Both Jews and Christians have used the story of
the brothers turned enemies typologically to depict group relations. Already in
the biblical book of Genesis, the story takes on a paradigmatic character in God's
statement to Rebecca, the mother of Jacob and Esau: "Two nations are in your
womb, / Two separate peoples shall issue from your body; / One people shall be
mightier than the other, / And the older shall serve the younger" (Gen. 25:23). In
Genesis, Jacob and Esau reconcile after Jacob flees to his uncle and later returns as a
rich man. However, God's oracle about future tensions between their descendants
(which is echoed by Isaac's blessings of his sons on his deathbed) still stands and
raises the question of what kind of antagonist Esau is, a potential ally or a particularly treacherous enemy. This ambiguity in the brothers' relationship explains,
perhaps, why the story of Jacob and Esau has become a privileged trope to figure
and refigure the relations between Jews and non-Jews. Rabbinic commentators
successively linked Esau to the Edomites, the Romans, and the Christians and con-
jured his image to warn their fellow Jews against the enemies of Israel. Christian
theologians identified Esau with the Jews and read the story as evidence that the
first-born Jews have to serve the later-born Christians. Enlightenment and emancipation gave birth to a number of retellings that were, however, still overwhelmingly focused on Esau's otherness. Among the few exceptions is Samson Raphael

---

24. The first poem, "Ruth," departs quite dramatically from the biblical narrative in its portrayal
of two lovers who cannot come together. The second poem, "Boaz," highlights the incompleteness of
Ruth's integration into the people of Israel. Its last lines describe the movement of Boaz's heart—here
figured as a stalk of grain—toward Ruth: "[Boaz's heart] sways so high / In his grain gardens / Toward
the foreign reaper." "[Boas Herz] wogt ganz hoch / In seinen Korngärten / Der fremden Schnitterin zu"
(165). Both the incompleteness of the heart's movement and Ruth's status as a foreigner suggest that the
process of rapprochement is still ongoing. The characterization of Ruth as a reaper or cutter of barley
(rather than a gatherer of leftovers) further casts her as an uprooting force, as she literally tears Boaz's
heart out of its native soil. While I won't interpret these two poems in more detail in this chapter, I will
show how other poems from *Hebrew Ballads* create a similar sense of separation in and through love.

25. When she first published *Hebrew Ballads,* Lasker-Schüler was involved in a relationship with
Gottfried Benn. They had met in the fall of 1912, around the time of Lasker-Schüler's divorce from
her second husband, Herwarth Walden. In 1913–14, Benn and Lasker-Schüler carried on a poetic dialogue, each writing several poems to or about each other. In retrospect, the relationship seems particularly fraught since Benn, who is regarded one of the greatest German poets of the twentieth century,
supported the Nazi regime in the early 1930s. Helma Sanders-Brahms 1997 film, *Mein Herz—Niemandem! (My Heart Is Mine Alone)*, uses their love affair as an allegory for German-Jewish relations. I
would argue that Lasker-Schüler's Benn poems continue the poetics of disjunction she developed earlier in *Hebrew Ballads.*

Hirsch's 1867 commentary on Genesis, which evinces optimism about the future of Christian-Jewish relations, based on the reconciliatory trajectory of the biblical story.[26] At the time, however, nobody had gone as far as Lasker-Schüler in depicting a peaceful harmony between the brothers.

Jacob and Esau

Rebecca's maidservant is a heavenly stranger
A garment of rose petals garbs the angel
And in her face a star.

She always looks to the light,
And her gentle hands enfold
A repast out of lentils gold.

Jacob and Esau blossom in her presence
And do not quarrel over the sweets
That in her lap she breaks to make the meal.

The brother leaves the chase to the younger
And his birthright for the maidservant's favor;
And wildly flings the thicket over his shoulder.

Jakob und Esau

Rebekkas Magd ist eine himmlische Fremde,
Aus Rosenblättern trägt die Engelin ein Hemde
Und einen Stern im Angesicht.

Und immer blickt sie auf zum Licht,
Und ihre sanften Hände lesen
Aus goldenen Linsen ein Gericht.

Jakob und Esau blühn an ihrem Wesen
Und streiten um die Süßigkeiten nicht,
Die sie in ihrem Schoß zum Mahle bricht.

Der Bruder läßt dem jüngeren die Jagd
Und all sein Erbe für den Dienst der Magd;
Um seine Schultern schlägt er wild das Dickicht.

(163)

---

26. On the different readings of the story of Jacob and Esau, see Malachi Haim Hacohen's *Jacob and Esau: Jewish European History between Nation and Empire* (New York: Cambridge University Press, forthcoming). I would like to thank Hacohen for sharing with me parts of the work in draft form and for responding to my queries.

Lasker-Schüler's most striking departure from the biblical story is the invention of the figure of Rebecca's maidservant, the "heavenly stranger" whose love generates more love and eases the competition between Jacob and Esau. What is most conspicuous about this figure is the ambiguity that surrounds her: Is she a human or an angel? A mother or a lover? Kin or stranger? The poem expands here on a sense of ambiguity already present in the Bible. There is no biblical model for the maidservant, but Rebecca herself is an Aramaic—and a member of Abraham's extended family—who comes to Canaan only after Abraham sends a servant to his former hometown to find a wife for his son.[27] Rebecca is thus both kin and a stranger, just as Jacob and Esau are both brothers and enemies. Here and elsewhere in the *Hebrew Ballads*, Lasker-Schüler elaborates on the rifts, ambiguities, and double entendres found in the original biblical stories. While the care Rebecca's maidservant lavishes on Jacob and Esau makes her a mother figure, the predicate "heavenly stranger" highlights her status as a foreigner. She is a "Gritli" figure whose ethnic or cultural otherness is the source of her positive transformative power. An ambiguous eroticism is part and parcel of this representation, notably when the brothers harmoniously share the sweets "that in her lap she breaks to make the meal."

At this moment of eroticization, however, love turns into a force that separates rather than unites, that brings the brothers together while creating new divisions between them. In the end only one of them receives the maidservant's "favor" (*Dienst*), and the poem concludes with a scene of departure rather than with reconciliation. The poem introduces here an interesting ambiguity: which of the brothers actually receives the maid's service or favor? The lines "The brother leaves the chase to the younger / And his birthright for the maidservant's favor" can be read in two different ways. First, as a scene of exchange: Esau gives Jacob his hunt and inheritance *in exchange for the maid's favor.* This reading would correspond to the biblical story, where Esau's marriage to two Canaanite women is said to be "a source of bitterness" for his parents (Gen. 26:35). The maidservant in the poem could be such a foreign woman who disrupts the family genealogy. However, a second scenario is suggested by the possibility of reading "for" (*für*) as a consecutive preposition. In this scenario, Esau gives his hunt and inheritance to Jacob *so that* Jacob can obtain the maidservant's favor, while Esau himself departs into the wilderness (*Dickicht*) with nothing at all. This would be a scene of radical departure rather than social exchange, an overturning of any quid-pro-quo logic. And Rebecca's maidservant would be another Ruth, the stranger-turned-kin who is absorbed into the family genealogy while inscribing a trace of otherness into it. These two readings are not mutually exclusive. Rather, the second reading brings out what is already implied in the first: that the rapprochement in and through love upsets the existing social order.

---

27. The Bible mentions a wet nurse and several maidservants who accompany Rebecca on her way to Isaac (Gen. 24.59, 61), but none of these play any role in the story of Jacob and Esau.

This disruption of the social also occurs on the level of representation. "Jacob and Esau" takes its figures out of the context of typological readings by undermining the historical thinking upon which such readings depend. Rather than point to later incarnations of the two brothers the poem maintains a strict focus on the present. Unlike the biblical prophecy, which anticipates later developments in the future tense, the poem creates a static present through locutions such as "She *always* looks to the light" (my emphasis) and the concluding evocation of a departure that leads nowhere. The image of Esau roaming alone through the wilderness and propelled out of each and every social order, however, takes nothing away from the poem's overall positive tone. Here and elsewhere in the *Hebrew Ballads*, Lasker-Schüler combines images of isolation, separation, even violence, with images of a social harmony based on love. The slippages between the familiar and the exotic, the divine and the erotic, are constitutive of the poems' social visions. The diffuse sensuality of the poems individualizes biblical figures and works against their deployment as social types or paradigms. While this representation participates in the modern discourse of love that pits individual freedom against social conventions, it ultimately serves to reimagine the social bond. The poems in *Hebrew Ballads* disrupt processes of social identification in order to create new connections between singularities.

Another biblical figure and social archetype that plays a particularly important role in Lasker-Schüler's imagination is Joseph. The biblical Joseph exemplifies the position of power to which a minority member may rise if protected by the majority ruler. Lasker-Schüler's poem "Pharaoh and Joseph" ("Pharao und Joseph") transforms this political partnership into a homoerotic bond. The poem stands at the beginning of her lifelong identification with Joseph, or more precisely, with the Prince Yussuf of Thebes, an imaginary figure that conflates aspects of Joseph and the Pharaoh. Whereas the biblical Joseph owes whatever power he has to the foreign sovereign, Yussuf is the sovereign ruler of Thebes, a priestly king who embodies absolute power.[28] In the poem, Pharaoh and Joseph are still two separate figures, yet united in love.

Pharaoh and Joseph

Pharaoh dismisses his blossoming wives—
They are fragrant as Amon's gardens.

His royal head rests on my shoulder,
That emanates the scent of grain.

---

28. The Arab spelling of his name already hints at the difference between Yussef and the biblical Joseph. Doerte Bischoff argues that the figure of the Pharaoh plays practically no role in Lasker-Schüler's prose because Yussef the Prince of Thebes unites all powers within himself. See Bischoff, *Ausgesetzte Schöpfung: Figuren der Souveränität und Ethik der Differenz in der Prosa Else Lasker-Schülers* (Tübingen: Max Niemeyer, 2002), 313.

Pharaoh is made of gold.
His eyes come and go
Like shimmering Nile waves.

His heart, though, lies in my blood—
Ten wolves went to my watering place.

Pharaoh always thinks
About my brothers,
Who threw me into the pit.

In sleep his arms become pillars—
And threaten.

But his dreamy heart
Ripples in my depths.

So my lips compose
Great sweets
In the wheat of our morning [tomorrow].

Pharao und Joseph

Pharao verstößt seine blühenden Weiber,
Sie duften nach den Gärten Amons.

Sein Königskopf ruht auf meiner Schulter,
Die strömt Korngeruch aus.

Pharao ist von Gold.
Seine Augen gehen und kommen
Wie schillernde Nilwellen.

Sein Herz aber liegt in meinem Blut.
Zehn Wölfe gingen an meine Tränke.

Immer denkt Pharao
An meine Brüder,
Die mich in die Grube warfen.

Säulen werden im Schlaf seine Arme
Und drohen.

Aber sein träumerisch Herz
Rauscht auf meinem Grund.

Darum dichten meine Lippen
Große Süßigkeiten
Im Weizen unseres Morgens.

To understand the dynamic of separation and entanglement in this poem we need to abandon any conception of love as fusion. As I have argued, Rosenzweig proposed an alternative conception of love that anticipates the more recent theories of Barthes, Agamben, and others. For these thinkers, love is an encounter that preserves the other's otherness, a form of recognition without knowledge. Knowing means to bestow a mental representation on something and make it commensurate with other things, whereas recognizing means to sense a presence without subsuming it to existing representational forms. In Rosenzweig's work, this form of encounter is realized in divine love and in neighbor-love, where contiguity outweighs similarity. Linguistic predication is disrupted in both cases. In neighbor-love the object is so indeterminate that its attributes no longer matter; in divine love the object is so specific that its attributes cannot be abstracted from it. Agamben and Barthes similarly postulate that love makes it impossible to separate the other's being from his or her attributes. In contrast to the pop-psychological notion that we are bound to fall for a certain "type," love in this view does not aim at the other's qualities in a way that would allow for categorization.

Lasker-Schüler realizes this idea of love in a poetic language that makes personal characteristics nontransferable, nondetachable from a particular person and a particular place. In "Pharaoh and Joseph," the process of substitution in which Joseph takes the wives' place changes the character of love. The poem shifts from metaphorical to metonymic constructions that embed a person's qualities in his or her being. The depiction of Pharaoh's wives by means of an attributive participle—"blossoming"—suggests that Pharaoh's love for them was based on properties such as beauty, youth, fragrance, and so on. In contrast, the synecdoche of the shoulder that emanates corn scent effectively fuses Joseph with the cornfield: Joseph does not smell like an ear of corn, he is one. The description of Pharaoh is similarly lacking in attributive structures that would allow a distinction between an individual and his or her properties. For instance, by omitting the definite article that most modern German Bible translations use before "Pharaoh," Lasker-Schüler transforms the political title into a proper name.[29] This change not only highlights the equality of Joseph and Pharaoh but also undermines the very function of political titles, which assign a social position rather than express a person's singularity. Furthermore, the depiction of Pharaoh as "of gold" ("von Gold" rather than the more idiomatic "aus Gold") emphasizes the material over the thing made of it. The Pharaoh appears to be a manifestation of goldenness rather than a person with the quality of goldenness.

The metonymic quality of the language contributes to a sense of persistent conflict in the poem. The vision of revenge in the sixth stanza, for instance, calls into

---

29. For instance, the 1905 edition of the Elberfelder Bible translation uses the definite article throughout, as does the 1951 edition of the Schlachter Bible translation (which first appeared in 1905). The 1912 edition of the Luther Bible uses the definite article only in some passages. See http://bibel-online.net.

question the opposition between militarist and loved-based communities posited by Miller and others. Just like "Jacob and Esau," "Pharaoh and Joseph" omits the conciliatory ending of the Bible, highlighting instead the conflict between Joseph and his brothers. The love between Joseph and Pharaoh seems only to deepen the rift between Joseph and his birth family. And even the symbiosis between Joseph and Pharaoh, which to some extent counteracts the atmosphere of menace, is not as seamless as it first looks. If this symbiosis culminates in the writing of poetry that expresses their harmonious union, the poem's possessive adjectives tell a slightly different story. While the "our" in the last line signals a newfound unity, it differs in tone and meaning from the other possessive adjectives in the poem. It is part of a genitive attribute and combined with an abstract noun, and a future-oriented one at that——since "unseres Morgens" can mean either "of our morning" or "of our tomorrow"—which gives the bond between Joseph and Pharaoh a fragile, utopian quality. This "our" cannot make the reader forget the physical separateness highlighted in the first seven stanzas, which relentlessly pit the possessive pronouns "his" and "my"—and the different body parts associated with them—against each other.

I wrote above that Rosenzweig rejects the Romantic idea of love as fusion, which in his mind ultimately leads to death and which materializes "if the little word 'and' is disavowed."[30] He considers the lack of fusion essential for any kind of interreligious rapprochement through love. It is interesting in that regard how Lasker-Schüler highlights the word "and" in the titles of *Hebrew Ballads*. Whereas most of the titles feature an individual biblical figure, some feature a couple, linking two proper names together with an "and." Yet as I have shown, the poems are marked by a sense of abiding separation and unfulfilled longing. While they blur the boundaries between the figures and blend their images, their abrupt and inconclusive endings undermine any rhetoric of fusion. The copula "and" in the titles anticipates the proliferation of differences in the main part of the poems. While conjoining the names, the "and" exhibits the space between them and draws attention to the disjunction created in love. This disjunctive effect also extends to the poems' structure of reference. Although the *Hebrew Ballads* actualize the biblical stories best known to both Christian and Jewish readers, they do not necessarily, as one critic contends, "foreground a common inheritance."[31] Rather, Lasker-Schüler's idiosyncratic take on biblical figures tears them out of their narrative context and singularizes them, thereby restoring the original function of proper names.[32]

---

30. Rosenzweig,"*Gritli"-Briefe*, 358. In *The Star of Redemption*, Rosenzweig also emphasizes that the "and" of revelation does not create a synthesis (255–26).

31. Miller, "Reading the Politics," 151.

32. It fits with this emphasis on singularity that Lasker-Schüler never attempted to create a narrative sequence out of the poems (this was done by her editors only after her death), although she repeatedly changed their order. In later editions, she used the metapoems to frame the ones on individual biblical figures, but she still avoided building a narrative sequence. Thus the poem "In the Beginning" ("Im Anfang") is the very last poem in the second edition of *Hebrew Ballads*, and the sixth-to-last poem in the third edition.

Revelatory Love and Antisemitic Violence

As we have seen, in *Hebrew Ballads* the view of love as reconciliation contrasts with a darker sense of exile and separation. Lasker-Schüler praises the conciliatory power of love while registering the irreducible distance between the lovers. I have suggested that this apparent contradiction resolves once we understand love along with Rosenzweig as revelatory. In both Rosenzweig and Lasker-Schüler, love connects singularities and in so doing proliferates the differences between them and within each of them. In this final section, I will explore the idea of revelatory love in one of Lasker-Schüler most openly political texts, "The Wonder-Working Rabbi of Barcelona." This is a story about a pogrom in medieval Spain, which the author probably wrote in response to the increase of antisemitism in her own time. The violence described in the text recalls the pogroms in Eastern Europe at the beginning of the twentieth century, about which the avid newspaper reader Lasker-Schüler was likely well informed, and the spread of antisemitic prejudice in Western Europe in the wake of the First World War. "The Wonder-Working Rabbi of Barcelona" also hints at several Jewish responses to antisemitism, including cultural and political Zionism, without clearly endorsing either of them.[33] Interspersed in this story about antisemitic violence is the love story of a Jewish girl and a Christian boy, who in the end escape the brutal pogrom with the help of a ship that mysteriously appears in the middle of the town. As I will show, their love is revelatory also in the sense that it allows the differences between them to emerge.

The language of revelation informs the text on several levels. In a letter to Karl Kraus, Lasker-Schüler describes her own writing process: "Now I wrote the Wonder-Rabbi, who came over me like a revelation, and I was shattered [*zerschlagen*]."[34] The word *zerschlagen* registers a violence that resonates with Rosenzweig when he describes revelatory love as a shattering, even traumatic event. Such love tears the subject out of self-containment, leading to a sudden change in consciousness: "And yet—love would not be the moving, the gripping, the searing experience that it is if the moved, gripped, seared soul were not conscious of the fact that up to this moment it had not been moved nor gripped. Thus a shock was necessary before the self could become beloved soul" (*The Star of Redemption*, 179). As I will show, in "The Wonder-Working Rabbi" interfaith romance effects just such a disruption, and—even more provocatively—antisemitism results from the failure to find an adequate response to such disruption. "The Wonder-Working Rabbi"

---

33. On the context of "The Wonder-Working Rabbi of Barcelona," see Sigrid Bauschinger, *Else Lasker-Schüler: Biographie* (Göttingen: Wallstein, 2004), 268–73. My reading of the text is indebted to two detailed interpretations that appeared in recent years. In *Jewish Pasts*, 105–46, Jonathan Skolnik offers a richly contextualized reading that emphasizes the story's critical engagement with nineteenth-century Jewish historical novels, and in particular with the representation of Spanish Jewry in these novels. In *Ausgesetzte Schöpfung*, 409–42, Doerte Bischoff focuses on figures of disruption in the story.

34. Lasker-Schüler, *Werke und Briefe*, 7:219.

is much more polemical than Lasker's Schüler's *Hebrew Ballads* or Rosenzweig's *Star of Redemption*. While Rosenzweig views Judaism and Christianity as two different but equally valid religions, Lasker-Schüler's "The Wonder-Working Rabbi" offers a trenchant critique of a specifically Christian concept of revelation. The story suggests that this concept is implicated in the antisemitism that suppresses revelatory love and the new forms of community such love entails. If revelatory love founds the possibility of an infinitely open neighborhood, the antisemitic violence depicted in "The Wonder-Working Rabbi" thwarts this possibility.

Although "The Wonder-Working Rabbi" lacks temporal markers, its portrayal of a Jewish community in Barcelona situates it in medieval times, before the 1492 expulsion of the Jews from Spain. The story's main theme is the precarious relationship between Jews and Christians at the time. While the title figure, a rabbi named Eleazar, commands the deep respect of both religious groups, conflicts regularly break out during Eleazar's annual journeys to Asia, when the Christians launch pogroms against the Jews. This year the Jewish elders decide to inform Rabbi Eleazar about the pogroms and to entreat him not to leave. In an allusion to the rising movement of Zionism, they begin to plan their departure to the Holy Land. One day a ship suddenly and inexplicably appears in the middle of the city. A delegation of Spaniards led by the mayor seeks Eleazar's advice about the ship, but he refuses to receive them. Roused by this refusal, the Christians launch a more murderous anti-Jewish pogrom than ever before, leaving behind them a scene of total destruction. As Eleazar becomes aware of the pogrom, he wrangles with God and then takes violent revenge on the Christians, who have begun to repent their deeds. Embedded in this story about interreligious conflict and violence is an interfaith love story. Amram, the daughter of the Jewish architect Arion Elevantos, and Pablo, the son of the Christian mayor of Barcelona, first meet when a fall from a ladder lands Amram at Pablo's feet. Still children at the time, they sustain their connection through dreams, visions, and conversations as they grow up. The appearance of the mysterious ship, which triggers the destruction of the communities into which Amram and Pablo were born, allows the couple to escape, although we do not know where to—they simply disappear from the text.

The three main plot elements—the Christian-Jewish conflict, the interfaith romance, and the journey of the mysterious ship—are structurally equivalent in that they all hark back to a single, enigmatic event. Initially, the narrator explains the pogroms that regularly befall the Jewish community in terms of sociopolitical conflicts: the Jews undercut the prices of the Christian merchants, they engage in protosocialist politics, and so on. But ultimately the violence goes back to a single event, the character of which remains unclear: "But no matter how the Jews behaved, they aroused resentment, which in truth originated from a single, disappointed Spaniard who once had had some sort of awkward conflict [*Auseinandersetzung*] with a Hebrew."[35] The word "disappointed" suggests a personal, emotional conflict that does not necessarily spring from larger sociopolitical tensions. The German word used here for conflict—*Auseinandersetzung*—literally means "setting apart" or "positing apart." All we know about the first Christian-Jewish conflict is that it created a tear in the social fabric.

The same is true of the Christian-Jewish love affair, which begins with an accident. After climbing up to the crest (in German, *Krone* or *Kuppel*) of the palace her father is building for Eleazar, Amram suffers a fall: "Descending the ladder that led from *the still unattached crest* [*der noch unbefestigten Krone*], little Amram in her haste fell from the sacred building on to a sandy hillock where Pablo, the little son of the mayor, was playing" (227/*11*; my emphasis). Significantly, the crest that arches over the building is unfinished, indicating a gap in the social order: there is no social authority that could initiate or validate the love between Pablo and Amram. More broadly speaking, Amram's accident or *Unfall* literalizes the contingency of the love event. We have seen in Rosenzweig that divine love (and its equivalent, erotic love) enigmatically seizes upon an object with little regard to its specific qualities. Neighbor-love, which aims at the person who is near me rather than like me, is likewise contingent—namely, upon proximity: the neighbor is whoever happens to be next to me. Amram's fall, which lands her in a place devoid of social meaning, captures such contingency. The sandy hills that receive Amran show no trace of human intervention; they are but the place next to Pablo.

As the loves story unfolds, it conveys a sense of what Franz Rosenzweig and Alain Badiou claim to be true of all love: that love creates a disjunction, a structure of Twoness. Love fails to build bridges between the religions in "The Wonder-Working Rabbi" not only because of the antisemitism of the Christian environment but also because of the divisive character of love itself. Amram first falls from the tower—and in love with Pablo—because there is no *Kuppel* (cupola) arching over the children, an image that also evokes the absence of *Kopplung* (coupling) and *Kuppelei* (matchmaking). At another time, Amram experiences a momentary estrangement from Pablo when drunken Christians knock on the door of the synagogue. The text portrays this estrangement in an image that repeatedly comes to describe Jewish difference—namely, the split gaze: "Amram felt a foreign continent growing between herself and Señor Pablo, the mayor's son. The commandments in the Jews' prayer books were read from the outside to the inside, and so, ever since their birth, their Jewish eyes had to be pointed in a different direction from those of all other nations. Eyes that dared not remain fixed on their object,

35. Else Lasker-Schüler, "The Wonder-Working Rabbi of Barcelona," in *The German-Jewish Dialogue: An Anthology of Literary Texts, 1749–1993*, ed. and trans. Ritchie Robertson (New York: Oxford University Press, 1999), 224–32; here 225 (trans. modified). For the original German, see Lasker-Schüler, "Der Wunderrabbiner von Barcelona," in *Werke und Briefe*, 4.1:9–17; here 9–10. Further citations from these editions will be included parenthetically in the text, with the page number in the English translation followed by the page number in the German edition in italics, as here (225/*9-10*).

eyes that hid in the book's stitching, and that always fled back to the split" (228/*13*; trans. modified). The sewing that is supposed to hold the book together is actually a gap that splits the book into two halves. The eyes that turn inside are lost in this inner split rather than securing a sense of self-identity. This scene is also significant because of what the eyes are *not* doing—namely, meeting the lover's eyes. In Romantic literature, the lovers' wordless exchange of glances suggests that love is a seamless, effortless communication that eschews the divisive medium of language. In contrast, in Lasker-Schüler the gaze of the beloved signifies the impossible union of the lovers and the equally impossible unity of the self.

The appearance of the ship that carries the lovers away is another instance in the series of enigmatic events that make up the story's plot. The ship appears suddenly in the middle of the marketplace, where it disrupts the usual exchange of commodities. At one point the narrator suggests that the ship was called forth by the lovers' longing for each other; the ship "had given ear to two people's yearning overnight" (229/*14*). Its movement, then, instantiates the ambiguous agency of individuals possessed by the erotic drive. As the lovers depart from the city, they are both active (since their love drives the ship) and passive (since they are carried away by the ship).[36] The disappearance of the couple is a loss for both Christians and Jews, and neither side seems to be responsible for it. Nor do we know what happens between the lovers, who remain hidden behind the ship's sail: "Transfigured by immense love, they remained invisible behind the wing of the sail" (229/*14*). The text's refusal to explain the events or depict the relationship is meaningful because the ship is an ancient metaphor of the metaphor, or the transport from one word or concept to another. The ship in this story, however, is coming from nowhere and going nowhere. As Bischoff notes, its movement articulates a "passage that cannot be described as regulated relationship between two sides, but as a radically discontinuous passage that unsettles all firm stances and perspectives (the Jewish and the Spanish)."[37]

What the major events in "The Wonder-Working Rabbi"—the first Christian-Jewish conflict, Amram's fall, and the appearance of the ship—have in common is that they disrupt patterns of social exchange. The text's greatest accomplishment, I would argue, is that it renders antisemitic violence legible as a *failed response* to such disruptions of social life. The cyclically recurring pogroms, for instance, are a ritualization and instrumentalization of the disappointment that first separated, or set apart, one Jew from one Christian. While the details of this first Christian-Jewish conflict are no longer known, the vague memories of it are used to stir up "resentment, which . . . was transferred to the people" (225/*9–10*), and to provide a pretext for the pogroms. Similarly, when their chance encounter establishes a

---

36. See also Markus Hallensleben, *Else Lasker-Schüler: Avantgardismus und Kunstinszenierung* (Tübingen: Francke, 2000), 221.

37. Bischoff, *Ausgesetzte Schöpfung*, 430.

telepathic connection between Amram and Pablo and allows their differences to emerge, the Christians of Barcelona are quick to translate these differences into cultural stereotypes. Thus Pablo's father, the mayor of Barcelona, labels the Jewish eyes that are hiding inside the Torah "'eyes that steal'" (228/*13*). And when Amram's love song conjures in Pablo's mind "signs . . . in ancient harp-writing" (227/*12*)—Lasker-Schüler's favorite metaphor for Hebrew letters—the Christian officials dismiss them as "the writing of dogged, obdurate Jews" (228/*12*). Like Pablo's father, the clerks translate the dream-like communication between the lovers into stock images of Jewish difference. They are unable or unwilling to understand that the love between Amram and Pablo developed outside of the social system that produced these stereotypes to begin with.

The starkest example of a failed response to social disruption is the final pogrom, in which the Christians brutally murder the Jews of Barcelona. The pogrom begins with an act of interpretive violence in which the Spaniards attempt but fail to make sense of the presence of the mysterious ship. As mentioned earlier, it remains unknown what actually happens on the ship, in part because there are no witnesses to its departure other than a stray dog (who is, ironically, named Abraham). The text's sudden change into the past perfect tense indicates that the moment of departure is unnarratable, that it has always already happened: "And only the dog *had witnessed* how the seas' enormous messenger . . . vanished through the gate as carefully as a solemn bridal carriage" (14/*229*; trans. modified; my emphasis). Meanwhile, the Christians begin to blame Rabbi Eleazar and Amram's father, Arion, for the appearance and disappearance of the ship; they gag Arion and smash the windows of his house. The violence escalates when Pablo's mother goads the others into killing Arion, whom she holds responsible for Amram's seduction of her son, that is, for being a *Kuppler*. However, it is clear that the Spaniards' outcry "'Kill him, the old procurer [*Kuppler*]'!!!" (229/*15*) misses what is most important about the encounter between Pablo and Amram: that no social or familial institution regulates the contact between them. If the text shows how the appearance of the ship gives rise to conspiracy fantasies, it repudiates these same fantasies on the level of imagery. For the *Kuppel* (cupola) that arches over Pablo and Amram is incomplete; it exposes but the gap that brings the lovers together.

The polemical thrust of "The Wonder-Working Rabbi" transpires most clearly in the act of revenge that ends the story. When Eleazar, who during the pogrom had been reading in the temple, finally turns his eyes toward Barcelona, the shock at the sight of the destruction splits his eye—an image that radicalizes the earlier image of Jewish eyes focused on the split in the Torah. Eleazar calls upon God, who awakens the Christians and causes them to repent. Unsatisfied with this repentance, Eleazar accuses God of rewarding the Christians' "'atrocities with enlightenment'" (231/*17*). Eleazar's final act of revenge, which evokes Jacob's wrestling with God and Samson's breaking of the pillars, puts an end to the endless repetition of violence. In lashing out against the Christians, Eleazar suspends the cycle of pogroms, or the state of exception that upheld the social order all along:

> All night [Eleazar] went out wrestling in riddles with God; darkened and broke away from Him. The priest shook the pillars of his house till they broke like arms. The roof rolled down in heavy blocks and shattered the houses in the street. An enormous quarry, He, the great wonder-working rabbi, a nation plunged from the sacred hill, which was transfigured by the golden fragments of the dome's mosaic, upon the Christians of Barcelona, who were penitently laying the last tortured Jew to rest, and extinguished their enlightenment [*erlosch ihre Erleuchtung*], crushed their bodies.
>
> (232/17; my emphasis)

It is noteworthy that Eleazar's revenge proceeds from the very site of Amram's fall, the sandy hill, and that this site has now become holy. This points to a deeper connection between the singularity of the love event and Eleazar's unique act of revenge. The curious phrase *erlosch ihre Erleuchtung* (extinguished their enlightenment) sums up the effect of Eleazar's act of violence, which is meant to end all violence. The immediate point of reference of this phrase is the idea that the murder of the Jews of Barcelona served the higher purpose of enlightening the Christians. The phrase also refers back to an earlier scene in which Eleazar, still unaware of the pogrom, reads about divine election in the fictional "atlas of creation" (230/15). The atlas describes how God took a star from his own dress and put it on the forehead of the Jewish people, thereby turning them into a people of enlightened prophets. This scene amalgamates ideas from several Judaic traditions.[38] However, any notion of Jews as enlighteners has now become implicated in the troublesome idea that the brutal pogrom served to "enlighten" the Christians, an idea to which Eleazar vehemently objects. Linguistically, the phrase *erlosch ihre Erleuchtung* stands out because it contains a paronomasia—that is, it combines words that are similar in sound but different in meaning—and a grammatical irregularity, since it uses the intransitive verb *erlöschen* transitively.[39] The irregular syntax and heightened rhetoricity draw the reader's attention to the phrase and, I would argue, to the true aim of Eleazar's act of revenge: the Christian ideology that bestows a redemptive meaning upon antisemitic violence.

---

38. The word *Entlichtung* (16; de-lightning) evokes the Jewish Mystical (Lurianic) concept of *tzimtzum*, according to which the creation of the world began with the self-contraction of the divine light that originally permeated everything. The scene also alludes to the idea of diaspora promoted by nineteenth-century German Reform Judaism, according to which the dispersed Jews have the mission to enlighten the Gentiles by setting an example of pure monotheistic faith. See Skolnik, *Jewish Pasts*, 140. Finally, the image of Jews carrying a star on their forehead also recalls Rosenzweig's notion, in *The Star of Redemption*, about the different roles of Jews and Christians in the divine economy.

39. There exists an older transitive form of *erlöschen*, but its past tense would be *erlöschte*. Skolnik points out that Lasker-Schüler's use of paronomasia and syntactic irregularities mimics stylistic features of Hebrew. See his *Jewish Pasts*, 132–33.

"The Wonder-Working Rabbi" can be read as a critical reworking of one strand in the tradition of literary representations of Christian-Jewish love. For the text explicitly associates interfaith romance with the Christian idea of revelation called *Erleuchtung* or *Erweckung*. Early on, the narrator depicts the Jews' attachment to Spain in the image of Jewish women who "with Jerusalem eyes had given Christians a painful awakening" (226/*10–11*). It is ambiguous who is feeling the pain—the Jewish women or the Christian men—but its mention recalls the literary cliché of the *belle juive*. Lasker-Schüler evokes here a stock character of nineteenth-century literature, the virtuous and beautiful Jewish woman whose suffering arouses compassion and love in Christians. The figure of Amram both evokes and thwarts this literary cliché. In her love song, Amram describes her role vis-à-vis Pablo in an image that recalls the idea of Jews as enlightened prophets: "But on your brow I want to plant my fortunate star, / Rob myself of my luminous blossom" (227/*12*). On another occasion, however, a bright-eyed Amram ("with light in her eye," 228/*13*) tells Pablo how she killed a Christian child molester. Amram, who bears a male name (the biblical name of the father of Moses and Aaron), engages in an act of destruction that recalls Moses's slaying of the Egyptian and anticipates Eleazar's act of revenge. The story's bold gender reversals transform the traditional *belle juive*, who enchants Christian men but in the end surrenders to her tragic fate, into a rather belligerent figure.

"The Wonder-Working Rabbi" does not simply reject the notion of the transformative power of love. After all, Amram and Pablo are able to leave the city. They alone are spared from death and destruction. Yet Lasker-Schüler prevents us from obtaining a facile meaning from their love, whether for purposes of scapegoating or of enlightenment. The modernist style of her prose works against any form of instrumentalization. As I have shown, the text is structured around a series of enigmatic events that are not further explained, described in detail, or causally connected to each other. They cannot even be clearly located in time: we learn that Amram each morning climbs up the new buildings with her father, when her fall is suddenly mentioned, without any indication about the timing. In the depiction of the lovers' departure from the city, the text's lapse into the past perfect tense suggests that the departure was not observable at the time of its occurrence. More than anything, Lasker-Schüler emphasizes the disruption brought about by these events, their ability to suspend cycles of repetitions or break a sense of stasis. The text's jumbled syntax, nonlinear narration, and oscillation between prose and poetry preserve the disruptive effect of an event on the level of form. In "The Wonder-Working Rabbi," Lasker-Schüler holds on to the idea of revelatory love—understood along with Rosenzweig as an encounter with the human-as-stranger that disrupts the existing sociopolitical order—while warning against the ideological narratives that come to fill the gaps thus created. She asks us to register the event of interfaith love without integrating it into any existing narrative, whether a cautionary or a redemptive one.

CONCLUSION

TOWARD THE PRESENT AND THE FUTURE

Gershom Scholem, Hannah Arendt,
Barbara Honigmann

This book has shown how at two transformative historical moments—around 1800 and around 1900—romantic love became a powerful model or metaphor for German-Jewish relations. If I have ended on two particularly emphatic visions of interreligious encounters in and through love, this is not to suggest any kind of teleology. Rather, chapter 6 once more conveys the precariousness of love as a model of interreligious or intercultural rapprochement. In Franz Rosenzweig and Else Lasker-Schüler, love indeed holds the promise of bringing people together across religious, national, and cultural boundaries. The romantic attraction between individuals gives rise to social structures—from the lovers' dyad to larger communities—that respect and in fact encourage the expression of difference. However, in "The Wonder-Working Rabbi of Barcelona," Lasker-Schüler uses an interreligious love story to comment on rising antisemitism. She depicts interfaith romance as a cause of social disruptions the Christians do not adequately process and to which they respond with violence. The novella preempts any view of love as a social panacea, while hinting at its capacity to establish new connections between different religious or ethnic groups. Before exploring how tropes of love were used to reimagine German-Jewish relations after the Holocaust, I would like to summarize once more the main arguments made in this book.

Since the Enlightenment, the literary dramatization of interreligious love has promoted the development of new concepts of pluralist communities. These include the Enlightenment conception of a secular state in which citizenship would be independent of religious affiliation; the early Romantic vision of communities that continue to absorb foreigners; and Franz Rosenzweig's notion of an infinitely open neighborhood. To highlight this political context, I have often read literary love stories together with the political writings of their authors or the movements they joined. In the late eighteenth century, Gotthold Ephraim Lessing's literary staging of new social bonds—or what I call "affective kinship"—between members of different religions complements the appeal to brotherly love in the political-theological writings of Moses Mendelssohn. Around 1900, modern German Jewish writers such as Ludwig Jacobowski, Max Nordau, and Georg Herrmann write literary love stories to probe the reasons for the faltering of Jewish emancipation. In so doing, they pursue political goals from repudiating racial antisemitism to advancing new visions of Jewish distinctiveness within the larger human community.

In order to grasp the political effects of representations of love we have to reconsider the meanings of "failure." Most of the literary love stories I have analyzed end unhappily. What message are we to take away from these unhappy endings? Sometimes they simply serve to bolster antisemitic claims about the impossibility of Jewish integration. This is the case in the later Romantic author Achim von Arnim, whose stories of failing Christian-Jewish love affairs illustrate the presumed dangers posed by Jews seeking integration into German society. There are modernist variants of this theme of which I have not yet made explicit mention. In Oskar Panizza's 1893 story, "The Operated Jew" ("Der operierte Jud'"), for example, a Jewish medical student who is portrayed in the worst antisemitic clichés undergoes a series of operations to acquire a Germanic body and soul: he lengthens his body through bone-stretching surgery, colors his hair blond, learns High German, and changes his name to Siegfried Freudenstern.[1] However, his fabricated German identity unravels on the night of his wedding to a woman of pure German stock, when his language reverts to gibberish, his body gradually disintegrates, and all of his hidden Jewish features reemerge. "The Operated Jew" illustrates the antisemitic tenet that intermarriage sets a limit on assimilation or reveals that assimilation has been a sham to begin with. As such, the story anticipates the protofascist novels of Artur Dinter and others, in which the failure of "interracial" marriages serves as proof of the alleged incompatibility of the races.[2]

---

1. See Oskar Panizza, "The Operated Jew," in Jack Zipes, *The Operated Jew: Two Tales of Anti-Semitism* (New York: Routledge, 1991), 47–74.

2. See Artur Dinter, *Die Sünde wider das Blut* (1918; Leipzig: Matthes and Thost, 1920).

Mixed Feelings certainly recognizes the possibility of such ideological usages of the motif of failing love. My main concern, however, has been with a different meaning of failure. The unhappy endings of love stories that cross religious, cultural, or "racial" boundaries do not have to reinforce a segregationist view. Rather, such endings can call for, gesture at, or otherwise help create new visions of sociopolitical integration. As I have argued, the impossibility of interfaith romance and the precariousness of affective kinship in Mendelssohn and Lessing give their writings a greater political urgency. Mendelssohn seeks to instill in his Christian readers the brotherly love he deems necessary yet still missing; Lessing makes it clear that a community in which the different religions would enjoy an equal status remains a desideratum. I have also suggested that in German Jewish modernism, the literary dramatization of failing "interracial" love relationships calls into question the racial ideology of the time. By having such relationships end before they produce children, modern German Jewish authors refuse to pass a final verdict on the compatibility or incompatibility of the "races." In all of these works, love becomes socially and politically significant as the figure of a promise still awaiting fulfillment. The simultaneous invocation and interruption of love open up a space in which German-Jewish relations can be reimagined.

In many of the love stories analyzed in this book, the lovers never really come together. One of my central arguments has been that some German Jewish writers turn this kind of "failure" into a structural feature of love. They conceptualize love as a structure of Twoness, an experience of indelible difference. Rather than as a fusion between two people, they see love as an opportunity for differentiation. Already around 1800, Dorothea Veit (much like her father, Moses Mendelssohn) evinces skepticism about the homogenizing effect of romantic love. In Veit's novel *Florentin*, the hero's pursuit of love and his quest for identity fail conspicuously, a failure that calls into question the Romantic love ideal and the reduction of difference it entails. Around 1900, when literary representations of Christian-Jewish love become central to the debates about Jewish acculturation, an alternative concept of love as a process of differentiation emerges. Modern German Jewish authors write stories and poems in which love both forges new connections between Jews and non-Jews and throws the differences between them into clearer relief. Thus Else Lasker-Schüler in several poems conjoins two biblical characters into a loving couple while highlighting the distance between them. The idea of love as a structure of Twoness finds its clearest articulation in Franz Rosenzweig, who in a letter to his Christian beloved posits that their love anchors each of them more firmly in their respective religious tradition rather than eliding the differences between them. In *The Star of Redemption*, Rosenzweig makes similar claims about neighbor-love, which links people in their irreducible singularity. The idea that love can establish new connections between the particular and the universal continues to be relevant in the present.

After 1945

I began this book by citing Gershom Scholem's famous critique, in his 1966 essay, "Jews and Germans," of the "one-sided love affair" between Jews and Germans before the Holocaust. Scholem argues that the often-professed love of Jews for German culture blinded them to the political realities of emancipation and even contributed to their destruction. One of my goals in this book has been to turn Scholem's verdict around and show that the *idea* of love—including of the idea of failed love—has in fact been highly productive. The invocation of love in German Jewish thought and literature generated new models of social integration and new modes of critical intervention. I would argue that this is true even in Scholem's own essay. Scholem wrote "Germans and Jews" to intervene in the memory culture of postwar West Germany and protest against the ongoing idealization of the purported "German-Jewish symbiosis" of the past. After emancipation has turned into its opposite—into exclusion, expulsion, and genocide—any remnants of love must be replaced by analytical clarity: "Love, insofar as it once existed, has been drowned in blood; its place must now be taken by historical knowledge and conceptual clarity—the preconditions for a discussion that might perhaps bear fruit in the future" (73). However, despite his critique of love past and present, Scholem incessantly, indeed obsessively, returns to the notion of love—in part, I would argue, because it fulfills an important rhetorical function in his own text. Throughout the essay, Scholem grapples with the question of what kind of relations between Germans and Jews are possible after the Holocaust. He posits the necessity of objectivity, distance, and rationality but realizes that the "burden of emotions" (71) renders such attitudes impossible. He nevertheless ends his essay by evoking the possibility of an entirely new beginning of German-Jewish relations, of a bridge built over an abyss, the depth of which cannot be fathomed. What does love have to do with this?

By casting the historical process of emancipation and assimilation as an unhappy love story, Scholem emphasizes two structural features of love: nonsynchronicity and nonreciprocity. Thus he writes about Friedrich Schiller, the German classical writer whom many German Jews loved passionately: "To Schiller, who never addressed them directly, the Jews did indeed respond" (79). This slightly paradoxical remark—how can we answer someone who does not speak to us?—suggests that love is unrequited in essence, a response to a call that never occurred. And this idea of love as nonreciprocal and nonsynchronous is crucial for Scholem's own attempt to imagine the resumption of German-Jewish relations after the radical rupture of the Holocaust. To be sure, Scholem himself rejects love and instead recommends respect, distance, openness, and goodwill as the foundation of a future German-Jewish dialogue. But it is not clear that any of these can accomplish what needs to be accomplished in a situation of radical dissociation. Respect requires mutuality and a common ground; distance keeps people apart but does not bring them together; openness can await but not initiate newness; goodwill requires concrete principles of action. The very mention of love, however, adds an element of drivenness, of unaccountable feeling and unsolicited calling. As such, it provides the extra energy needed to establish a new connection between radically distanced partners or, in Scholem's words, to bridge an abyss. Arguably, his allusion to the possibility of a new beginning of German-Jewish relations derives its power from the very affect he attempts to purge.

More explicitly than Scholem, Hannah Arendt revalorizes love as a mode of German-Jewish rapprochement. Born in 1906 into an assimilated German Jewish family, Arendt studied philosophy and wrote her dissertation on the concept of love in Saint Augustine. In 1933 she fled from Nazi Germany first to France, where she worked for several Jewish organizations, and then to the United States, where she eventually became one of the leading political theorists of the twentieth century. In the four years before her departure from Germany, already apprehensive of Hitler's ascension to power, Arendt began to write a book in which she reassessed the past 150 years of Jewish emancipation and assimilation: *Rahel Varnhagen: The Life of a Jewess*.[3] Rahel Varnhagen, the admired hostess of one of the Jewish salons of the Romantic era, was involved in several love affairs with Gentile men that garnered the attention of contemporaries and historians alike, although none of them made it the focal point of her life in the way that Arendt did.[4] In her biography of Rahel, Arendt both critiques the pursuit of love as a strategy of social integration and promotes a certain kind of love—the pariah's love—as a source of political solidarity.[5]

This latter claim may sound surprising, since Arendt is known for excluding emotions as a source of politics in favor of a strict separation between private and public domains. In her later work, she presents the Greek polis as a model of a

---

3. See Hannah Arendt, *Rahel Varnhagen: The Life of a Jewess*, ed. Liliane Weissberg, trans. Richard Winston and Clara Winston (Baltimore: Johns Hopkins University Press, 1997). All further citations of *Rahel Varnhagen* refer to this edition and will be included parenthetically in the text. Arendt wrote most of the book between 1929 and 1933 and added the last two chapters, in which she elaborates the distinction between pariah and parvenu, in the late 1930s. However, the book was published only many years later, in English translation in 1957, and in the German original in 1959. For a detailed history of the biography's composition and publication history, see Weissberg's introduction to the book, "Introduction: Hannah Arendt, Rahel Varnhagen, and the Writing of (Auto)biography)," 3–69.

4. In the mid-1920s, Arendt herself had been involved in an (adulterous) love affair with the German philosopher Martin Heidegger, which later became notorious because of Heidegger's support of the Nazi regime in the early 1930s. In what follows, I do not read *Rahel Varnhagen* in this context, in part because Arendt's physical affair with Heidegger was over, and they were rarely in contact when she researched the book and completed the draft. Furthermore, reading Arendt's book as a response to the affair would potentially reduce her complex account of Jewish assimilation to a mere gloss of her biography.

5. The best way to refer to Rahel Levin Varnhagen is an open question because she bore many names in her life, including Rahel Levin, Rahel Robert, Rahel Varnhagen, and Antonie Friedericke Varnhagen von Ense. See Weissberg, "Introduction," 12 and n. 30. "Rahel Levin Varnhagen," as she is often called today, is in fact an artificial construction, a combination of her Jewish patronym and the surname of her Christian husband. For lack of a clear alternative, many contemporary scholars continue to refer to her by her first name "Rahel." I will do the same, following Arendt's own usage throughout the biography.

transparent public space whose participants disengage from purely private interests.[6] However, Seyla Benhabib has traced an alternative conception of the public in Arendt's work and located its beginnings in the conception of salon culture in *Rahel Varnhagen*. According to Benhabib, Arendt's appreciation of the salon as a site of sociability that celebrates individual differences in tastes, manners, and lifestyles contrasts with her later valorization of the Greek polis.[7] Along similar lines, I will argue that *Rahel Varnhagen* conjures a different kind of connection between love and politics than Arendt's subsequent critique of emotional politics suggests. Her biography of the Jewish *salonnière* is structured around the opposition between two types of sociopolitical behavior—that of the pariah and that of the parvenu—which are associated with two kinds of love. Arendt's central argument is that Rahel retained the pariah's love for humanity even after she became a parvenu enamored with social power, and that she inspired political rebels such as Heinrich Heine.

Rahel Varnhagen is initially quite critical of the idea of love as a mode of interreligious or intercultural rapprochement. Rahel's various attempts to assimilate to German society through love and marriage epitomize the individualist model of Jewish emancipation Arendt rejects. Rahel's choices show the inability of Jews to seek political emancipation *as Jews*, their tendency toward an abstract individualism that left no ties among them but "that questionable solidarity which survives among people who all want the same thing: to save themselves as individuals" (87). Love is a key component in a strategy of social climbing Arendt associates with the parvenu. Rahel's Gentile husband, Karl August Varnhagen, who had a tendency to adore his employers and thus advance his career, exemplifies this behavior. Arendt generalizes: "All parvenus are familiar with Varnhagen's impulse, all those who must climb by fraud into a society, a rank, a class, not theirs by birthright. Making a strenuous effort to love, where there is no alternative but obedience, is more

---

6. In several of her later books, Arendt is critical of the infusion of emotions—and especially of love—into politics. She criticizes the French Revolution for being inspired by compassion for the poor, in contrast to the American Revolution, which aimed at the creation of a democratic public space. See Hannah Arendt, *On Revolution* (New York: Penguin, 2006), 56–88. Arendt reasserted the distinction between love and politics in a public dispute with Scholem. When Scholem reproached her after the publication of her *Eichmann in Jerusalem* of lacking *Ahavath Yisrael*, or "love of the Jewish people," Arendt responded that she indeed loved only her friends, and that she reserved her love for individuals rather than collectives. See Gershom Scholem, "Letter to Hannah Arendt," trans. John Mander, in *On Jews and Judaism in Crisis*, 300–306; here 303; Hannah Arendt, "The Eichmann Controversy: A Letter to Gershom Scholem," in Arendt, *The Jewish Writings*, ed. Jerome Kohn and Ron H. Feldman, 465–71 (New York: Schocken, 2007), here 466–67. If politics needs to be protected from personal feelings, the reverse is also true. In a 1959 commentary on racial tensions in the United States, Arendt suggests repealing the existing laws against interracial marriage because they constitute an inappropriate political intervention into personal lives. See the summary of the article and the surrounding debate in Elisabeth Young-Bruehl, *Hannah Arendt: For Love of the World* (New Haven, Conn.: Yale University Press, 1982), 309–10.

7. See Seyla Benhabib, *The Reluctant Modernism of Hannah Arendt* (Thousand Oaks, Calif.: Sage Publications, 1996), 19–20.

productive of good results than simple and undisguised servility" (237). Jews, who were forced to become "parvenus par excellence" (238), were particularly prone to such an affective attachment to the institutions of power. Rahel was no exception. Arendt can hardly conceal her disdain when she describes Rahel's enthusiasm for the rise of German nationalism and her efforts to help during the wars against Napoleon: "She became thoroughly stupid and commonplace out of sheer wild delight that she was graciously being allowed to help, that she had something to do, that waiting and being a spectator had ceased" (234). Much like Scholem, Arendt suggests that the love of Jews for things German blinded them to the precariousness of their own situation and rendered them incapable of acting in solidarity with other Jews in times of crisis.

Rahel Varnhagen offers a succinct analysis of the historical settings and social dynamics of love. With utmost verbal economy, Arendt depicts Rahel's first love affair as a long-awaited chance to "escape from Judaism" (103). The introduction of her husband-to-be Varnhagen is similarly lacking in emotional intensity: "In the spring of 1808 Rahel met August Varnhagen in Berlin, and a few months later became his mistress" (194). This laconic sentence downplays feelings in a manner characteristic of the biography as a whole. Arendt, who always believed in the power of storytelling and chose to tell Rahel's life as a string of stories,[8] refrains from telling persuasive love stories. She uses literary techniques of foreshadowing to have the love stories end before they even begin. The abstractness of her style, the lack of dialogue, descriptive detail, and character development, further undermine the power of narration. Instead of storytelling she offers a critical analysis of the sociohistorical dimensions of love. Rahel met her first great love, the Christian count Karl von Finckenstein, in 1795 at a time of increased social mobility and uncertainty. For her, a Jewish woman living in a period in which the dissolution of Jewish collectivity had begun yet Jewish acceptance into German society lagged, the prospect of marriage to a Gentile of high standing promised a place in society. For him, the representative of a class that had lost much of its political significance, the relationship with a poor yet high-spirited Jewish woman was a chance to experiment with new forms of individual freedom and cross-class sociability. Their love failed because the pull of their different backgrounds proved too strong. Unable to define himself as an individual and to thwart the expectations of his family that he marry within his class and religion, Finckenstein slowly but surely withdrew from Rahel, leaving her more isolated and vulnerable than before (103–21). Love as a strategy of social integration thus failed Rahel in two ways. First, it blinded her to the sociohistorical reality of acculturation. Second, it did not even grant her the illusion of social integration, since all her love affairs ended unhappily.

However, Arendt ultimately salvages Rahel's life and love by separating love from marriage, and the pariah's love of humanity from the parvenu's love for

---

8. On Arendt's use of storytelling, see Weissberg, "Introduction," 21–23.

social superiors. It is crucial to her conception that Rahel did not love the man she ultimately married and that she never became a complete parvenu. At the moment when baptism and marriage to a Gentile secured her a place in society, Rahel adopted an altogether different attitude, an embrace of social ostracism and solidarity with other outsiders. She contacted her old friend Pauline Wiesel, whose bohemian lifestyle made her a persona non grata in respectable society, and stayed in close contact with her for the rest of her life. As Arendt puts it, Rahel remained a sometime pariah when she could have become a complete parvenu. Arendt took the term *pariah* from Bernard Lazare (1865–1903), a legal adviser to the Dreyfus family and author of a book on the causes of antisemitism. Lazare regarded the Jews as a whole as a pariah people and called "conscious pariahs" those who turned the experience of social exclusion into principles of political action.[9] Rahel's greatest merit, Arendt concludes in her biography, was her recognition of the pariah's truth in the midst of a parvenu's existence. Rahel's insights prepared the ground for more self-conscious pariahs, such as the writer Heinrich Heine, who turned their social ostracism into social critique and picked up the political struggle Rahel avoided.

When turning to the pariah qualities Rahel retained behind her parvenu appearance, Arendt discovers a love altogether different from the parvenu's infatuation with social superiors. Quoting from Rahel's letters and diaries, she calls this love: "the deeply humane love of all outcasts from society for the 'true realities'—'a bridge, a tree, a ride, a smell, a smile'" (245) and the pariah's "'love for free existence'" (249). These descriptions are quite vague, and it is perhaps best to broach the pariah's love by stating what it is not: a ploy in the search for social advancement. If the parvenu improves his chances for social advancement by idolizing his superiors, this is precisely what Rahel was unable or unwilling to do. She resisted instrumentalizing love in this way. Toward the end of her life "she discovered that it was necessary for the parvenu—but for him alone—to sacrifice every natural impulse, to conceal all truth, to misuse all love, not only to suppress all passion, but worse still, to convert it into a means for social climbing" (244). According to Arendt, Rahel refused to do the same. Rahel's ability to remain true to herself, which Arendt emphasizes throughout the biography, included an understanding of the social game of love and an unwillingness to play along. She held onto her knowledge of the mechanisms of social exclusion and her appreciation of everything human at the very moment when marriage to Varnhagen finally secured her a place in higher society.

Whereas the parvenu's love leads to social acquiescence, the pariah's love potentially leads to political rebellion and political solidarity. Arendt continues here a line of thought she first developed in her dissertation on Saint Augustine, especially in the discussion of neighbor-love. Neighbor-love, which is grounded in

9. See Weissberg, "Introduction," 4; and Arendt, "The Jew as Pariah: A Hidden Tradition," in Kohn and Feldman, *The Jewish Writings*, 275–97.

the memory of one's origin and gratefulness for one's God-given life, allows for a human togetherness based on an equality of situation rather than a similarity of traits.[10] This idea returns in *Rahel Varnhagen* in the depiction of political alliances that evolve not from a shared identity, but from the shared experience of marginalization. The pariah's love for things in and of themselves is the basis of an alternative model of politicization. Whereas the parvenu manages to fend off the claims of others and his own impulses, the pariah remains vulnerable and exposed, but for that reason also able to form new bonds with others, including political alliances with other oppressed people. The pariah's self-exposure in love, of which Rahel's unhappy loves are a prime example, enables the formation of such rainbow coalitions. Arendt writes of the aging Rahel: "It had been her privilege to have preserved a 'soft heart, of flesh and blood,' to have remained eternally vulnerable, to have admitted each weakness to herself, and thus, only thus, to have acquired experience" (244). Its excessive character prevents the pariah's love from becoming a mere means to an end.

The pariah's love allows for new connections between the particular and the universal. The political message of Arendt's biography is that Jews should demand political rights *as Jews* and form alliances with other marginalized groups rather than seek social integration at all costs. However, as Richard Bernstein notes, it is unclear what exactly it would mean to demand rights *as Jews*, for Arendt rejected most existing definitions of Jewishness in religious, ethnic, or national terms.[11] This is why the pariah's love becomes so important. It allows Arendt to conjure a model of political solidarity that begins in concrete existence and ends in abstract potentiality. For the pariah embodies a specific mode of thought and perception, a combination of attention to details and an ability to generalize. This mind-set transpires in the descriptions of the objects of her love, which include abstractions such as "'free existence'" (249) and simple things such as "'a bridge, a tree, a ride, a smell, a smile'" (245). This series of mundane things, stripped of all attributes and combined with indefinite articles, conveys a sense of uniqueness in generality. The pariah loves things outside of systems of social signification and relates to people in much the same way. She is conscious of the mechanisms of social exclusion and perceives the universally human behind the plurality of human beings, all the while insisting on her own difference and avoiding any pretense to social equality. The pariah embodies a universalism "from below," as opposed to the universalism "from above" promoted by the German Enlightenment with its pedagogical impetus and its quid-pro-quo model of Jewish emancipation.

---

10. See Hannah Arendt, *Love and Saint Augustine*, ed. Joanna Vecchiarelli Scott and Judith Chelius Stark (Chicago: University of Chicago Press, 1996), 100. The English translation is not the original dissertation, but a revision Arendt began in the mid-1960s and left unfinished. For a summary of the dissertation, see Young-Bruehl, *Hannah Arendt*, 490–500.

11. See Richard J. Bernstein, *Hannah Arendt and the Jewish Question* (Cambridge, Mass.: MIT Press, 1996), 26–29.

I have attempted to do on a larger scale what Arendt accomplished for a specific case: recuperate love as a category for the study of German Jewish culture. Like Arendt, I do not suggest that loving and marrying across religious and cultural divides provides a "solution" to the "problem" of an increasingly pluralist society. As we have seen, intermarriage in particular can be a model with problematic totalizing implications, one to which German Jewish writers from Moses Mendelssohn to Georg Hermann objected. It is outside of fixed social forms—in erratic affects, momentary encounters, inevitable failures—that love unfolds its power to stimulate our sociopolitical imagination.

After 1990

The decade after the 1990 reunification of Germany saw a surge of interest in the topic of German-Jewish love. At this time of national renewal, the question of what it means to be German acquired new urgency, as did the question of how to publicly acknowledge German responsibility for the Second World War and the Holocaust. At this moment of re-remembrance, stories of Jewish-Gentile love were deployed in two different ways, which roughly correspond to earlier conceptions of love as fusion and love as differentiation. On the one hand, a number of German feature films dramatize interreligious love to highlight moments of solidarity between Jews and non-Jews during the Third Reich. On the other hand, the German Jewish writer Barbara Honigmann depicts the memory of the National Socialist past as a lasting obstacle to Jewish-Gentile love relationships. Whereas the films use love stories to project the possibility of German-Jewish reconciliation into the past, Honigmann uses such stories for the opposite end, to show how conflicts of the past continue into the present. But as I will argue, this is not a simple negation of love as a trope of interreligious or intercultural mediation. Love remains an important trope in Honigmann, one that allows her to imagine a new kind of German Jewish diaspora.

Lutz Koepnick has aptly spoken of a wave of "heritage films" that hit the German movie theaters starting in the late 1990s. The term *heritage film* was originally coined for late twentieth-century British films that cast the English past in a nostalgic light. While the new German films on the Third Reich can hardly be called nostalgic, they send a positive message in the sense that they "reclaim sites of multicultural consensus from a history of intolerance and persecution."[12] These films construct a usable past that can be easily consumed and enjoyed by contemporary viewers, without reminders of trauma and irredeemable dispersion. Interreligious love stories play a crucial role in this representation. Thus Max Färberbock's *Aimée & Jaguar* evolves around a lesbian love affair between a Jewish woman and

---

12. Lutz Koepnick, "Reframing the Past: Heritage Cinema and Holocaust in the 1990s," *New German Critique* 87 (2002): 47–82; here 57.

the "Aryan" wife of a German soldier, and Joseph Vilsmaier's *Comedian Harmon-ists*, which recounts the rise and fall of a popular German musical band during the 1930s, features three Jewish-Gentile couples. Both films depict the increasing oppression and persecution of Jews under the Nazi regime but shy away from a direct discussion of the Holocaust. Instead they focus on private dramas of love, jealousy, and reconciliation. The depiction of love affairs in which non-Jews stead-fastly hold onto their Jewish partners, despite insults, threats, and dangers to their own life and liberty, adds to the feel-good quality of the films. Their central mes-sage is that romantic love inspired acts of solidarity and resistance that could have forestalled genocidal terror had they only occurred with greater frequency and on a larger scale.

This conciliatory message culminates in Margarethe von Trotta's 2003 film *Rosenstrasse*, which turns love into a political program. The film dramatizes a real historical event, one of the very few instances of public protest against the anti-Jewish policies of Nazi Germany. When, in March 1943, Jewish men living in intermarriage—a status that had thus far protected them from deportation—were arrested, their non-Jewish wives and relatives gathered and protested until the men were released. The film *Rosenstrasse* focuses on the story of Ruth, a Jewish woman living in New York City who as a child in Nazi Germany had been rescued by one of the women participating in the protest. She has never talked about this until her daughter Hannah flies to Germany and, in a series of interviews with the woman who saved her mother, reconstructs her mother's story as well as the history of the protest. The film evokes the idea of a "resistance of the heart," as the title of a book on the protest by the historian Nathan Stoltzfus reads, and intimates that if such behavior had occurred on a broader scale, it could have curbed or even prevented the Nazi persecution of the Jews. Historians are actually still debating the effective-ness of the protest: it is unclear, for instance, whether the Jewish men were actually facing deportation, and if yes, whether it was the protest that prevented it.[13] But the film quite unambiguously suggests that the wives' love, devotion, and courage saved the husbands. According to its logic, intermarriage is a good thing because it creates kinship networks that protect minorities against persecution.

Even more problematic than the film's rather facile celebration of love as politi-cal resistance is its implication that Jews objecting to intermarriage might be to blame for their own persecution. This message is conveyed by the frame narra-tive, which shows how Ruth after her husband's death suffers from psychical symptoms including anxiety, flashbacks, and overly ritualistic behavior during the *shiva*, the weeklong Jewish mourning ritual. Among other things, she suddenly

---

13. The film begins by announcing "the events that unfolded on Rosenstrasse in Berlin from Feb-ruary 27 till March 6, 1943 are a historical fact," yet it distorts historical reality in several ways. See Beate Meyer, "Geschichte im Film: Judenverfolgung, Mischehen und der Protest in der Rosenstraße 1943," *Zeitschrift für Geschichtswissenschaft* 1 (2004): 23–36.

and vehemently rejects Hannah's fiancée because he is not Jewish. During her trip to Germany, Hannah learns what must be the reason for her mother's strained behavior: Ruth herself had a non-Jewish father, who during the Third Reich abandoned her and her mother, thereby indirectly causing the deportation of her mother. Upon her return to the United States, Hannah apparently persuades Ruth to recognize the story of her life and remember the bond with her adoptive Gentile mother.[14] This restoration of trust—made possible by the memory of the Gentile women who courageously stood by their Jewish husbands—seems to have a curative effect on Ruth, who in the final scene can be seen happily attending Hannah's wedding and blessing her son-in-law.[15]

By framing the history of the public protest with the story of a Jewish woman who learns to overcome her objections to intermarriage, *Rosenstrasse* at best pathologizes the victims and at worst blames them for their own persecution. The film suggests that Ruth's opposition to intermarriage is a pathological condition, a symptom of post-traumatic stress disorder rather than, for instance, a theologically justifiable position. *Rosenstrasse* leaves no room for expressions of particularity such as the commandment to marry within the faith, which is important in traditional Judaism. In its portrayal of Ruth, a Jewish woman who rejects the claims of love in favor of a rigid adherence to traditional rules and customs, the film revives one of the oldest religious stereotypes: the opposition between Jewish law and Christian love. In casting romantic love as the fusion of opposites, and Judaism as a source of stubborn resistance to such fusion, *Rosenstrasse* harks back to the early Romantic thought of F. Schlegel and G. F. W. Hegel. In what follows, I will contrast this view with that of Barbara Honigmann, who belongs to a new generation of German Jewish authors that began to emerge during the 1980s. Perhaps more than anyone else today, Honigmann continues to elaborate the trope of the German-Jewish love affair. Akin to earlier German Jewish writers such as Rosenzweig and Lasker-Schüler, she depicts love as a deepening of difference—in her case, between the descendants of victims and perpetrators of the Holocaust. And like these earlier writers, she ascribes to love a certain cultural productivity—in her case, the capacity to spawn a new German Jewish diaspora literature.

---

14. On the significance of mother-daughter relationships in the film, see Anna M. Parkinson, "Neo-feminist *Mütterfilm*? The Emotional Politics of Margarethe von Trotta's *Rosenstrasse*," in *The Collapse of Conventional German Film and Its Politics at the Turn of the Twenty-First Century*, ed. Jaimey Fisher and Brad Prager (Detroit: Wayne State University Press, 2010), 109–35.

15. As Sara Horowitz points out, the wedding is only ambiguously coded as Jewish. It contains some elements of a Jewish ceremony, especially the breaking of a glass, but not others, notably the canopy. The film leaves open the question of whether Luis converted to Judaism or whether the couple is having an interfaith ceremony, thus continuing the themes of intermarriage and hybridity through the end. See Sara R. Horowitz, "Lovin' Me, Lovin' Jew: Gender, Intermarriage, and Metaphor" in *Antisemitisim and Philosemitism in the Twentieth and Twenty-first Centuries:Representing Jews, Jewishness, and Modern Culture*, ed. Phyllis Lassner and Lara Trubowitz (Newark: University of Delaware Press, 2010), 196–216; here 211.

Barbara Honigmann was born in 1949 to Jewish parents who had returned to East Germany in 1947 after years of exile in Paris and London. While Judaism in a religious or cultural sense played no role in her parents' home, Honigmann herself began in the 1970s what she describes as a "search for a minimum of Jewish identity in my life."[16] She started learning Hebrew, got married in a Jewish ceremony, and in 1984 left the GDR for Strasbourg, a French city close to the German border that is home to a sizable and vibrant Jewish community, with members of various geographical origins and religious orientations.[17] It is here that she wrote her first collection of prose, which upon its publication in 1986 became an instant success on the German book market. Honigmann would stage and restage this central fact of her life—that she became a German-language writer at the very moment she left Germany—in a series of autofictional texts. One of the main motives of her literary oeuvre is the birth of writing out of the spirit of exile; another is the failing love between Jews and non-Jews.

In Honigmann's *A Love Made Out of Nothing* (*Eine Liebe aus nichts*, 1991), the narrator, a young Jewish woman working at a theater, leaves the GDR for Paris in the hope of gaining new experiences and perspectives. The novel figures her need for distance from her native Germany, among other things, through an impossible love story. While still in Berlin, the narrator has an oddly secretive and distanced relationship with a theater director named Alfried. Even when together, they cannot look into each other's eyes; they communicate mostly through brief written notes; the narrator can barely get herself to say her lover's overly Germanic name. Her sense of incompatibility culminates in a nightmarish vision of a monstrously divided child that would be born to them: "I saw the child in nightmares, the way it was put together loosely from individual pieces and then came undone and fell apart and couldn't stand upright."[18] The involuntary bond between Alfried and the narrator—she calls their love a "connection or even an adhesion that we couldn't pull away from" (33/46)—epitomizes what Dan Diner has called the "negative symbiosis" between Jews and Germans after Auschwitz. Since 1945, Diner argues, German and Jewish identities have largely been constituted in relation to the Holocaust and the, naturally opposed, traumas it inflicted on the collective of the perpetrators and that of the victims. This situation has created a new, negative interdependency of postwar Jews and Germans, who need

---

16. Barbara Honigmann, "Selbstporträt als Jüdin," in *Damals, dann, danach* (Munich: Carl Hanser, 1999), 11–18; here 15.

17. On the heterogeneous character of Strasbourg's Jewish community and Honigmann's conception of diasporic writing, see also Christina Guenther, "Exile and the Construction of Identity in Barbara Honigmann's Trilogy of the Diaspora," *Comparative Literature Studies* 40, no. 2 (2003): 215–31.

18. Barbara Honigmann, *A Love Made Out of Nothing* and *Zohara's Journey*, trans. John Barrett (Jaffrey, N.H.: Godine, 2003), 33. For the original German, see Barbara Honigmann, *Eine Liebe aus nichts* (Reinbek: Rowohlt, 1993), 46. Further citations from these editions will be included parenthetically in the text, with the page number in the English translation followed by the page number in the German edition in italics, as here (33/46).

each other to work through the "screen memories" that cover up the core of each collective's trauma.[19] What happens, however, if one conveys this idea through an impossible love story rather than a theoretical concept such as "negative symbiosis" or "distanced dialogue"? In other words, what is the theoretical, artistic, or political purchase of love?

One of the things the rhetoric of love does for Honigmann is help carve out a space for diasporic writing. In an essay titled "On My Great-Grandfather, My Grandfather, My Father, and Me" ("Von meinem Urgroßvater, meinem Groß-vater, meinem Vater und von mir," 1995) she recalls her family's commitment to German culture in terms quite similar to those of Gershom Scholem. She describes how her ancestors' models of acculturation—including her great grandfather's struggle for political rights, her grandfather's commitment to academia, and her father's membership in the East German Communist Party—were fueled by love for German culture. All of these ancestors were, in addition to their professional occupations, authors of literary texts. Like Scholem, Honigmann believes that the devotion of Jews to German culture did not help them but only blinded them to the precariousness of their situation. Her ancestors "desired [the German culture], reached out for it, and stretched and contorted themselves unbelievably in order to unite themselves with it. Instead of unification, they mostly experienced denial and repulsion, and my father was given the privilege of witnessing the final destruction of German-Jewish history with his own eyes."[20] Honigmann decides to distance herself from this model of acculturation, conceptually by giving up the idea of a social avant-garde and geographically by moving from Germany to France.

However, she finds that she remains connected to Germany through her writing in two ways. First, all of her writing circles around the failed hopes and the unrequited love experienced by her ancestors. She may no longer try to spearhead ideas as they did, instead recycling and recharging the words of everyday life, but she nevertheless remains thematically focused, even fixated, on her family's failed love affair with German culture. Second, and more important, she uses the rhetoric of love to depict her own development as a writer. The primary scene of her literary work—how she became a German writer by going into exile—is now recast as a romantic breakup. Her writing is a form of farewell from Germany, comparable to the letters composed by lovers after a separation. This separation, she conjectures, guarantees an abiding attachment. Her writing is still a form of love, now

---

19. See Dan Diner, "Negative Symbiosis: Germans and Jews after Auschwitz," in *The Holocaust: Theoretical Readings*, ed. Neil Levi and Michael Rothberg (New Brunswick, N.J.: Rutgers University Press, 2003), 423–30.

20. Barbara Honigmann, "On My Great-Grandfather, My Grandfather, My Father, and Me," trans. Meghan W. Barnes, *World Literature Today* 69, no. 3 (1995): 512–16; here 513. For the original German, see Honigmann, *Damals, dann, danach*, 45. Further citations from these editions will be included parenthetically in the text, with the page number in the English translation followed by the page number in the German edition in italics, as here (513/*45*).

understood as a desperate appeal to an Other, who may or may not be listening. Here is this passage, quoted at some length:

> But perhaps writing was also something like homesickness and an assurance that we really did belong together, Germany and I, that we, as they say, could not get away from each other, especially not now, after everything that had happened.... My writing had in effect come from a more or less fortuitous separation, just as couples write each other love letters at the very beginning of their infatuation and then not again until their breakup....
>
> I wanted to present myself completely differently than my great-grandfather, my grandfather, and my father, and now I saw myself, just like them, speaking again to the Other, hoping to be heard, perhaps even to be understood, calling to him, "Look at me! Listen to me, at least for five minutes." ...
>
> I understood that writing means being separated and is very similar to exile, and that it is in this sense perhaps true that being a writer and being a Jew are similar as well, in the way they are dependent upon the Other when they speak to him, more or less despairingly. It is true of both that approaching the Other too closely is dangerous for them and that agreeing with him too completely will bring about their downfall.
>
> (513f./46–47)

While the connection Honigmann establishes here between writing, exile, and Jewishness is not an entirely new idea, the rhetoric of love adds an interesting twist, as it creates a sense of continuity with the earlier tradition of German Jewish literature. Even if Honigmann's German-language texts are farewell letters to a lover rather than the wooing calls uttered by her ancestors, they are still driven by the same impulse. In fact, they for the first time render this impulse fully tangible. According to Honigmann, writing means to sustain a tension between distance and proximity, to endure the dependence on another whom one addresses but from whom one remains separated. All writing is a desperate call across a necessary distance, a one-directional communication with someone who potentially misunderstands everything. As a self-professed diasporic writer, Honigmann does in a conscious and critical manner what her forefathers did unconsciously, desperately, and futilely.

Here we find one reason interreligious love is so important in Honigmann, although she mostly stages its failure. Love is central to Honigmann's conception of the relationship between self and other in the diaspora. Love stories capture the constant negotiation between proximity and distance, recognition and rejection, collaboration and conflict, in the diaspora. In that process, love itself becomes redefined as a force of disruption rather than of fusion. Another novel by Honigmann that is structured around a failing relationship between a Jewish woman and a Gentile man depicts the gradual surfacing of ever more differences between the two. Furthermore, one of the novel's central lines—"Where there is love there is also betrayal"[21]—posits that love is inherently disruptive. I would argue that the repeated failures of Jewish-Gentile love affairs in Honigmann are a sign of this disruptive potential rather than the result of psychological incompatibility, irresolvable historical conflict, or anything along these lines. I would further argue that this inherent negativity of love is part of its appeal as a trope for interreligious relations—for Honigmann as well as for contemporary critics in search of new models of particularity and universality. When we understand love as a force that proliferates differences rather than creates a union, it makes for not quite so cheesy a metaphor, not quite so conciliatory a story.

This alternative conception of love can also change our understanding of what the interaction between ethnic or religious groups might look like. Rather than a union or dialogue, such interaction may take the form of a disjointed, noncontemporaneous exchange between multiple parties. Honigmann's essay "On My Great-Grandfather" itself provides an example of such a disjointed exchange. This essay has a frame narrative I have thus far neglected. Honigmann's meditation on her family's past is triggered by her encounter with a German Turkish (presumably Muslim) family that now lives in Strasbourg and that confronts her with some well-worn stereotypes about Jews. When the family wonders why Honigmann and her husband do not have a shop like all the other Jews, she is mentally transported to her ancestors' decidedly intellectual pursuits. After telling the story of her ancestors, she reminds the reader that she did this only in her head and avoided responding to the question of the Turkish family in reality. Instead of attempting to overcome the barriers between her and her Turkish neighbors, she decides to play ball with one of the children:

> I walk a ways and play with [the Turkish child] . . . because I find doing so less stressful than explaining to his parents why we have no shop, less stressful than setting straight their picture of Jews—a picture which is apparently just as distorted as ours is of them—less stressful than clearing away all the misunderstandings that emerge between us in just this one afternoon and telling them the whole story of my great-grandfather, my grandfather, my father, and me.
>
> (516/55)

Ironically, what the narrator refuses to do for her Turkish neighbors—to explain her family's background—she has just done for her German readers, from whom she presumably feels no less separate. This is an example of how one failed dialogue generates another form of exchange, one that is written rather than spoken, distanced rather than immediate, unidirectional rather than reciprocal. We can see the potential of this model by looking at the actual effect of Honigmann's

---

21. Barbara Honigmann, *Alles, alles Liebe* (Munich: Carl Hanser, 2000), 103, 160.

essay. While the essay itself describes her unwillingness to engage with her Turkish neighbors, to dispel their prejudices and establish a common ground, it sub-
sequently became an inspiration for the contemporary German Turkish writer
Zafer Şenocak. Şenocak cites Honigmann's text in one of his own essays, which
traces points of contact between Turkish Islam and the secularized Christianity
of the German Enlightenment. Among other things, he recounts how his Turkish
ancestors, who were pious Muslims, eagerly read the German classics, which one
of them adorned with jottings in Arabic script. Şenocak also writes that life stories
and family genealogies such as Honigmann's inspired him to reconstruct this history of transreligious and transcultural exchange. According to him, cultures open
up to each other in the singularity of personal experience, which registers but also
exceeds cultural influences. For Şenocak, the German Jewish experience described
in Honigmann and others becomes a model of Turkish German transculturation.[22]
In other words, the failed Turkish-Jewish encounter *described* in Honigmann's
essay generates the indirect Jewish-German exchange that *is* Honigmann's essay,
which in turn generates the complex Turkish-German-Jewish exchange that is
Şenocak's essay. I would venture to say that here we have another explanation
as to why love supplants dialogue as a privileged trope of mediation in Scholem,
Arendt, and Honigmann: love—and especially unrequited love—can inaugurate
potentially infinite chains of encounters.

---

22. Zafer Şenocak, "Mein Erbe spricht auch Deutsch: Vergessene deutsch-türkische Verwandtschaften," in *Deutschsein: Eine Aufklärungsschrift* (Hamburg: Edition Körber-Stiftung, 2011), 172–90,
esp. 180–82. One may add here that the history of German-Turkish relations is long and complex, and
their character not uncontroversial. The political alliance between the Wilhelminian and Ottoman em-
pires, the flight of German Jewish academics to Turkish universities in the 1930s, and the influx of
Turkish *Gastarbeiter* (guest workers) into postwar German society provided much intercultural contact
yet were far from being equal exchanges. A firm believer in Enlightenment principles, Şenocak tends
to idealize German-Turkish relations and to downplay the anti-Muslim biases of many German intellectuals. One may even speak here of another "one-sided love affair" between twentieth-century Turkish and German thinkers. I believe, however, that this takes nothing away from Şenocak's point that
German Turkish writers in search of new models of transculturation may draw inspiration from German Jewish writers.

Bibliography

Abels, Norbert. *Sicherheit ist nirgends: Judentum und Aufklärung bei Arthur Schnitzler*. Königstein im Taunus: Athenäum, 1982.

Adelung, Johann Christoph. *Grammatisch-kritisches Wörterbuch der hochdeutschen Mundart*. Leipzig: Johann Gottlob Immanuel Breitkopf und Compagnie, 1793.

———. *Grammatisch-kritisches Wörterbuch der hochdeutschen Mundart*. Vienna: Bauer, 1811.

Agamben, Giorgio. *The Coming Community*. Translated by Michael Hardt. Minneapolis: University of Minnesota Press, 1993.

———. *The Time That Remains: A Commentary on the Letter to the Romans*. Translated by Patricia Dailey. Stanford, Calif.: Stanford University Press, 2005.

Ahlwardt, Hermann. *Der Verzweiflungskampf der arischen Völker mit dem Judentum*. Berlin: Grobhäuser, 1890.

Anderson, Mark M. "'Jewish' Mimesis? Imitation and Assimilation in Thomas Mann's 'Wälsungenblut' and Ludwig Jacobowki's *Werther, Der Jude*." *German Life and Letters* 49, no. 2 (April 1996): 193–204.

Arendt, Hannah. *The Jewish Writings*. Edited by Jerome Kohn and Ron H. Feldman. New York: Schocken, 2007.

———. *Love and Saint Augustine*. Edited by Joanna Vecchiarelli Scott and Judith Chelius Stark. Chicago: University of Chicago Press, 1996.

———. *On Revolution*. New York: Penguin, 2006.

———. *Rahel Varnhagen: The Life of a Jewess*. Edited by Liliane Weissberg. Translated by Richard Winston and Clara Winston. Baltimore: Johns Hopkins University Press, 1997.

Arnim, Achim von. *Gentry by Entailment*. Translated by Alan Brown. London: Atlas Press, 1990.

———. *Werke in sechs Bänden*. Edited by Roswitha Burwick et al. Frankfurt am Main: Deutscher Klassiker Verlag, 1989–94.

Aschheim, Steven E. "German History and German Jewry: Boundaries, Functions, and Interdependence." *Leo Baeck Institute Yearbook* 43 (1998): 315–22.

———. *Scholem, Arendt, Klemperer: Intimate Chronicles in Turbulent Times*. Bloomington: Indiana University Press, 2001.

Badiou, Alain. *Saint Paul: The Foundation of Universalism*. Translated by Ray Brassier. Stanford, Calif.: Stanford University Press, 2003.

———. "What Is Love?" Translated by Justin Clemens. *Umbr(a): A Journal of the Unconscious* 1 (1996): 37–53.

Badiou, Alain, with Nicolas Truong. *In Praise of Love*. Translated by Peter Bush. New York: The New Press, 2012.

Bambus, Willy. "Die Mischehe." *Zion: Monatsschrift für die nationalen Interessen des jüdischen Volkes* 4, no. 5 (1898): 19–21.

Barthes, Roland. *A Lover's Discourse: Fragments*. Translated by Richard Howard. New York: Farrar, Straus and Giroux, 1979.

Batnitzky, Leora Faye. *Idolatry and Representation: The Philosophy of Franz Rosenzweig Reconsidered*. Princeton, N.J.: Princeton University Press, 2000.

Battegay, Caspar. *Das andere Blut: Gemeinschaft im deutsch-jüdischen Schreiben 1830–1930*. Cologne: Böhlau, 2011.

Bauman, Zygmunt. *Modernity and Ambivalence*. Ithaca, N.Y.: Cornell University Press, 1991.

Baumbach, Clara. "Glaube und Liebe." *Allgemeine Zeitung des Judentums* 68, nos. 20–24 (1904): 239–40, 248–50, 261–63, 272–75, 286–88. http://sammlungen.ub.uni-frankfurt.de/cm/periodical/titleinfo/3228581.

Baumgart, Hildegard. "Arnim's 'Judengeschichte': Eine biographische Rekonstruktion." In *Arnim und die Berliner Romantik: Kunst, Literatur und Politik*, edited by Walter Pape, 71–94. Tübingen: Max Niemeyer, 2001.

Bauschinger, Sigrid. *Else Lasker-Schüler: Biographie*. Göttingen: Wallstein, 2004.

Becker-Cantarino, Barbara. "'Die wärmste Liebe zu unsrer litterarischen Ehe': Friedrich Schlegels *Lucinde* und Dorothea Veits *Florentin*." In *Bi-Textualität: Inszenierungen des Paares*, edited by Annegret Heitmann, 131–41. Berlin: Erich Schmidt, 2001.

———. "Dorothea Veit-Schlegel als Schriftstellerin und die Berliner Romantik." In *Arnim und die Berliner Romantik: Kunst, Literatur und Politik*, edited by Walter Pape, 123–34. Tübingen: Max Niemeyer, 2001.

———. "'Feminismus' und 'Emanzipation'? Zum Geschlechterdiskurs der deutschen Romantik am Beispiel der *Lucinde* und ihrer Rezeption." In *Salons der Romantik: Beiträge eines Wiepersdorfer Kolloquiums zu Theorie und Geschichte des Salons*, edited by Hartwig Schultz, 22–44. New York: Walter de Gruyter, 1997.

Beller, Steven. "Otto Weininger as Liberal?" In *Jews & Gender: Responses to Otto Weininger*, edited by Nancy A. Harrowitz and Barbara Hyams, 91–101. Philadelphia: Temple University Press, 1995.

———. *Vienna and the Jews, 1867–1938: A Cultural History*. New York: Cambridge University Press, 1989.

Benhabib, Seyla. *The Reluctant Modernism of Hannah Arendt*. Thousand Oaks, Calif.: Sage Publications, 1996.

Bernstein, Richard J. *Hannah Arendt and the Jewish Question*. Cambridge, Mass.: MIT Press, 1996.

Bhabha, Homi K. *The Location of Culture*. New York: Routledge, 1994.

Biale, David. *Eros and the Jews: From Biblical Israel to Contemporary America*. New York: Basic Books, 1992.

Biemann, Asher D. *Dreaming of Michelangelo: Jewish Variations on a Modern Theme*. Stanford, Calif.: Stanford University Press, 2012.

Bischof, Jakob. *Dina, das Judenmädchen aus Franken: Ein tragisches Familiengemälde*. Fürth: Bureau für Literatur, 1802.

Bischoff, Doerte. *Ausgesetzte Schöpfung: Figuren der Souveränität und Ethik der Differenz in der Prosa Else Lasker-Schülers*. Tübingen: Max Niemeyer, 2002.

Blumenthal, W. Michael. *The Invisible Wall: Germans and Jews; A Personal Exploration*. Washington, D.C.: Counterpoint, 1998.

Bohnert, Christiane. "Enlightenment and Despotism: Two Worlds in Lessing's *Nathan the Wise*." In *Impure Reason: Dialectic of Enlightenment in Germany*, edited by Daniel Wilson and Robert C. Holub, 344–61. Detroit: Wayne State University Press, 1993.

Braun, Christina von. "Antisemitismus und Misogynie: Vom Zusammenhang zweier Erscheinungen." In *Von einer Welt in die andere: Jüdinnen im 19. und 20. Jahrhundert*, edited by Jutta Dick and Barbara Hahn, 179–96. Vienna: Christian Brandstätter, 1993.

———. "*Blutschande:* From the Incest Taboo to the Nuremberg Racial Laws." In *Encountering the Other(s): Studies in Literature, History, and Culture*, edited by Gisela Brinker-Gabler, 127–48. Albany: State University of New York Press, 1995.

———. "Ist die Sexualwissenschaft eine 'jüdische Wissenschaft'? Säkularisierung und die Entstehung der Sexualwissenschaft." In *Preußens Himmel breitet seine Sterne . . . : Beiträge zur Kultur-, Politik- und Geistesgeschichte der Neuzeit*, vol. 2, edited by Willi Jasper and Joachim H. Knoll, 697–714. New York: Georg Olms, 2002.

———. "Zur Bedeutung der Sexualbilder im rassistischen Antisemitismus." In *Jüdische Kultur und Weiblichkeit in der Moderne*, edited by Inge Stephan, Sabine Schilling, and Sigrid Weigel, 23–49. Cologne: Böhlau, 1994.

Brenner, Michael. *The Renaissance of Jewish Culture in Weimar Germany*. New Haven, Conn.: Yale University Press, 1996.

Brunner, Otto, Werner Conze, and Reinhart Koselleck, eds. *Geschichtliche Grundbegriffe: Historisches Lexikon zur politisch-sozialen Sprache in Deutschland*. 8 vols. Stuttgart: Klett-Cotta, 1972–97.

Butler, Judith, Jürgen Habermas, Charles Taylor, and Cornel West. *The Power of Religion in the Public Sphere*. Edited by Eduardo Mendieta and Jonathan VanAntwerpen. New York: Columbia University Press, 2011.

Butler, Judith, Ernesto Laclau, and Slavoj Žižek. *Contingency, Hegemony, Universality: Contemporary Dialogues on the Left*. New York: Verso, 2000.

Caspary, Arpe. "Usumes Maske: Vom gesichterten und ungesichterten Schreiben." In *Aber ihr Ruf verhallt ins Leere hinein: Der Schriftsteller Georg Hermann (1871 Berlin–1943 Auschwitz)*, edited by Kerstin Schoor, 57–86. Berlin: Weidler, 1999.

Chamberlain, Houston Stewart. *Die Grundlagen des 19. Jahrhunderts*. 4th ed. Vol. 1. Munich: Bruckmann, 1903.

Coontz, Stephanie. *Marriage, a History: How Love Conquered Marriage*. New York: Penguin, 2006.

Daub, Adrian. *Uncivil Unions: The Metaphysics of Marriage in German Idealism and Romanticism*. Chicago: University of Chicago Press, 2012.

De Man, Paul. "The Rhetoric of Temporality." In *Blindness and Insight: Essays in the Rhetoric of Contemporary Criticism*, 2nd rev. ed., 187–228. Minneapolis: University of Minnesota Press, 1983.

Derrida, Jacques. *The Politics of Friendship*. Translated by George Collins. London: Verso, 1997.

Diner, Dan. "Negative Symbiosis: Germans and Jews after Auschwitz." In *The Holocaust: Theoretical Readings*, edited by Neil Levi and Michael Rothberg, 423–30. New Brunswick, N.J.: Rutgers University Press, 2003.

Dinter, Artur. *Die Sünde wider das Blut*. 1918. Leipzig: Matthes and Thost, 1920.

Dippel, John Van Houten. *Bound upon a Wheel of Fire: Why So Many German Jews Made the Tragic Decision to Remain in Nazi Germany*. New York: Basic Books, 1996.

Dohm, Christian Wilhelm von. "Concerning the Amelioration of the Civil Status of the Jews." In *The Jew in the Modern World: A Documentary* History, edited by Paul R. Mendes-Flohr and Jehuda Reinharz, 27–34. New York: Oxford University Press, 1980.

Duncan, Bruce. "Die Versöhnung in der Sommerfrische: Eine ungedruckte Erzählung Achim von Arnims." *Aurora* 40 (1980): 100–146.

Engelstein, Stefani. "The Allure of Wholeness: The Eighteenth-Century Organism and the Same-Sex Marriage Debate," *Critical Inquiry* 39, no. 4 (Summer 2013): 754–76.

——. "Civic Attachments & Sibling Attractions: The Shadows of Fraternity." *Goethe Yearbook* 18 (2011): 205–21.

——. *Sibling Action: The Genealogical Structure of Modernity*. New York: Columbia University Press, forthcoming.

——. "Sibling Incest and Cultural Voyeurism in Günderode's *Udohla* and Thomas Mann's *Wälsungenblut*." *The German Quarterly* 77, no. 3 (2004): 278–99.

Erb, Rainer, and Werner Bergmann. *Die Nachtseite der Judenemanzipation: Der Widerstand gegen die Integration der Juden in Deutschland 1780–1860*. Berlin: Metropol, 1989.

Erdle, Birgit. "'Über die Kennzeichen des Judenthums': Die Rhetorik der Unterscheidung in einem phantasmatischen Text von Achim von Arnim." *German Life and Letters* 49, no. 2 (1996): 147–58.

Erspamer, Peter R. *The Elusiveness of Tolerance: The "Jewish Question" from Lessing to the Napoleonic Wars*. Chapel Hill: University of North Carolina Press, 1997.

Euchel, Isaac. *Reb Henoch, oder, Woss tut me damit: Eine jüdische Komödie der Aufklärungszeit*. Edited by Marion Aptroot and Roland Gruschka. Hamburg: Helmut Buske, 2006.

Falk, Johann Daniel. "Der Jahrmarkt zu Plundersweilern." In *Die ästhetische Prügeley: Streitschriften der antiromantischen Bewegung*, edited by Rainer Schmitz, 81–114. Göttingen: Wallstein, 1992.

Feiner, Shmuel. *Moses Mendelssohn: Sage of Modernity*. Translated by Anthony Berris. New Haven, Conn.: Yale University Press, 2010.

Fischer, Barbara. *Nathans Ende? Von Lessing bis Tabori: Zur deutsch-jüdischen Rezeption von "Nathan der Weise."* Göttingen: Wallstein, 2000.

Foucault, Michel. *The History of Sexuality*. Vol. 1, *An Introduction*. Translated by Robert Hurley. New York: Pantheon, 1978.

Freud, Sigmund. *The Standard Edition of the Complete Psychological Works of Sigmund Freud*. Edited and translated by James Strachey. London: Hogarth Press, 1953–74.

Friedländer, David, Friedrich Schleiermacher, and Wilhelm Abraham Teller. *A Debate on Jewish Emancipation and Christian Theology in Old Berlin*. Edited and translated by Richard Crouter and Julie A. Klassen. Indianapolis: Hackett Publishing, 2004.

Friedrichsmeyer, Sara. *The Androgyne in Early German Romanticism: Friedrich Schlegel, Novalis, and the Metaphysics of Love*. New York: Peter Lang, 1983.

———. "Romantic Nationalism: Achim von Arnim's Gypsy Princess Isabella." In *Gender and Germanness: Cultural Productions of Nation*, edited by Patricia Herminghouse and Magda Mueller, 51–65. Providence: Berghahn Books, 1997.

Frühwald, Wolfgang. "Antijudaismus in der Zeit der deutschen Romantik." In *Conditio Judaica: Judentum, Antisemitismus und deutschsprachige Literatur vom 18. Jahrhundert bis zum Ersten Weltkrieg*, edited by Hans Otto Horch and Horst Denkler, 2:72–91. Tübingen: Max Niemeyer, 1989.

Fuhrmann, Inken. *Die Diskussion über die Einführung der fakultativen Zivilehe in Deutschland und Österreich seit Mitte des 19. Jahrhunderts*. Frankfurt am Main: Peter Lang, 1998.

Furst, Lilian R. *Fictions of Romantic Irony*. Cambridge, Mass.: Harvard University Press, 1984.

Garloff, Katja. "Femininity and Assimilatory Desire in Joseph Roth." *Modern Fiction Studies* 51, no. 2 (Summer 2005): 354–73.

———. "Figures of Love in Romantic Antisemitism." *The German Quarterly* 80, no. 4 (Fall 2007): 427–48.

———. "Interreligious Love in Contemporary German Film and Literature." In *Judaism, Christianity, and Islam: Collaboration and Conflict in the Age of Diaspora*, edited by Sander L. Gilman, 153–64. Hong Kong: University of Hong Kong Press, 2014.

———. "Kafka's Racial Melancholy." In *Kafka for the Twenty-First Century*, edited by Stanley Corngold and Ruth V. Gross, 89–104. New York: Camden House, 2011.

———. "Sublimation and Its Discontents: Christian-Jewish Love in Lessing's *Nathan der Weise*." *Lessing Yearbook* 36 (2004–5): 51–68.

———. "Unrequited Love: On the Rhetoric of a Trope from Moritz Goldstein to Hannah Arendt." *Nexus: Essays in German Jewish Studies* 1 (2011): 47–65.

Gay, Peter. *Freud, Jews, and Other Germans: Masters and Victims in Modernist Culture*. New York: Oxford University Press, 1978.

Geiger, Ludwig. "Henriette Jacoby." *Allgemeine Zeitung des Judentums* 72, no. 23 (1908): 271–73. http://sammlungen.ub.uni-frankfurt.de/cm/periodical/titleinfo/3228822.

———. "Jettchen Gebert." *Allgemeine Zeitung des Judentums* 70, no. 49 (1906): 585–87. http://sammlungen.ub.uni-frankfurt.de/cm/periodical/titleinfo/3228740.

Gelber, Mark H. *Melancholy Pride: Nation, Race, and Gender in the German Literature of Cultural Zionism*. Tübingen: Max Niemeyer, 2000.

Geller, Jay. "The Conventional Lies and Paradoxes of Jewish Assimilation: Max Nordau's Pre-Zionist Answer to the Jewish Question." *Jewish Social Studies* 1, no. 3 (Spring 1995): 129–60.

———. *On Freud's Jewish Body: Mitigating Circumcisions*. New York: Fordham University, Press, 2007.

Giddens, Anthony. *The Transformation of Intimacy: Sexuality, Love, and Eroticism in Modern Societies*. Stanford, Calif.: Stanford University Press, 1992.

Gillman, Abigail. *Viennese Jewish Modernism: Freud, Hofmannsthal, Beer-Hofmann, and Schnitzler*. University Park: Pennsylvania State University Press, 2009.

Gilman, Sander L. *Love + Marriage = Death: And Other Essays on Representing Difference*. Stanford, Calif.: Stanford University Press, 1998.

Goethe, Johann Wolfgang von. *The Sufferings of Young Werther*. Translated by Stanley Corngold. New York: W. W. Norton, 2012.

Goetschel, Willi. "Lessing and the Jews." In *A Companion to the Works of Gotthold Ephraim Lessing*, edited by Barbara Fischer and Thomas C. Fox, 185–210. Rochester, N.Y.: Camden House, 2005.

———. *Spinoza's Modernity: Mendelssohn, Lessing, and Heine*. Madison: University of Wisconsin Press, 2004.

Goldstein, Moritz. "Deutsch-Jüdischer Parnaß." *Der Kunstwart* 25, no. 11 (1912): 281–94.

Gordon, Peter Eli. *Rosenzweig and Heidegger: Between Judaism and German Philosophy*. Berkeley: University of California Press, 2003.

Graetz, Heinrich Hirsch. *History of the Jews*. Vol. 5. Philadelphia: Jewish Publication Society of America, 1895.

Grimm, Jacob, and Wilhelm Grimm. *Deutsches Wörterbuch*. 33 vols. Leipzig: S. Hirzel, 1854–1961. http://dwb.uni-trier.de/de/.

Guenther, Christina. "Exile and the Construction of Identity in Barbara Honigmann's Trilogy of the Diaspora." *Comparative Literature Studies* 40, no. 2 (2003): 215–31.

Gustafson, Susan E. *Absent Mothers and Orphaned Fathers: Narcissism and Abjection in Lessing's Aesthetic and Dramatic Production*. Detroit: Wayne State University Press, 1995.

Habermas, Jürgen. *An Awareness of What Is Missing: Faith and Reason in a Post-Secular Age*. Translated by Ciaran Cronin. Malden, Mass.: Polity Press, 2010.

———. "Pre-Political Foundations of the Democratic Constitutional State?" In *Dialectics of Secularization: On Reason and Religion*, edited by Florian Schuller, translated by Brian McNeil, 19–52. San Francisco: Ignatius Press, 2006.

Hacohen, Malachi Haim. *Jacob and Esau: Jewish European History between Nation and Empire*. New York: Cambridge University Press, forthcoming.

Hahn, Barbara. *The Jewess Pallas Athena: This Too a Theory of Modernity*. Translated by James McFarland. Princeton, N.J.: Princeton University Press, 2005.

Hallensleben, Markus. *Else Lasker-Schüler: Avantgardismus und Kunstinszenierung*. Tübingen: Francke, 2000.

Halle-Wolfssohn, Aaron. *Leichtsinn und Frömmelei: Ein Familiengemälde in drei Aufzügen*. Edited by Gunnar Och and Jutta Strauss. St. Ingbert: Röhrig, 1995.

Harden, Maximilian. "Sem." In *Apostata: Neue Folge*, 155–56. Berlin: Stilke, 1893.

Härtl, Heinz. "Romantischer Antisemitismus: Arnim und die 'Tischgesellschaft.'" *Weimarer Beiträge* 33, no. 7 (1987): 1159–73.

Hartwich, Wolf-Daniel. *Romantischer Antisemitismus: Von Klopstock bis Richard Wagner*. Göttingen: Vandenhoeck and Ruprecht, 2005.

Hegel, Georg Wilhelm Friedrich. "The Spirit of Christianity and Its Fate." In *On Christianity: Early Theological Writings by Friedrich Hegel*, translated by T. M. Knox, 182–301. Gloucester, Mass.: Peter Smith, 1970.

Helfer, Martha B. "'Confessions of an Improper Man': Friedrich Schlegel's *Lucinde*." In *Outing Goethe and His Age*, edited by Alice Kuzniar, 174–93. Stanford, Calif.: Stanford University Press, 1996.

———. "Dorothea Veit-Schlegel's *Florentin*: Constructing a Feminist Romantic Aesthetic." *The German Quarterly* 69, no. 2 (1996): 144–60.

———. *The Word Unheard: Legacies of Anti-Semitism in German Literature and Culture*. Evanston, Ill.: Northwestern University Press, 2011.

Henckmann, Gisela. "Das Problem des 'Antisemitismus' bei Achim von Arnim." *Aurora* 46 (1986): 48–69.

Henel, Heinrich. "Arnims Majoratsherren." In *Romantikforschung seit 1945*, edited by Klaus Peter et al., 145–67. Königstein: Athenäum, Hain, Scriptor, Hanstein, 1980.

Hermann, Georg. "Camille Pisarro." *Ost und West* 4, no. 1 (1904): 13–22. http://sammlungen. ub.uni-frankfurt.de/cm/periodical/titleinfo/2589658

——. "Max Liebermann." In *Juedische Kuenstler*, edited by Martin Buber, 107–35. Berlin: Juedischer Verlag, 1903.

——. "Max Liebermann." *Ost und West* 3, no. 6 (1903): 377–98. http://sammlungen.ub.uni-frankfurt.de/cm/periodical/titleinfo/2587257

——. *Werke und Briefe: Henriette Jacoby.* Edited by Gert Mattenklott and Gundel Mattenklott. Vol. 3. Berlin: Das Neue Berlin, 1998.

——. *Werke und Briefe: Jettchen Gebert.* Edited by Gert Mattenklott and Gundel Mattenklott. Vol. 2. Berlin: Das Neue Berlin, 1998.

Hertz, Deborah Sadie. *How Jews Became Germans: The History of Conversion and Assimilation in Berlin.* New Haven, Conn.: Yale University Press, 2007.

——. *Jewish High Society in Old Regime Berlin.* 2nd ed. Syracuse, N.Y.: Syracuse University Press, 2005.

Herzl, Theodor. *The Jewish State.* Based on a revised translation published by Scopus Publishing. Further revised and edited by Jacob M. Alkow. New York: Dover Publications, 1988.

Hess, Jonathan M. "Fictions of a German-Jewish Public: Ludwig Jacobowski's *Werther the Jew* and Its Readers." *Jewish Social Studies* 11, no. 2 (2005): 202–30.

——. *Germans, Jews, and the Claims of Modernity.* New Haven, Conn.: Yale University Press, 2002.

——. "Lessing and German-Jewish Culture: A Reappraisal." In *Lessing and the German Enlightenment,* edited by Ritchie Robertson, 179–204. Oxford: Voltaire Foundation, 2013.

——. *Middlebrow Literature and the Making of German-Jewish Identity.* Stanford, Calif.: Stanford University Press, 2010.

Hoffmann, Volker. "Künstliche Zeugung und Zeugung von Kunst im Erzählwerk Achim von Arnims." *Aurora* 46 (1986): 158–67.

Holland, Jocelyn. "*Lucinde*: The Novel from 'Nothing' as Epideictic Literature." *Germanisch-Romanische Monatsschrift* 54, no. 2 (2004): 163–76.

Honigmann, Barbara. *Alles, alles Liebe.* Munich: Carl Hanser, 2000.

——. *Damals, dann, danach.* Munich: Carl Hanser, 1999.

——. *Eine Liebe aus nichts.* Reinbek: Rowohlt, 1993.

——. *A Love Made Out of Nothing* and *Zohara's Journey.* Translated by John Barrett. Jaffrey, N.H.: Godine, 2003.

——. "On My Great-Grandfather, My Grandfather, My Father, and Me." Translated by Meghan W. Barnes. *World Literature Today* 69, no. 3 (1995): 512–16.

Horch, Hans-Otto. "Über Georg Hermann: Plädoyer zur Wiederentdeckung eines bedeutenden deutsch-jüdischen Schriftstellers." *Bulletin des Leo Baeck Instituts* 77 (1987): 73–94.

Horowitz, Sara R. "Lovin' Me, Lovin' Jew: Gender, Intermarriage, and Metaphor." In *Antisemitisim and Philosemitism in the Twentieth and Twenty-First Centuries: Representing Jews, Jewishness, and Modern Culture,* edited by Phyllis Lassner and Lara Trubowitz, 196–216. Newark: University of Delaware Press, 2010.

Hull, Isabel V. *Sexuality, State, and Civil Society in Germany, 1700–1815.* Ithaca, N.Y.: Cornell University Press, 1996.

Jacobowski, Ludwig. *Gesammelte Werke in einem Band: Jubiläumsausgabe zum 100. Todestag.* Edited by Alexander Müller and Michael Matthias Schardt. Oldenburg: Igel Verlag Literatur, 2000.

Janik, Allan. "Weininger's Vienna: The Sex-Ridden Society." In *Vienna: The World of Yesterday, 1889–1914,* edited by Stephen Eric Bronner and F. Peter Wagner, 43–62. Atlantic Highlands, N.J.: Humanities Press, 1997.

Jellinek, Adolph. *Der jüdische Stamm: Ethnographische Studien.* Vienna: Herzfeld and Bauer, 1869.

Jenisch, Daniel. *Diogenes Laterne.* Leipzig, 1799.

Kampits, Peter. "Otto Weininger und das Sein zum Tode." In *Otto Weininger: Werk und Wirkung,* edited by Jacques Le Rider and Norbert Leser, 167–77. Vienna: Österreichischer Bundesverlag, 1984.

Kaplan, Benjamin J. *Divided by Faith: Religious Conflict and the Practice of Toleration in Early Modern Europe.* Cambridge, Mass.: Harvard University Press, 2007.

Katz, Jacob. *Tradition and Crisis: Jewish Society at the End of the Middle Ages.* Translated by Bernard Dov Cooperman. New York: New York University Press, 1993.

Kittler, Wolf. *Die Geburt des Partisanen aus dem Geist der Poesie: Heinrich von Kleist und die Strategie der Befreiungskriege.* Freiburg: Rombach, 1987.

Kluckhohn, Paul. *Die Auffassung der Liebe in der Literatur des 18. Jahrhunderts und in der deutschen Romantik.* 3rd ed. Tübingen: Max Niemeyer, 1966.

Knaack, Jürgen. *Achim von Arnim—nicht nur Poet: Die politischen Anschauungen Arnims in ihrer Entwicklung.* Darmstadt: Thesen, 1976.

Koepnick, Lutz. "Reframing the Past: Heritage Cinema and Holocaust in the 1990s." *New German Critique* 87 (2002): 47–82.

Kraus, Karl. *Die Fackel* 11 (1899). http://corpus1.aac.ac.at/fackel/.

Kremer, Detlef. "Kabbalistische Signaturen: Sprachmagie als Brennpunkt romantischer Imagination bei E. T. A. Hoffmann und Achim von Arnim." In *Kabbala und die Literatur der Romantik: Zwischen Magie und Trope,* edited by Eveline Goodman-Thau, Gert Mattenklott, and Christoph Schulte, 197–221. Tübingen: Max Niemeyer, 1999.

Krobb, Florian. *Die schöne Jüdin: Jüdische Frauengestalten in der deutschsprachigen Erzählliteratur vom 17. Jahrhundert bis zum Ersten Weltkrieg.* Tübingen: Max Niemeyer, 1993.

Laclau, Ernesto, and Chantal Mouffe. *Hegemony and Socialist Strategy: Towards a Radical Democratic Politics.* 2nd ed. New York: Verso, 2014.

Landgraf, Edgar. "Romantic Love and the Enlightenment: From Gallantry and Seduction to Authenticity and Self-Validation." *The German Quarterly* 77, no. 1 (Winter 2004): 29–46.

Langmuir, Gavin I. *Toward a Definition of Antisemitism.* Berkeley: University of California Press, 1990.

Lasker-Schüler, Else. *Gesichte: Essays und andere Geschichten.* Berlin: Paul Cassirer, 1913.

——. *Hebrew Ballads and Other Poems.* Translated by Audri Durchslag and Jeanette Litman-Demeestère. Philadelphia: Jewish Publication Society of America, 1980.

——. *Star in My Forehead: Selected Poems.* Translated by Janine Canan. Duluth, Minn.: Holy Cow! Press, 2000.

——. *Werke und Briefe: Kritische Ausgabe.* Edited by Norbert Oellers, Heinz Rölleke, and Itta Shedletzky. 11 vols. Frankfurt am Main: Jüdischer Verlag im Suhrkamp Verlag, 1996–2010.

——. "The Wonder-Working Rabbi of Barcelona." In *The German-Jewish Dialogue: An Anthology of Literary Texts, 1749–1993,* edited and translated by Ritchie Robertson, 224–32. New York: Oxford University Press, 1999.

Le Rider, Jacques. *Modernity and Crises of Identity: Culture and Society in Fin-de-Siècle Vienna.* Translated by Rosemary Morris. New York: Continuum, 1993.

Lessing, Gotthold Ephraim. *Nathan the Wise.* Translated by Ronald Schechter. Boston: Bedford/St. Martins, 2004.

———. *Nathan the Wise, Minna von Barnhelm, and Other Plays and Writings*. Edited by Peter Demetz. New York: Continuum, 1991.

———. *Werke*. Edited by Herbert G. Göpfert. 8 vols. Munich: Carl Hanser, 1970–79.

Levenson, Alan T. "Jewish Reactions to Intermarriage in Nineteenth-Century Germany." PhD diss., Ohio State University, 1990.

Lévi-Strauss, Claude. *The Elementary Structures of Kinship*. Translated by James Harle Bell, John Richard von Sturmer, and Rodney Needham. Rev. ed. Boston: Beacon Press, 1969.

Lezzi, Eva. "'. . . ewig rein wie die heilige Jungfrau . . .' Zur Enthüllung des Jüdschen in der Rezeption von deutschsprachigen Romanen um 1800." In *Juden und Judentum in der deutschsprachigen Literatur*, edited by Willi Jasper, Eva Lezzi, Elke Liebs, and Helmut Peitsch, 61–86. Wiesbaden: Harrassowitz, 2006.

———. *"Liebe ist meine Religion!": Eros und Ehe zwischen Juden und Christen in der Literatur des 19. Jahrhunderts*. Göttingen: Wallstein, 2013.

Librett, Jeffrey S. *The Rhetoric of Cultural Dialogue: Jews and Germans from Moses Mendelssohn to Richard Wagner and Beyond*. Stanford, Calif.: Stanford University Press, 2000.

Lipphardt, Veronika. *Biologie der Juden: Jüdische Wissenschaftler über "Rasse" und Vererbung 1900–1935*. Göttingen: Vandenhoeck and Ruprecht, 2008.

Lotich, Johann Karl. *Wer war wohl mehr Jude?* Leipzig: Friedrich Gotthold Jacobäer, 1783.

Lowenstein, Steven M. *The Berlin Jewish Community: Enlightenment, Family, and Crisis, 1770–1830*. New York: Oxford University Press, 1994.

———. "Jewish Intermarriage and Conversion in Germany and Austria." *Modern Judaism* 25, no. 1 (2005): 23–61.

Luft, David S. *Eros and Inwardness in Vienna: Weininger, Musil, Doderer*. Chicago: University of Chicago Press, 2003.

Luhmann, Niklas. *Love as Passion: The Codification of Intimacy*. Translated by Jeremy Gaines and Doris L. Jones. Stanford, Calif.: Stanford University Press, 1998.

Lund, Hannah Lotte. *Der Berliner "jüdische Salon" um 1800: Emanzipation in der Debatte*. Berlin and Boston: Walter De Gruyter, 2012.

Mack, Michael. *German Idealism and the Jew: The Inner Anti-Semitism of Philosophy and German Jewish Responses*. Chicago: University of Chicago Press, 2003.

Marcuse, Ludwig. *Obszön: Geschichte einer Entrüstung*. Munich: Paul List, 1962.

Marcuse, Max. *Vom Inzest*. Halle: Carl Marhold Verlagsbuchhandlung, 1915.

Matysik, Tracie. *Reforming the Moral Subject: Ethics and Sexuality in Central Europe, 1890–1930*. Ithaca, N.Y.: Cornell University Press, 2008.

Meir, Ephraim. *Letters of Love: Franz Rosenzweig's Spiritual Biography and Oeuvre in Light of the Gritli Letters*. New York: Peter Lang, 2006.

Meiring, Kerstin. *Die christlich-jüdische Mischehe in Deutschland 1840–1933*. Hamburg: Dölling und Galitz, 1998.

Mendelssohn, Moses. *Brautbriefe*. Berlin: Schocken, 1936.

———. *Gesammelte Schriften: Jubiläumsausgabe*. Edited by Alexander Altmann, Michael Brocke, Daniel Krochmalnik, and Eva J. Engel. 39 vols. Stuttgart-Bad Cannstatt: Frommann-Holzboog, 1972–.

———. *Jerusalem, or on Religious Power and Judaism*. Translated by Allan Arkush. Hanover, N.H.: University Press of New England, 1983.

———. *Writings on Judaism, Christianity, and the Bible*. Edited by Michah Gottlieb. Lebanon, N.H.: Brandeis University Press, 2011.

Mendelssohn Veit Schlegel, Dorothea. *Florentin: A Novel*. Translated by Edwina Lawler and Ruth Richardson. Lewiston: Edwin Mellen Press, 1988.

Mendes-Flohr, Paul R. *Divided Passions: Jewish Intellectuals and the Experience of Modernity*. Detroit: Wayne State University Press, 1991.

——. "Franz Rosenzweig and the Crisis of Historicism." In *The Philosophy of Franz Rosenzweig*, edited by Paul R. Mendes-Flohr, 138–61. Hanover, N.H.: University Press of New England, 1988.

——. *German Jews: A Dual Identity*. New Haven, Conn.: Yale University Press, 1999.

Meyer, Beate. "Geschichte im Film: Judenverfolgung, Mischehen und der Protest in der Rosenstraße 1943." *Zeitschrift für Geschichtswissenschaft* 1 (2004): 23–36.

Meyer, Imke. *Männlichkeit und Melodram: Arthur Schnitzlers erzählende Schriften*. Würzburg: Königshausen and Neumann, 2010.

Meyer, Michael A., ed., with the assistance of Michael Brenner. *German-Jewish History in Modern Times*. 4 vols. New York: Columbia University Press, 1996–98.

Michaelis, Johann David. "Arguments against Dohm." In *The Jew in the Modern World: A Documentary History*, edited by Paul R. Mendes-Flohr and Jehuda Reinharz, 36–38. New York: Oxford University Press, 1980.

Miller, Cristanne. "Reading the Politics of Else Lasker-Schüler's 1914 *Hebrew Ballads*." *Modernism/Modernity* 6, no. 2 (1999): 135–59.

Miron, Dan. *From Continuity to Contiguity: Toward a New Jewish Literary Thinking*. Stanford, Calif.: Stanford University Press, 2010.

Mosès, Stéphane. *The Angel of History: Rosenzweig, Benjamin, Scholem*. Translated by Barbara Harshaw. Stanford, Calif.: Stanford University Press, 2009.

——. "On the Correspondence between Franz Rosenzweig and Eugen Rosenstock-Huessy." In *The German-Jewish Dialogue Reconsidered: A Symposium in Honor of George L. Mosse*, edited by Klaus L. Berghahn, 109–23. New York: Peter Lang, 1996.

Moßmann, Susanna. "Das Fremde ausscheiden: Antisemitismus und Nationalbewußtsein bei Ludwig Achim von Arnim und in der 'Christlich-deutschen Tischgesellschaft.'" In *Machtphantasie Deutschland: Nationalismus, Männlichkeit und Fremdenhass im Vaterlandsdiskurs deutscher Schriftsteller des 18. Jahrhunderts*, edited by Hans Peter Herrmann, Hans-Martin Blitz, and Susanna Moßmann, 123–59. Frankfurt am Main: Suhrkamp, 1996.

Mücke, Dorothea E. von. *The Seduction of the Occult and the Rise of the Fantastic Tale*. Stanford, Calif.: Stanford University Press, 2003.

Nielaba, Daniel Müller. "'Die arme Recha, die indes verbrannte!' Zur Kombustibilität der Bedeutung in Lessings *Nathan der Weise*." In *Neues zur Lessing-Forschung: Ingrid Strohschneider-Kohrs zu Ehren am 26. August 1997*, edited by Eva J. Engel and Claus Ritterhoff, 105–25. Tübingen: Max Niemeyer, 1998.

Nienhaus, Stefan. *Geschichte der deutschen Tischgesellschaft*. Tübingen: Max Niemeyer, 2003.

Nietzsche, Friedrich Wilhelm. *On the Genealogy of Morality*. Translated by Maudemarie Clark and Alan J. Swensen. Indianapolis: Hackett Publishing, 1998.

Nordau, Max. *Die conventionellen Lügen der Kulturmenschheit*. Leipzig: B. Elischer Nachfolger, 1883.

——. *Doktor Kohn: Bürgerliches Trauerspiel aus der Gegenwart in vier Aufzügen*. 2nd ed. Berlin: Ernst Hofmann, 1899.

——. *Erinnerungen*. Translated by S. O. Fangor. Leipzig: Renaissance, 1928.

——. *Zionistische Schriften*. 2nd expanded ed. Berlin: Jüdischer Verlag, 1923.

Och, Gunnar. "'Gewisse Zauberbilder der jüdischen Kabbala'—zur Aneignung kabbalist-ischer Stoffe bei Achim von Arnim und Clemens Brentano." In *Kabbala und die Literatur der Romantik: Zwischen Magie und Trope*, edited by Eveline Goodman-Thau, Gert Matten-klott, and Christoph Schulte, 179–95. Tübingen: Max Niemeyer, 1999.

Oesmann, Astrid. "*Nathan der Weise*: Suffering Lessing's 'Erziehung.'" *Germanic Review* 74, no. 2 (Spring 1999): 131–45.

Oesterle, Günter. "'Illegitime Kreuzungen': Zur Ikonität und Temporalität des Grotesken in Achim von Arnim's *Die Majoratsherren*." *Études Germaniques* 43, no. 1 (March 1988): 25–51.

———. "Juden, Philister und romantische Intellektuelle: Überlegungen zum Antisemitismus in der Romantik." *Athenäum* 2 (1992): 55–91.

Panizza, Oskar. "The Operated Jew." In Jack Zipes, *The Operated Jew: Two Tales of Anti-Semitism*, 47–74. New York: Routledge, 1991.

Parkinson, Anna M. "Neo-feminist *Mütterfilm*? The Emotional Politics of Margarethe von Trotta's *Rosenstrasse*." In *The Collapse of Conventional German Film and Its Politics at the Turn of the Twenty-First Century*, edited by Jaimey Fisher and Brad Prager, 109–35. Detroit: Wayne State University Press, 2010.

Pateman, Carole. *The Sexual Contract*. Stanford, Calif.: Stanford University Press, 1988.

Perry, Ruth. *Novel Relations: The Transformation of Kinship in English Literature and Culture, 1748–1818*. New York: Cambridge University Press, 2004.

Pnevmonidou, Elena. "Die Absage an das romantische Ich: Dorothea Schlegels *Florentin* als Umschrift von Friedrich Schlegels *Lucinde*." *German Life and Letters* 58, no. 3 (2005): 271–92.

Presner, Todd S. *Mobile Modernity: Germans, Jews, Trains*. New York: Columbia University Press, 2007.

Puschner, Marco. *Antisemitismus im Kontext der politischen Romantik: Konstruktionen des "Deutschen" und des "Jüdischen" bei Arnim, Brentano und Saul Ascher*. Tübingen: Max Niemeyer, 2008.

Ragins, Sanford. *Jewish Responses to Anti-Semitism in Germany, 1870–1914: A Study in the History of Ideas*. Cincinnati: Hebrew Union College Press, 1980.

Reinhard, Kenneth. "The Ethics of the Neighbor: Universalism, Particularism, Exceptionalism." *Journal of Textual Reasoning* 4, no. 1 (November 2005): 1–21.

———. "Universalism and the Jewish Exception: Lacan, Badiou, Rosenzweig." *Umbr(a): A Journal of the Unconscious* 1 (2005): 43–71.

Reitter, Paul. *On the Origins of Jewish Self-Hatred*. Princeton, N.J.: Princeton University Press, 2012.

Richarz, Monika. "Demographic Developments." In *German-Jewish History in Modern Times*, edited by Michael A. Meyer, with the assistance of Michael Brenner, 3:734. New York: Columbia University Press, 1996.

Riedl, Peter Philipp. "'. . . das ist ein ewig Schachern und Zänken . . .': Achim von Arnims Haltung zu den Juden in den Majorats-Herren und anderen Schriften." *Aurora* 54 (1994): 72–105.

Robertson, Ritchie. "Historicizing Weininger: The Nineteenth-Century German Image of the Feminized Jew." In *Modernity, Culture, and "the Jew,"* edited by Bryan Cheyette and Laura Marcus, 23–39. Stanford, Calif.: Stanford University Press, 1998.

———. *The "Jewish Question" in German Literature, 1749–1939: Emancipation and Its Discontents*. New York: Oxford University Press, 1999.

Rodlauer, Hannelore. "Fragments from Weininger's Education (1895–1902)." In *Jews & Gender: Responses to Otto Weininger*, edited by Nancy A. Harrowitz and Barbara Hyams, 35–58. Philadelphia: Temple University Press, 1995.

Rosenzweig, Franz. *Der Mensch und sein Werk: Gesammelte Schriften* I, *Briefe und Tagebücher*. Vol. 2, *1918–1929*. Edited by Rachel Rosenzweig and Edith Rosenzweig-Scheinmann, with the cooperation of Bernhard Casper. The Hague: Martinus Nijhoff, 1979.

———. *Der Mensch und sein Werk: Gesammelte Schriften* III, *Zweistromland: Kleinere Schriften zu Glauben und Denken*. Edited by Reinhold Mayer and Annemarie Mayer. Dordrecht: Martinus Nijhoff, 1984.

———. *Der Stern der Erlösung*. 3rd ed. Frankfurt am Main: Suhrkamp, 1990.

———. *Die "Gritli"-Briefe: Briefe an Margrit Rosenstock-Huessy*. Edited by Inken Rühle and Reinhold Mayer. Tübingen: Bilam, 2002.

———. *The Gritli Letters (Gritli Briefe)*. Transcribed by Ulrike von Moltke. Edited by Michael Gormann-Thelen and Elfriede Büchsel. http://www.argobooks.org/gritli/.

———. *The Star of Redemption*. Translated by William Hallo. Notre Dame, Ind.: University of Notre Dame Press, 1985.

Rozenblit, Marsha L. *The Jews of Vienna, 1867–1914: Assimilation and Identity*. Albany: State University of New York Press, 1983.

Sanders-Brahms, Helma. *Mein Herz—Niemandem!* Helma Sanders-Brahms Filmproduktion GmbH, 1997. (Film.)

Santner, Eric L. "Miracles Happen: Benjamin, Rosenzweig, Freud, and the Matter of the Neighbor." In *The Neighbor: Three Inquiries in Political Theology*, by Slavoj Žižek, Eric Santner, and Kenneth Reinhard, 76–133. Chicago: University of Chicago Press, 2005.

———. *On the Psychotheology of Everyday Life: Reflections on Freud and Rosenzweig*. Chicago: University of Chicago Press, 2001.

Sasse, Günter. *Die aufgeklärte Familie: Untersuchungen zur Genese, Funktion und Realitätsbezogenheit des familialen Wertsystems im Drama der Aufklärung*. Tübingen: Max Niemeyer, 1988.

Schlegel, Dorothea. *Dorothea v. Schlegel geb. Mendelssohn und deren Söhne Johannes und Philipp Veit: Briefwechsel*. Edited by J. M. Raich. Mainz: Franz von Kirchheim, 1881.

———. *Florentin*. Edited by Wolfgang Nehring. Stuttgart: Reclam, 1993.

———. *Florentin: A Novel*. Translated by Edwina Lawler and Ruth Richardson. Lewiston, N.Y.: Edwin Mellen Press, 1988.

———. *Florentin: Roman, Fragmente, Varianten*. Edited by Liliane Weissberg. Berlin, Ullstein, 1987.

Schlegel, Friedrich. *Friedrich Schlegel's "Lucinde" and the Fragments*. Translated by Peter Firchow. Minneapolis: University of Minnesota Press, 1971.

———. *Friedrich Schlegel: Kritische Ausgabe seiner Werke*. Edited by Ernst Behler, with the collaboration of Jean-Jacques Anstett and Hans Eichner. Paderborn: Schöningh, 1958–.

Schleiermacher, Friedrich. *On Religion: Speeches to Its Cultured Despisers*. Translated and edited by Richard Crouter. New York: Cambridge University Press, 1996.

Schmitz, Rainer, ed. *Die ästhetische Prügeley: Streitschriften der antiromantischen Bewegung*. Göttingen: Wallstein, 1992.

Schneider, Helmut J. "Der Zufall der Geburt: Lessings *Nathan der Weise* und der imaginäre Körper der Geschichtsphilosophie." In *Körper/Kultur: Kalifornische Studien zur deutschen Moderne*, edited by Thomas W. Kniesche, 100–124. Würzburg: Königshausen and Neumann, 1995.

Schnitzler, Arthur. *Der Weg ins Freie*. Frankfurt am Main: Fischer Taschenbuch, 1990.

———. *The Road into the Open.* Translated by Roger Byers. Berkeley: University of California Press, 1992.

———. *Tagebuch.* Edited by Werner Welzig et al. 10 vols. Vienna: Verlag der Österreichischen Akademie der Wissenschaften, 1981.

Scholem, Gershom. *On Jews and Judaism in Crisis: Selected Essays.* Edited by Werner J. Dannhauser. New York: Schocken, 1976.

———. *Von Berlin nach Jerusalem: Jugenderinnerungen.* Frankfurt am Main: Suhrkamp, 1977.

Schulte, Christoph. *Psychopathologie des Fin de siècle: Der Kulturkritiker, Arzt und Zionist Max Nordau.* Frankfurt am Main: Fischer Taschenbuch, 1997.

Şenocak, Zafer. "Mein Erbe spricht auch Deutsch: Vergessene deutsch-türkische Verwandtschaften." In *Deutschsein: Eine Aufklärungsschrift*, 172–90. Hamburg: Edition Körber-Stiftung, 2011.

Shapiro, Susan E. "The Status of Women and Jews in Moses Mendelssohn's Social Contract Theory: An Exceptional Case." *The German Quarterly* 82, no. 3 (Summer 2009): 373–94.

Sigusch, Volkmar. *Geschichte der Sexualwissenschaft.* Frankfurt am Main: Campus, 2008.

Simplicissimus. "Ueber Mischehen und jüdisch-nationale Gesinnung." *Jüdische Rundschau* 18 (May 1904): 189–90. http://sammlungen.ub.uni-frankfurt.de/cm/periodical/titleinfo/2651360.

Skolnik, Jonathan. *Jewish Pasts, German Fictions: History, Memory, and Minority Culture in Germany, 1824–1955.* Stanford, Calif.: Stanford University Press, 2014.

Sombart, Werner. *Die Zukunft der Juden.* Leipzig: Duncker and Humblot, 1912.

Sombart, Werner, et al. *Judentaufen.* Munich: Georg Müller, 1912.

Sorkin, David. "Emancipation and Assimilation: Two Concepts and Their Application to German-Jewish History." *Leo Baeck Institute Yearbook* 35 (1990): 17–33.

———. *Moses Mendelssohn and the Religious Enlightenment.* Berkeley: University of California Press, 1996.

———. *The Transformation of German Jewry, 1780–1840.* New York: Oxford University Press, 1987.

Spector, Scott. "Forget Assimilation: Introducing Subjectivity to German-Jewish History." *Jewish History* 20, nos. 3–4 (2006): 349–61.

Stanislawski, Michael. *Zionism and the Fin-de-Siècle: Cosmopolitanism and Nationalism from Nordau to Jabotinsky.* Berkeley: University of California Press, 2001.

Steinberg, Karl. "Menschen und Menschen Situationen, oder die Familie Grunau." *Deutsche Schaubühne* 4 (1792): 1–180.

Stephan, Inge. "Weibliche und männliche Autorschaft: Zum *Florentin* von Dorothea Schlegel und zur *Lucinde* von Friedrich Schlegel." In *"Wen kümmert's, wer spricht": Zur Literatur und Kulturgeschichte von Frauen aus Ost und West*, edited by Inge Stephan, Sigrid Weigel, and Kerstin Wilhelms, 83–98. Cologne: Böhlau, 1991.

Stern, Carola. *"Ich möchte mir Flügel wünschen": Das Leben der Dorothea Schlegel.* Reinbek bei Hamburg: Rowohlt, 1990.

Stern, Fred B. *Ludwig Jacobowski: Persönlichkeit und Werk eines Dichters.* Darmstadt: Joseph Melzer, 1966.

Stieglitz, Charlotte. *Geschichte eines Denkmals.* Edited by Susanne Ledanff. Frankfurt am Main: Ullstein, 1986.

Stoltzfus, Nathan. *Resistance of the Heart: Intermarriage and the Rosenstrasse Protest in Nazi Germany.* New York: W.W. Norton, 1996.

Suchy, Barbara. "The *Verein zur Abwehr des Antisemitismus* (I): From Its Beginnings to the First World War." *Leo Baeck Institute Yearbook* 28 (1983): 205–39.

Szondi, Peter. "Friedrich Schlegel and Romantic Irony, with some Remarks on Tieck's Comedies." In *On Textual Understanding and Other Essays*, translated by Harvey Mendelsohn, 57–73. Minneapolis: University of Minnesota Press, 1986.

Taylor, Michael Thomas. "Same/Sex: Incest and Friendship in Lessing's *Nathan der Weise*." *Seminar* 48, no. 3 (2012): 333–47.

———. "'Was heißt Aufklärung?' Eine Fußnote zur Ehekrise." In *Vor der Familie: Grenzbedingungen einer modernen Institution*, by Albrecht Koschorke et al., 51–95. Munich: Konstanz University Press/Wilhelm Fink, 2010.

Theisen, Bianca. "Chaos—Ordnung." In *Ästhetische Grundbegriffe: Historisches Wörterbuch in sieben Bänden*, edited by K. H. Barck, 751–71. Stuttgart: Metzler, 2000.

Treitschke, Heinrich von. "Noch einige Bemerkungen zur Judenfrage." In *Der Berliner Antisemitismusstreit*, edited by Walter Boehlich, 77–90. Frankfurt am Main: Insel, 1965.

Urang, John Griffith. *Legal Tender: Love and Legitimacy in the East German Cultural Imagination*. Ithaca, N.Y.: Cornell University Press, 2010.

van Liere, Cornelis Geerard. *Georg Hermann: Materialien zur Kenntnis seines Lebens und seines Werkes*. Amsterdam: Rodopi, 1974.

van Rahden, Till. "Verrat, Schicksal oder Chance: Lesarten des Assimilationsbegriffs in der Historiographie zur Geschichte der deutschen Juden." *Historische Anthropologie* 13, no. 2 (2005): 245–64.

———. "Weder Milieu noch Konfession: Die situative Ethnizität der deutschen Juden im Kaiserreich in vergleichender Perspektive." In *Religion im Kaiserreich: Milieus—Mentalitäten—Krisen*, edited by Olaf Blaschke and Frank-Michael Kuhlemann, 409–34. Gütersloh: Gütersloher Verlagshaus, 1996.

Volkov, Shulamit. *Germans, Jews, and Antisemites: Trials in Emancipation*. New York: Cambridge University Press, 2006.

Wassermann, Jakob. *Die Juden von Zirndorf*. Munich: Albert Langen, 1897.

———. *My Life as German and Jew*. Translated by Salomea Neumark Brainin. New York: Coward-McCann, 1933.

Weigel, Sigrid. "Wider die romantische Mode: Zur ästhetischen Funktion des Weiblichen in Friedrich Schlegels *Lucinde*." In *Die verborgene Frau: Sechs Beiträge zu einer feministischen Literaturwissenschaft*, 67–82. Berlin: Argument, 1983.

Weil, Kari. *Androgyny and the Denial of Difference*. Charlottesville: University Press of Virginia, 1992.

Weininger, Otto. *Sex and Character: An Investigation of Fundamental Principles*. Translated by Ladislaub Löb. Bloomington: Indiana University Press, 2005.

Weissberg, Liliane. Afterword to *Florentin: Roman, Fragmente, Varianten*, by Dorothea Veit. Berlin: Ullstein, 1987.

———. "Introduction: Hannah Arendt, Rahel Varnhagen, and the Writing of (Auto)biography)." In Hannah Arendt, *Rahel Varnhagen: The Life of a Jewess*, edited by Liliane Weissberg, translated by Richard Winston and Clara Winston, 3–69. Baltimore: Johns Hopkins University Press, 1997.

———. "Schreiben als Selbstentwurf: Zu den Schriften Rahel Varnhagens und Dorothea Schlegels." *Zeitschrift für Religions- und Geistesgeschichte* 47, no. 3 (1995): 231–53.

Wilson, W. Daniel. *Humanität und Kreuzzugsideologie um 1780: Die "Türkenoper" im 18. Jahrhundert und das Rettungsmotiv in Wielands "Oberon," Lessings "Nathan" und Goethes "Iphigenie."* New York: Peter Lang, 1984.

Wistrich, Robert S. *The Jews of Vienna in the Age of Franz Joseph*. New York: Oxford University Press, 1989.

Young-Bruehl, Elisabeth. *Hannah Arendt, for Love of the World*. New Haven, Conn.: Yale University Press, 1982.

Zank, Michael. "The Rosenzweig-Rosenstock Triangle, or What Can We Learn from Letters to Gritli? A Review Essay." *Modern Judaism* 23, no. 1 (2003): 74–98.

Ziegelhauser, Gottfried Julius. *Die Juden: Eine bürgerliche Scene in einem Aufzuge*. Vienna: Johann Baptist Wallishausser, 1807.

Žižek, Slavoj. *The Sublime Object of Ideology*. New York: Verso Books, 1998.

Žižek, Slavoj, Eric L. Santner, and Kenneth Reinhard. *The Neighbor: Three Inquiries in Political Theology*. Chicago: University of Chicago Press, 2005.

Zudrell, Petra. *Der Kulturkritiker und Schriftsteller Max Nordau: Zwischen Zionismus, Deutschtum und Judentum*. Würzburg: Königshausen and Neumann, 2003.

INDEX

CPSIA information can be obtained
at www.ICGtesting.com
Printed in the USA
BVOW08*2019091116
467374BV00003B/6/P